Messiahs

The Visions and Prophecies
for the Second Coming

Messiahs

The Visions and Prophecies for the Second Coming

JOHN HOGUE

ELEMENT

Shaftesbury, Dorset • Boston, Massachusetts • Melbourne, Victoria

© Element Books Limited 1999
Text © John Hogue 1999

First published in Great Britain in 1999 by
ELEMENT BOOKS LIMITED
Shaftesbury, Dorset SP7 8BP

Published in the USA in 1999 by
ELEMENT BOOKS INC
160 North Washington Street, Boston MA 02114

Published in Australia in 1999 by
ELEMENT BOOKS
and distributed by Penguin Australia Ltd
487 Maroondah Highway, Ringwood, Victoria 3134

Designed and created with
The Bridgewater Book Company Limited

ELEMENT BOOKS LIMITED
Editorial Director Sue Hook
Senior Commissioning Editor Caro Ness
Group Production Director Clare Armstrong
Production Manager Stephanie Raggett

THE BRIDGEWATER BOOK COMPANY
Art Director Sarah Howerd
Designer Jane Lanaway
Editorial Director Fiona Biggs
Managing Editor Anne Townley
DTP Designer Chris Lanaway
Illustrators Catherine McIntyre, Sandy Gardner
Picture Research Liz Eddison

Printed and bound in Great Britain by
Butler & Tanner Ltd

British Library Cataloging in Publication
data available

Library of Congress Cataloging in Publication
data available

ISBN HB 1-86204-442-2
PB 1-86204-549-6

Picture Acknowledgments

The Bridgeman Art Library London/New York pp / Albright Knox Art Museum, Buffalo, New York 80 / Museo National de Antropologia, Mexico City, Mexico 125bl / Museo de Bellas Artes, Seville, Spain 179c / Biblioteca Nazionale Centrale, Florence, Italy 113br / Bibliothèque Nationale, Paris, France 222br / Birmingham Museums & Art Gallery, UK 61 / Branacacci Chapel, Santa Maria del Carmine, Florence, Italy 122-123b / British Library, London, UK 34cr, 178br, 218 / British Museum, London, UK 34bl & 132bl / Brooklyn Museum of Art, New York, USA 78b, 238bl / Christie's Images 36tr, 82, 85tr, 86-87 / Royal Library of Copenhagen, Denmark 24tr / Courtauld Gallery, London, UK 124 / Crown Estate, Institute of Directors, London, UK 171tr / Musée D'Orsay, Paris, France 107 / Hermitage, St Petersburg, Russia 162-163t / National Museum of India, New Delhi 8tr & 35 / Louvre, Paris, France 171b / Santa Lucia dei Magnoli, Florence, Italy 58 / The De Morgan Foundation 212c / Museo dell'Opera del Duomo, Siena, Italy 73 / Oriental Museum, Durham University, UK 59 / Phillips, The Fine Art Auctioneers, UK 83, 84-85b / Prado, Madrid, Spain 21bl / Private Collection 84cl, 112, 169tr, 231 / Pushkin Museum, Moscow, Russia 167 / Central Museum of the Revolution, Moscow, Russia 17tr / RSA, London, UK 120 / Musée Rodin, France 178tl / Museo de Santa Cruz, Toledo, Spain 90bl / Sotheby's, London, UK 169bl / Stapleton Collection, UK 121t / Taipei Nationa Palace Museum, Taiwan 204cl / Musée d'Unterlinden, Colmar, France 60bl, 150b / Rafael Valls Gallery, London, UK 86br / Johnny van Haeften Gallery, London, UK 226-227b / Victoria & Albert Museum, London, UK 100, 106, 161t, 168, 216-217b / National Gallery of Art, Washington DC, USA 26br / York City Art Gallery, North Yorkshire, UK 21t;

Corbis pp 24bl, 28br, 38-39, 39bl, 49cr, 68-69b, 150-151, 151t, 186-187, 190-191 / AFP 17cl & 48tl, 45cr / Delmi Alvarez 51 / B.D.V 157bl / Gianni Baldizzone 31tr, 66tl / Bettmann 28cl, 29, 29cr, 38tl, 62tr, 62b, 63br, 74tr, 74c, 104tl, 104br, 105cr, 108bl, 110-111c, 123tr, 130tl, 130cl, 130tr, 132-133, 133br, 141tr, 219tr / Jacques M Chenet 157tl / Sheldan Collins 108t, 108cr / Dean Conger 79br / Henry Diltz 154bl / Ed Eckstein 154-155c, 155tr / Jack Fields 170bl / Owen Franken 60tr / Michael Freeman 170-171t / Chris Gertenberg 88cl / Philip Gould 49bl / Hulton Deutsch 33bl, 37, 57bl, 104cl, 105t, 130br, 152, 205tr, 206-207, 214t / Zen Icknow 125tr / Yevgeny Khaldei 88tr / Christine Kolisch 35br / Mikik Kratsman 91, 130cl / David Lees 50bl / Charles Lenar 27t / Craig Lovell 21br & 66br / Richard Nowitz 89 / Neal Preston 75tr / Eldad Rafaeli 44cl / Enzo & Paolo Ragazzini 31bl, 42bl / Chris Rainier 176-177 / Roger Ressmeyer 74bl / Bob Rowan 218l / David Rubinger 129cr / Sakamoto Photo Research Laboratory 219br / Phil Schermeister 78-79 / Janez Skok 219tl / Paul A Souders 26tl / Keren Su 108-109 / Peter Turnley 74br / Brian Vikander 43t / Patrick Ward 65b / Michael S Yamashita 216tr;

ET Archive pp 8cl & 172, 204-205b;

Sarah Howerd p 72bl;

Hulton Getty p 105br;

The Image Bank pp 178 / Color Day 195cr / David De Lossy 195br, 220br / Yuri Doje 9bl / Thierr Dosogne 3 & 9tr / David Gaz 19 & 20 / Don Klumpp 194 / Butch Martin 221 bc / Carlos Navarjas 36 & 222-223 / Hans Neleman 220 cl / Piecework Product 242-243 / Tomek Sikora 1;

The Kobal Collection pp 44bl, 142b, 143t, 143b, 144-145t, 161bl, 210tl, 210c, 210br, 211;

Rex Features pp 213b, 215cl, 238-239 / ATF 130cr / Australian TV 75bl / Dieter Ludwig 109b, 110tl, 11br, 213t / SIPA 25br, 173 &215, 206tl, 206b, 214-215/ Tom Treick 179 & 236-237, 237b, 240-241c / Xip Rano 237t;

Science Photo Library p 182;

Tony Stone Images pp 69c, 196-197 / Bruce Ayers 126-127c / Sandra Baker 232-233 / A Berger 128tl / Lynn Butler 99 & 160 / Peter Cade 56t / Richard A Cooke III 25 & 230 / James Darell 220-221 / Cameron Davidson 54-55bc / Chuck Davis 54-55 / Deborah Davis 54bl / Nicholas DeVore 156 / Paul Edmondson 26 / Richard Elliot 212-213 / Richard Evers 233tl / Ken Fisher 98 & 128-129 / Bruce Forster 55tr / Ernst Haas 47 / Andrew Hall 227-228 / Joerg Hardtke 63t / James Harrington 234 / Pal Hermansen 14-15 / Frank Herholdt 190t / Alan Kler 46tl / Klaus Lahnstein 64br / Yann Layma 55cr / John Lund 17b & 52-53b / Anthony Marsland 69t / Joe McBride 48b / Will & Deni McIntyre 50 / Roger Mear 104-105 / Ralph Merecr 57br / Laurence Monneret 122t / Euan Myles 221tl / Donald Nausbaum 153 / Derke O Hara 68-69 & 144-145, 140-141 / Frank Orel 49br / Richard Passmore 64tl / Joseph Pobereskin 64-65 / Ed Pritchard 44-45, 45c, 232l & 233r / RKG Photography 53tr / Magnus Rew 183 / Tamara Reynolds 72 / Andreas Rudolf 45bl / Andy Sacks 46tr / Mark Segal 22-23 / Manoj Shah 90 & 166 / Chris Simpson 235 / A & L Sinibaldi 248-249 & 250-251 / Hugh Sitton 33tr / Don Spiro 140-141bc / Vera Storman 137t, 142-143 / James Stracchan 42-43 / Stephen Studd 10-11, 131 & 136-137 / Chris Thomaidis 79c / Tim Thompson 56b / Alan Thornton 207c / Darryl Torckler 16 / Nabeel Turner 67 / Penny Tweedie 48 / Olney Vasan 113 / Nick Verdos 128-129b / Paul Webster 46br / Ralph H Wetmore II 81;

Superstock p 195tr.

Every effort has been made to trace all copyright holders and obtain permissions. The publishers sincerely apologise for any inadvertent errors and will be happy to correct them in future editions.

CONTENTS

FOREWORD

Going Beyond Sibylline Rivalry and Pulpit Fiction 8

INTRODUCTION

A Note to the Reader 10
The Call of the Messiahs 11
A Key to the Prophecy Source Abbreviations 12

PART ONE
THE SECOND COMING SYNDROME

INTRODUCTION 16
THE MESSIAHS GALLERY 18

Immanuel, "The" Messiah 22

Jesus Christ, the Messiah of the Gentiles 23

Balder, the Viking Redeemer 24

The Maori Messiah 24

The Sinful Messiah 25

Jesus Christ, the Mormon Messiah 26

The "Pale-Faced" Prophet 26

Pahána, the Hopi Messiah 27

Quetzalcoatl, the Mesoamerican Savior 28

The Eskimo Messiah 28

The Iroquois Messiah 29

The Great Plains Messiah 29

The Ghost Dancers' Messiah 29

The King of Shambhala,
the Himalayan Avatar 30

The White Burkhan 31

Saoshyant, the Second Coming of
Zoroaster 31

Muntazar, the Final Prophet of
Sunni Islam 32

The Twelfth Imam,
the Last Prophet of Shi'ite Islam 32

Khidr, the Sufi Final Lawgiver 33

Osiris, the Egyptian Savior 33

The Aeon, the Occult Messiah 33

The Return of Krishna 34

Kalki, the Last Avatar of Hinduism 34

Maitreya the Buddha 35

Amida Buddha 35

The Japanese Messiah 36

The Spiritual King,
the Indonesian Messiah 36

The Nazi Messiah 37

Ruth Montgomery's New Age Messiah 38

The Idiotic Messiahs 39

SIGNS OF THE END TIMES 42

The Kali Yuga: Age of Iron and Chaos   44   The Forerunners   60

Holy Mothers to the Rescue   58   The Final Signs   62

COUNTERFEIT CHRISTS 72

The Antichrist Is a Nerd   76   Who Is Imitating Immanuel?   88

Christ, the False Prophet of the Christians   78   Righteous Wrongs   92

Immanuel, the False Prophet of the Jews   84

THE ADVENT 98

Salvation Rides a White Horse   99   Saviors for the Birds...   113

The Man from the East   102   ...Coming from the Clouds   114

Maitreya the Transmigrant   112   A Wish List of Woes before "He" Returns   116

FROM PROPHEGANDA TO ARMAGEDDONOMICS 120

Brainwashed to Make Doomsday Happen   122   His Terrible Swift Sword   132

THE GREAT ESCAPE 134

Saved by a UFO   138   Castles in the Clouds   144

Destination: The Pearly Gates
or Heaven's Gate?   140   Saved from Myself   145

THE 1,000-YEAR REICH OF THE SAVIOR 146

A New Heaven, a New Earth,   The Dictatorship of the Forgiven   153

a New World Order   150   Sing Praises Forever, or Else...   156

A THIEF IN THE NIGHT 158

Messiahs Missed   162   Dangerous Beings   166

A Plague of Parrot Punditry   164   New Eyes, New Ears   174

PART TWO
THE APOCALYPSE OF THE AWAKENED ONES

INTRODUCTION 182
NOAH'S ARK OF CONSCIOUSNESS 186

The Coming Mind Broil 190
Sh*t Happens to Sleepwalkers 194
Samsara's Tornado 198
Safe Is the Center of the Cyclone 204

THE UNBEARABLE LIGHTNESS OF BEING ORDINARY 210

The Man Behind the God-Man Myth 212
I-diocy the Empty Sky? 216
The Path of Trust 218
Many Candles – One Flame 226

THE BUDDHAFIELD 230

Escaping the Misery Field 232
The Coming of the
    Transpersonal Messiah 234
The Great Paradox 244

EPILOGUE: CHILDHOOD'S END 246
SEERS' ENCYCLOPEDIA 248

Selected Bibliography 252
Index 254
Acknowledgments 256

FOREWORD
GOING BEYOND SIBYLLINE RIVALRY AND PULPIT FICTION

Messiahs...

It is not a word you often find in plural form. Yet there are over 700 prophecies from around the world that cast their oracular gaze into the 21st century to capture the promised advent of more than 30 world saviors pledging spiritual revolution and redemption.

Certainly there have been and will be plenty of books focusing exclusively on the return of Jesus, or Buddha, and their predicted appearance. But to this day no one has written a comprehensive book on all the messiahs who have promised to grace our earth in the opening decades of the new millennium. One reason for this is the religious volatility of this subject. Every religion believes there can be only one Messiah – theirs.

ABOVE **The Buddha is just one of many Messiahs predicted to return and redeem humankind.**

No other subject in prophecy suffers from more religious myopia. The very nature of the messianic genre nourishes in its interpreters the judgment that the savior from their particular faith is the only

ABOVE **Vishnu, shown here creating the cosmic order, is the creator god of the Hindu pantheon.**

"true" redeemer. I have come across this difficulty firsthand over the last few decades, when I traveled around the world collecting the 777 prophecies for this book. While living in India I came to understand that the Hindu pundit was just as divinely assured that the Avatar Krishna would return as Kalki, the true Messiah, as were the Christians convinced their Jesus is the only true redeemer. While living in Buddhist lands, the monks there counseled me with equal assurance that no Krishna or Christ would return to save the world, but rather that an incarnation of Lord Buddha, called "Maitreya," was at hand. Moreover, he was as "real" a savior to my Buddhist contacts as the 12th Imam was to my Shi'ite Muslim sources. They vigorously brushed aside any assertions by Buddhists, Hindus, and Christians and placed their cherished Imam on the table as the only true prophet.

And so it continued as I traveled from one country to the next. Each believer saw their deliverer from this dark age of sinfulness as the only true catalyst of God's plan. All the other candidates were either politely rejected as deluded, or righteously condemned as evil deceivers – antichrists.

A new millennium demands a new perspective on the messianic prophecy genre. It must be freed from the straitjacket of religious conditioning and expectations of religious traditions. A fresh examination has to put aside all preconceived notions of good messiahs as opposed to bad antichrists.

Messiahs levels Armageddon's playing field where the sons and incarnations of God compete to save humanity. Waiting for you in the following pages is a strange gathering of equals. At the dawning of the 1,000-year rule of the savior, the returned Christian Prince of Peace vies to sit on the same throne as the Himalayan King of Shambhala. Prophecies of a final Imam of Islam inter-act with those of Maitreya, the returned Buddha. The red-robed Buddhist monk will find that his deliverer is the same man from the East forecast by the Indians of North and Central America. The blood-stained sleeve of the Jewish Christ will even rub against the blood-flag swastika armbands of a Nazi Messiah, and the savior of the skinheads will confront a real Aryan savior from the Hindu East who isn't blond and blue-eyed, but a blue-skinned and brown-eyed God-man riding a horse as white and imposing as the one the Christians describe for the Second Coming of their savior in the Book of Revelation.

ABOVE **Images of Christ on the cross are a reminder of his death but also of the prospect of his long-expected Second Coming.**

Messiahs blends the prophecies of diverse messianic traditions, and every declaration taken as dogma is questioned. Through this process we may come to understand that all of the polarized points of view about final prophets share not only many common prejudices, but also a common vision of salvation. By exploring all the apocalyptic shades of messianic vision, we might crystallize our understanding of what motivates such prophecies and gain a clearer insight into who, or "what," is coming to save the world.

BELOW **People from all cultures have their own vision of the new Messiah.**

Often what we expect from the future does not happen. The savior does not live up to our hopes. Historically he has almost always stood against our traditions and presented a new vision. We usually call that vision "antichrist," because for most of us a fresh and revolutionary understanding of divine mystery is terrifying. Even so, prophets from many traditions around the world declare that a new dispensation is coming. We are at the threshold of the Aquarian Age. Messianic catalysts will come who will excite our understanding of God and religion, just as Buddha, Muhammad, and Christ did in previous ages.

All bets are off on a future based on the old traditional views. Even the most hallowed of prophetic subjects – the Messiah – will undergo a death and resurrection.

A NOTE TO
THE READER

Messiahs: The Visions and Prophecies from the Second Coming is Book Two of my planned four-part 777-prophecy series. The previous 777 predictions in Book One, The Millennium Book of Prophecy (HarperCollins, 1994), examined collective visions of doomsday and of "bloomsday" – the flowering of a new civilization beginning sometime in the 21st century.

How the prophecy indexing works

To streamline my interpretation of a prophecy, or to explain, clarify, or correct a quotation's grammar, I sometimes insert words or phrases in the quoted predictions. These insertions always appear in brackets – for example:

The [12th] Iman will return at a time when a thing called an "attenna" is on the way.

The name of the prophet appears in capital letters after every prophecy, followed by the actual or estimated composition date of the prediction in parentheses. For example:

ST. JOHN OF PATMOS (81–96 C.E.)

Prophets or their followers often collected and indexed their predictions in books and religious scriptures. In such cases you will find the name and date of the prediction, followed by an abbreviated code for the book's title and the prediction's indexing. For instance:

ST. JOHN OF PATMOS (81–96 C.E.) RV 16:12

("Rv 16:12" stands for St. John's Book of Revelation, Chapter 16, Verse 12.)

To decode the abbreviated indexing, refer to the "Key to Prophecy Abbreviations" on the following pages. There you can also find the source of the prediction quoted for further reading. The "Seers' Encyclopedia" at the back of the book contains a short biography of each prophet.

INTRODUCTION:
THE CALL OF THE MESSIAHS

Believe in me and I will save you from yourself.
I am the Avatar, the only begotten Son of God.
I am called your dear leader, your Savior.
I am your Führer.
Let me take your burden, let me show you the Way,
Let me lead you to the New Age,
The Thousand-Year Reich,
Nirvana.

I will appear dressed and masked according to your
   hopes, fears, visions, and divine expectations.
To those who follow me,
I am the Second Coming of Christ, the Maitreya,
   the Krishna.
I am your Final Prophet.
To those who disbelieve in me,
I am the Antichrist,
The False Prophet.

Few recognize me when I walk the Earth.
They expect the Messiahs of the past to return
   in their future.
They do not clear the dust of their expectations off
   their ancient prophecies to see me as I am.
They expect me to strengthen their traditions,
   but I always come as a destroyer of their past.
I come to preach a new law, a new dispensation,
   a new world order.
I am the Apocalypse, the Holocaust, the End
   of History.

I am your Messiah,
Born of many virgins from many lands and
   historical times.
I am foretold in the Bible, the Gita, the Torah.
I lurk in The Book of Revelation and hide in the
   Little Red Book of Mao.
I have been many in the past, and your prophecies
   from around the world depict me returning by
   the dozens in the near future.
I am coming back.
In your dreams, in your nightmares,
   in your Tomorrows.

A KEY TO THE PROPHECY SOURCE ABBREVIATIONS

'Abdu'l-Bahá
NWER   *Bahá'u'lláh and the New Era*, 1950
PARIS   *Paris Talks*, 1911-1912
PRM   *Promulgation of Universal Peace*, 1982
SLC   *Selections from the Writings of 'Abdu'l-Bahá*, 1978

Adi Da Samraj (aka Bubba Free John, Da Free John, Da Love Ananda, Da Kalki, and Da Avabhasa)
EGOI   *The ego-'I,'* 1980
GARB   *Garbage and the Goddess*, 1974
HBUS   *Handle Business*, 1987
WYIT   *The Way I Teach*, 1977

Anandamayi Ma
MATRI   *Matri Darshan*, 1983

Sri Aurobindo
LFDV   *Life Divine*, 1996

Bahá'u'lláh
GLE   *Gleanings from the Writings of Bahá'u'lláh*, 1983
IQN   *Kitáb-Í-Íqán (The Book of Certitude)*, 1950

Bible: Old Testament (King James version)
DEUT   Deuteronomy
DN   Daniel
EZ   Ezekiel
IS   Isaiah (First, Second, and Third)
MAL   Malachi
MI   Micah
ZEC   Zechariah (First and Second)

Bible: New Testament (King James version)
1 COR   1 Corinthians (First letter of St. Paul to the Corinthians)
1 JN   1 John (First letter of John)
1 PT   1 Peter (First letter of Peter)
1 THES   1 Thessalonians (First letter of St. Paul to the Thessalonians)
2 THES   2 Thessalonians (Second letter of St. Paul to the Thessalonians)
2 TM   2 Timothy (Second letter of St. Paul to Timothy)
JN   John
LK   Luke
MK   Mark
MT   Matthew
ROM   Romans
RV   Revelation

Gnostic Bible (Nag Hammadi Library)
BKTC   The Book of Thomas the Contender, 1977
GOFT   The Gospel of Thomas, ibid.

Christian Apocrypha (New Testament Apocrypha, Vol. 2)
AOFT   Apocalypse of Thomas, 1963

H. P. Blavatsky
SCDOC   *The Secret Doctrine*, 1888

Buddha Gautama (Juan Mascaró translation)
DHM   *The Dhammapada*, c. 480 B.C.E.

Edgar Cayce
Note on the Readings: Cayce's 14,246 trance sessions are indexed by the subject's case number and the hyphenated number of the reading, for example: No. 301-4. For further investigation of the readings contact the Edgar Cayce Foundation, Virginia Beach, VA, U.S.A.

Cheiro (Keiro)
CWP   *Cheiro's World Predictions*, 1926 (Revised 1931)

Peter Deunov

DIVT   *Divine Thought*, as it appears in *Prophet for Our Times*, by David Lorimer, Element 1991

EVRY   *Everyday Thoughts*, ibid.

NWDY   *The New Day*, ibid.

ROYL   *The Royal Path of the Soul*, ibid.

G. I. Gurdjieff

MIRA   *In Search of the Miraculous*, by P. D. Ouspensky, 1915-1917 (Statements of Gurdjieff recorded and edited by P. D. Ouspensky)

VWS   *Views from the Real World: Early Talks of Gurdjieff*, 1914-1924

Hermes Trismegistus

ASC 21-29   *The Coptic Asclepius 21-29*. A dialogue between Hermes Trismegistus and his disciple, Asclepius: c. 150-270 C.E.

Adolf Hitler

SCRTC   *Hitler's Secret Conversations* (1941-1944), 1953

Krishna (Juan Mascaró translation)

GITA   *The Bhagavad Gita*

J. Krishnamurti

FTNW   *The Future Is Now*, 1989

LIAH   *Life Ahead*, 1963

URTHW   *You Are the World*, 1972

Muhammad

QUR   The Holy Qur'an, 7th century C.E.

Ruth Montgomery

ALNS   *Aliens Among Us*, 1985

AMG   *Strangers Among Us*, 1979

WBF   *The World Before*, 1976

Osho

BYND   *Beyond Enlightenment*, 1986

CMC   *Come, Come, Yet Again, Come*, 1980

DMBY   *Dimensions Beyond the Known*, 1971

DMPDA   *The Dhammapada: The Way of Buddha*, 1979

DTOD   *From Death to Deathlessness*, 1985

FTOT   *From the False to the True*, 1985

GATE   *I Am the Gate*, 1971

GLM   *Glimpses of a Golden Childhood*, 1981

GTN   *The Great Nothing*, 1976

HAL   *Hallelujah!*, 1978

INVT   *The Invitation*, 1987

LTG   *Let Go!*, 1978

MRCL   *The Miracle!*, 1980 (unpublished)

MST   *The Mustard Seed*, 1974

MTOE   *From Misery to Enlightenment*, 1984

MYST   *The Mystic Experience*, 1970

NEWD   *The New Dawn*, 1987

PHLS   *Philosophia Perennis*, 1980

PTHM   *The Path of Meditation*, 1965

RAZR   *The Razor's Edge*, 1987

SHWR   *Showering Without Clouds*, 1976

SRM   *Sermons in Stones*, 1986

TAH   *Ta Hui*, 1988

TITE 1   *Take It Easy*, Vol. I, 1978

WHIS   *What Is Is What Ain't Ain't*, 1977

WHT   *The White Lotus*, 1979

ZARD   *Zarathustra, the God that Can Dance*, 1987

ZNM   *The Zen Manifesto*, 1989

Padmasambhava

STUPA   *The Legend of the Great Stupa*, 1973

The Hindu Puranas

VIS-P   *Vishnu Purana*, c. 900 C.E.

Quetzalcoatl (Kate Zahl)

HEW   *He Walked the Americas*, by L. Tayor Hansen, 1997

Prophecy of Shambhala

ALTAI   *Altai-Himalaya: A Travel Diary*, by Nicholas Roerich, 1929 (reprinted 1983)

SHMB   *Shambhala*, by Nicholas Roerich, 1930 (reprinted 1990)

Tamo-san

LOOK   *Look Here!* (a Discourse), Summer 1960

MOOR   *Moor the Boat*, 1957

Rabbi Hile Wechsler

EWM   *Ein Word der Mahnung (A Word of Warning)*, 1881; reprinted in Rosenbaums of Zell, 1962

Paramhansa Yogananda

AUTO   *Autobiography of a Yogi*, 1945 (first edition)

PART ONE

THE SECOND COMING SYNDROME

PART ONE
THE SECOND COMING SYNDROME

When righteousness is weak and faints and
unrighteousness exults in pride, then my Spirit
arises on earth. For the salvation of those who
are good, for the destruction of evil in men, for
the fulfillment of the kingdom of righteousness,
I come to this work in the ages that pass.

KRISHNA (*c.* 3000 B.C.E.), GITA 4:7–8

I am the resurrection, and the life: he that
believeth in me, though he were dead, yet shall
he live: And whosoever liveth and believeth in
me shall never die. Believest thou this?

Y'SHUA (*c.* 30 C.E.), JN 11:25–26

Part One begins with a brief introduction of the messiahs themselves and illuminates the promises and exclusive claims for the world's salvation promoted by their followers. When these claims are seen gathered together as a group, some readers may find that their savior appears to share a common agenda with others to save and heal the righteous (believers) and to punish the wicked (nonbelievers).

Messianic traditions are chock full of shared visions of social breakdown, climatic disaster, wars and rumors of wars as precursors to the appearance of the Savior. We will look into the signs and portents that support the common belief that a redeemer will come to clean house, destroy evil, and dictate a new and benevolent world order sometime within the next 50 years.

ABOVE **A vision of the end times – American high school pupils mourn the death of friends after a mass shooting.**

I will propose that there is a dark lining to every silver cloud of salvation promoted by the religions – that between the lines of the proclamations of forgiveness hides a lust for revenge against all those who do not submit (or are not privy) to the divine mystery. The benevolent reign of the Messiah on earth promises a life of happiness and bliss only for those who believe the doctrines and follow the rules of the faith. Those who do not are threatened with forced conversion and a thousand-year repression.

ABOVE **Revolutions and social upheavals are eagerly seized upon as evidence of the Second Coming.**

Perhaps the most dangerous aspect of this Second Coming syndrome is its repeated programming of people for thousands of years to mindlessly believe that the world has to be practically destroyed before the Savior can arrive. I will show parallels with current events and prophecies that reveal a disturbing pattern. We may be unconsciously steering civilization toward a breakdown over the next few decades simply because the wrong interpretations of the Bible, the Gita, the Qur'an and other scriptures "tell us so."

At the end of Part One, I set aside all the finger-pointing and Antichrist-calling of every messianic tradition to argue that something spiritually unique, even messianic, is coming our way in the 21st century, but we run the danger of misinterpreting the signs. Past experience shows us that most people do not recognize the true messiahs when they walk the earth. Perhaps the adopted expectations and projections of religious leaders distort our capacity to see him in the flesh.

Are we being programmed to miss the Messiah again?

Perhaps not, if we have the courage to confront the Second Coming syndrome.

BELOW **Climatic disasters seem to be on the increase and are read as omens of the world's end.**

JESUS NAZARENUS
REX JVDEORVM

†HE MESSIAHS GALLERY

Surely I am coming soon.

Y'SHUA (Jesus) RV 22:20-21

And when I am no longer needed,

after my mission is accomplished,

then I shall be called away.

ADOLF HITLER

THE MESSIAHS GALLERY

LEFT **John the Baptist prepared the way for the Christian Messiah, the anointed one.**

The prime definition of the title "Messiah" is "deliverer," or "the anointed one." He is generally conceived as a kind of superman, God's "god-man" on earth. The word "Messiah" comes from the Aramaic *mashiah*, "the anointed." It conjures up visions of John the Baptist pouring muddy waters on the Christ, who does not know that he is the chosen one until the slap of the Baptist's water awakens the "Messiah" within. In a splash Y'shua bar Yosseph, the carpenter from Galilee, becomes the Greek pseudonym "Christ."

The labels "Christ" and "Messiah" are docile bullocks of etymology. They both trace their source meaning all the way back to a "raging bull" from the Sumerian language. The Sumerian root of the Judeo-Christian savior's title describes exactly "what" is anointing the Christ/Messiah. Simply put, he is one who is "smeared with semen." Thus there was a need to unman the word. God forbid that reproductive body fluids are the stuff of holy monikers for the highest incarnations of God!

The secondary definition of Messiah is "spiritual and temporal king." Technically

LEFT **The heroic Christ, the bringer of salvation through death, is only one among many saviors.**

speaking, the current Dalai Lama as ruler of Tibet is more a messiah in the Jewish definition than anyone else alive today. He is the spiritual and political king of his people. However, he flunks out in the last category set by the Jews for their "spiritual king": a messiah must be born from the bloodline of the Jewish King David.

Jews and Christians see their savior coming like a new dawn from the East, but they do not say how far eastward is his source. Just how far do we go on chasing the eastern horizon? Beyond the River Jordan the dawn of salvation strikes the skies of Persia with the expected coming of Saoshyant. Go farther east and there are people sweltering under the hazy dawn skies of South Asian valleys – or shivering in the shade of Himalayan peaks kissed by a solar first blush – who watch for the coming of the Avatar Kalki and the Lord of Shambhala. Before dawn touches these places it warms the jungles and rice paddies of the Far East, where people await the appearance of Lord Maitreya. Follow the eastern horizon across the vast Pacific, beyond where Polynesians await their atoll Avatars, and dawn's earlier landfall brings us to the shores of North America, where the light of dawn will paint a new era red with American Indian messiahs.

It seems that our pilgrimage to catch first sight of a savior arising in the East can keep us spinning around the earth forever. Who therefore is the savior of the world?

There is a whole gallery of messiahs to choose from. What follows is a brief overview and illustrated examination of the chief saviors expected to arrive in the next 30 to 50 years.

BELOW **The Dalai Lama is the spiritual leader of Tibet, and hence a Messiah.**

IMMANUEL, "THE" MESSIAH

I will raise them up a Prophet from among their brethren, like unto thee, and will put my words in his mouth; and he shall speak unto them all that I shall command him.

DEUT. 18:18

The Old Testament foresees the Jewish Messiah, Immanuel, as the true messenger of Yahweh, the God of the Jews. He is a theocratic king yet to be born in Bethlehem (whether it becomes a borough in a future Palestinian state or not). He is from the bloodline of King David. Immanuel will restore the Jewish people to their status as the Chosen People and will rule over the nations of earth as God's arbiter and lawgiver. It is said that we will know his time has come when the foretold Jewish Diaspora ends and the state of Israel is restored in the Holy Land. (This took place in 1948.) Next we will see a red heifer born among the Jews. This bovine's burnt offerings will ceremoniously pave the way for new *cohanim* (priests) to rebuild the Temple of Herod.

The spirit of the Lord shall rest upon him, the spirit of wisdom and understanding, the spirit of counsel and might, the spirit of knowledge and the fear of the Lord....With righteousness shall he judge the poor, and reprove the equity for the meek of the earth: and he shall smite the earth with the rod of his mouth, and with the breath of his lips shall he slay the wicked. And righteousness shall be the girdle of his loins, and faithfulness the girdle of his reins.

FIRST ISAIAH (783–687 B.C.E.), IS. 11:2–5

And he shall judge among the nations, and shall rebuke many people: and they shall beat their swords into plowshares, and the spears into pruning hooks: nation shall not lift up sword against nation, neither shall they learn war any more.

FIRST ISAIAH (783–687 B.C.E.), IS 2:4

JESUS CHRIST, THE MESSIAH OF THE GENTILES

The best known messianic tradition of a savior is the Christian "Christ," Jesus, son of the Virgin Mary, and the only-begotten son of God. He laid claim to the title of Jewish Messiah, but crucifixion cut his ministry down to a mere three years in length. A cult of his promised Second Coming spread rapidly after his purported resurrection and disappearance from the face of the earth. His salvation scenario foresees a descent from the clouds in glory after a seven-year tribulation on earth. He will return after sinful humanity suffers the horrors of unprecedented wars, social and ecological breakdown, and natural disasters.

At the onset of this time of troubles many believe Christ will take a minimum of 144,000 converted Jews and thousands of Christian devotees, body and soul, into the clouds in the "twinkling of an eye." After this "Rapture" liftoff, and at the close of the final battle of Armageddon, Christ will return to earth from the clouds. He won't be meek or mild-mannered this time. He'll come to "kick butt" and will lead an army of those delivered up in the Rapture to triumph over evil and rule the earth in a new Jerusalem for a thousand years. His Second Coming is widely expected by all Christian sects during or shortly after the year 2000.

> There shall come in the last days scoffers, walking after their own lusts, and saying, Where is the promise of his coming?
>
> SIMON THE ZEALOT (c. 64 C.E.), 2 PT 3:3–4

> I pray God your whole spirit and soul and body be preserved blameless unto the coming of our Lord Jesus Christ.
>
> SAUL OF TARSUS (c. 51 C.E.), 1 THES 5:23

> "Surely, I am coming soon!" Amen. Even so come, Lord Jesus! The Grace of the Lord Jesus be with you all.
>
> ST. JOHN OF PATMOS (81–96 C.E.), RV 22:20–21

BALDER, THE VIKING REDEEMER

In Viking lore, Balder, the son of Odin, the king of the Viking gods who dwell in Asgard, is comparable to Christ, the son of the Christian God who dwells in Heaven. Balder is handsome, wise, and gentle. You might say he is a Nordic, blond, goatee-adorned Jesus in Viking horns and armor. He also faces his own betrayal and crucifixion, not by an errant Judas or a heavy wooden cross but through the intrigues of Loki, the god of mischief, who discovered Balder's only weakness – the poisonous prick of a mistletoe thorn. Once poked, Balder dies and his soul is sent to dwell in the trunk of Yggdrasill, the world ash tree that balances all the worlds of the Viking universe upon her branches. Balder will return again after Asgard, Earth, and Hel (Hell) are destroyed in the Ragnarök (the Destruction of the Powers). After this Viking version of Armageddon takes place, Balder leads the surviving children of the gods out of the wreckage of Yggdrasill, and together they will build a new and better world.

RIGHT **The Christlike Nordic God Balder was also sacrificed for the sake of his chosen people.**

THE MAORI MESSIAH

LEFT **The Maoris not only wholeheartedly adopted the Christian faith but even proclaimed themselves prophets of the white man's Messiah.**

If the Japanese can adapt Western technologies and improve them, then the first white settlers of New Zealand saw the native Maoris try the same upgrade of the Westerners' Christian cult of the Messiah.

From 1820 through 1920 over a dozen Maori men and women abandoned their own pagan prophecies and gathered their people to hear the "good news" that they had become the forerunners and prophets of the coming Judeo-Christian Messiah foretold by the whites. Indeed, they believed they were more zealous in following the commands of the Old and New Testaments than were their white missionary neighbors. The Maori prophets translated the whites' Bible into Polynesian, and for a hundred years many spiritual communities thrived on the expectation of imminent salvation from Polynesian paradise. Eventually most of the movements died out, and the whites suppressed those that stubbornly remained active through legal action, police raids, and mass arrests.

THE SINFUL MESSIAH

A Pentecostal prophet or messianic figure appears in the final days before the Apocalypse. Unlike Christ, this savior from the Protestant fringe is not without sin. Rather, he is comparable to the Catholic Elias and Enoch prophecies. These concern two Christlike figures martyred by a world-dominating false Christ, or Antichrist, unleashed on the earth by Satan to lead people astray in the final days.

David Koresh (a.k.a. Vernon Wayne Howell), leader of a Christian apocalyptic cult known to themselves as the Students of the Seven Seals – and incorrectly labeled by the press as the Branch Davidians – believed he was this sinning Savior. He became sexually involved with many of his celibate male followers' wives and girlfriends in order to beget a new race of spiritual adepts to preach the message of the Seven Seals prophecies of the Book of Revelation (Chapters 6–8). February 1993 saw this lusty lawgiver and over 80 of his followers immolated in their Waco, Texas, compound after a long and protracted siege with federal agents. Some believe it was self-immolation – Koresh's stab at self-fulfillment of a prophecy wherein he predicted his and his followers' ascent into heaven by fire. Others say that members of a siege army of ATF and FBI agents flung the match into the Waco funeral pyre. Also gone up in flames was this functionally illiterate messiah's attempt to revise interpretations of the mysterious Seven Seals to help give humanity the keys to unlocking the messianic kingdom to come.

ABOVE **David Koresh giving instruction to the Students of the Seven Seals, before his followers went up in smoke at Waco.**

JESUS CHRIST, THE MORMON MESSIAH

A newer testament was added to the New Testament in 1823, in New York State of all places, when Joseph Smith unearthed a set of golden tablets containing "reformed Egyptian" hieroglyphs. Smith, who would go on to become the forerunner prophet of Mormonism, claimed that the angel Moroni led him to the scripture's burial site near Palmyra, New York. Smith later translated the tablets with the help of Moroni. After compiling their revelations in the *Book of Mormon*, a religious movement sprang up.

The scripture contends that two lost tribes of Israel populated the New World from 600 B.C.E. to 400 C.E. Jesus Christ visited these pre-Columbian Israelites shortly after his ascent into heaven from Jerusalem (*c.* 33 C.E.). Mormonism's Christ later ascended into heaven after promising to return.

Like Joseph Smith, the Mormons, also known as the Latter-Day Saints, believe they are paving the way for Christ's return to rule for 1,000 years. The Mormon Church will act as Christ's government for God's kingdom on earth.

The Mormons believe that even the dearly departed can be baptized and saved if the genealogical records of their existence can be confirmed. The Latter-Day Saints have compiled the world's foremost genealogical records department, where a global census slots the world's departed sinners for baptism by proxy in the Mormon way, so they can stand in the presence of God at Judgment Day.

LEFT **The angel Moroni stands proudly on the roof of the Washington Mormon Temple. Joseph Smith, founder of the Mormons, claimed that the angel delivered the faith to him.**

THE "PALE-FACED" PROPHET

Joseph Smith was not the first person to promote the idea of a great white mystic appearing in the land of the Native American Indian. From native nations of North and South America come a number of parallel legends of a great white teacher (or teachers) who disembarked from boats on the Pacific shores of pre-Columbian Peru around 2,000 years ago. He was pale in complexion like a Caucasian. His hair was the color of ripe corn, and on his chin was a short yellow beard. Rumor had it that he had come into the world by virgin birth. He preached from nation to nation, heading north along the foothills of the Andes. The Maya and the ancestors of the Aztecs noted his passage. Verbal records of his wanderings and his power to heal the sick and raise the dead reach as far north as the Pueblo and the Plains Indians.

Other legends say he was one of a band of white mystics traveling through Central America and Mexico who caused a schism by teaching a gospel of peace and love.

One story tells of this man being cast out of Mexico for his teachings. He set sail for the northwest and was last seen being carried by the Gulf Stream toward the Atlantic shores of Roman-dominated Europe. The Pale-Faced Prophet augured the coming Native American apocalypse before he left, after which he promised his return to redeem the lost spiritual soul of the Native American peoples.

RIGHT **Joseph Smith's idea about the great white hope bringing salvation from the East had been around in native traditions for years.**

PAHÁNA, THE HOPI MESSIAH

ABOVE **The Pueblo peoples built the cliff Palace in Colorado, U.S.A. around 700 C.E. American Hopi Indians claim descent from the Pueblo civilizations.**

One sees a common messiah/deliverer prophecy-coming from Native American nations that have widely diverse cultures and languages. To some extent this strange coincidence may be said to support the hypothesis that there is a root source for such predictions. The Hopi Indians of the southwestern United States believe they are that source, claiming their descent from the most ancient Pueblo civilizations in the Americas. If this claim is true, then their legends and prophecies are the principal source for Native American religion.

All Native American tribes have a variation on the following prophecy:

The forefathers of the Hopi nation said that at the dawn of the creation of the current fourth world, there were two brothers. The younger brother was red-skinned; the older was as white as a European. The Great Spirit had a stone tablet with the sign of a circle on it. Breaking the tablet in two, the Great Spirit gave each brother half, to help them remember him and to guide them. The Great Spirit instructed the older, white-skinned brother to lead his people to a distant land, where he would develop the power of reason and human material powers. The younger, red-skinned brother would stay in ancient America, where he would be a caretaker of the land and develop human spiritual powers. A day would come when the older white brother would return from the East to his red brother, and they would share their material and spiritual powers to make a balanced paradise on earth.

However, the prophecy warned of the appearance of a false white brother, whose "return" would be marked by a cross (instead of a circle) on his tablet. This one would bring devastation to Native Americans, and would use his material magic to destroy the balance of nature. His rape of the land would eventually bring about the destruction of the world, and a great purification by fire.

Yet just when the red brother's people's extinction seems most assured, the new age of the fifth world will arise from the ashes of the old. Then *Pahána*, the True White Brother, will return from the East, descending from the sky in a flying boat. He will be wearing a red cap and cloak, and at his side will stand two helpers holding the sacred symbols: the swastika, the cross, and the power symbol of the sun. Pahána will restore the native Indian and the white brother to righteousness and balance and create a brotherhood of human beings across the entire earth.

The signs of the (Christian) cross, the swastika (Nazi Germany), and the red ball sun sign of Imperial Japan have already appeared in our time. The power of a sun weapon, the atomic bomb, brought the white man's world war to an end. Therefore we are well into the Hopi latter days before the return of the True White Brother.

QUETZALCOATL, THE MESOAMERICAN SAVIOR

The Mayans call him Kukulcan, the Toltecs call him Kate-Zahl, and Aztecs call him the True White Brother, Quetzalcoatl. They share the belief that he is the fair foreigner who sailed across the Pacific to bless their land with his divine presence. He claimed to be born of a virgin and was the founding father of most of ancient Central America's scriptures and laws.

Aztec, Toltec, and Mayan prophecies promise his return from the East during a time of great troubles to restore the law of the red man to North America.

Generally speaking, Quetzalcoatl translates as "plumed serpent," but it can also mean "rare bird-serpent" or even "twin brother." The latter suggests the popular myth shared by ancient peoples of godlike twin brothers: one is divine and true, but the other is all too human and false. In 1519, King Moctezuma of the Aztecs overlooked this less auspicious possibility when he approached the white and bearded Spanish conquistador Hernando Cortés, believing he was the True White Brother Quetzalcoatl. Cortés, a formidably cunning and money-grabbing "serpent" if ever there was one, used the prophecy like a weapon alongside his "thunder sticks" – cannons – and cold steel to conquer and pillage the Aztec Empire. "Quetzalcoatl" Cortés did not show a tablet with a cross to Moctezuma, but the Christian cross *was* emblazoned on the breastplates and flags of his Christian army.

Some visions of the true Quetzalcoatl's return portray him as an olive-skinned man with a long white beard, descending from the eastern skies in a great air canoe. This vision's fulfillment will come after the dark age begun by Cortés burns itself out and nearly annihilates the Native American.

LEFT **The arrival of Westerners brought carnage to Native North America.**

THE ESKIMO MESSIAH

The prophets of the native peoples of the Arctic foresee the Messiah to be an olive-skinned man with a long beard and white hair who comes from the East.

In 1912 a number of Eskimo shamans claimed to share a visionary dream of a "strange and wondrous white figure" – a Godzilla-sized being of love "towering over all humanity, with special servants under him, guiding the masses of the people to God."

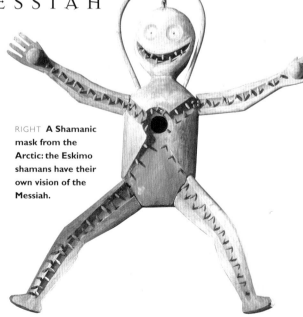

RIGHT **A Shamanic mask from the Arctic: the Eskimo shamans have their own vision of the Messiah.**

THE IROQUOIS MESSIAH

In the 1500s – roughly one century before the white man's invasion of New York – the Iroquois-speaking Huron Indian Deganawida gave a warning of the white man's arrival. He described it in his famous prophecy as a three-way struggle between red and white serpents and a black snake – the latter representing evil. The red snake and the white would exhaust themselves in battle. Then a light coming from the East would vanquish the black snake. The white snake would recognize the red as his long-lost brother, and they would live in harmony. Subsequently a savior of the tribes of modern-day New York, New England, and eastern Canada would come from the East in glory. What makes this account unique is Deganawida's contention that it was he himself who would return, risen from the spirit world.

THE GREAT PLAINS MESSIAH

A man in a red cloak, coming from the East, will restore the law of the Native American to North America. In 1872, the Sioux medicine man Black Elk declared that the great suffering of the Sioux Indians at the hands of the whites would continue until a message came to the Indian nations through a prophet who comes from the East. This messenger would be "painted bright red."

RIGHT **The sufferings of the Sioux, such as the massacre at Wounded Knee, were held to presage the coming of the prophet from the East.**

THE GHOST DANCERS' MESSIAH

The rape of the Native American culture after Columbus reached its peak by the end of the 19th century, by which time the Native American messianic tradition had been supplanted by Christian eschatology. In the late 19th century the Paiute Indian prophet Wowoka He (1858–1932) revised the Pale-Faced Prophet legend. He saw a vision of an earthly paradise, with game and buffalo rising from the dead to crowd the plains once again. He saw the red and white peoples living as brothers who would restore nature's balance. They would establish a golden age by purifying themselves of negativity through participation in a sacred dance that would link the living with the souls of all those lost in the Native American apocalypse.

The Ghost Dancer movement spread across the American West and stirred for a time the broken hearts of Native American survivors who were enslaved in "reservations." However, most Native Americans grew impatient with Wowoka's call for a gradual healing of their relationship with whites. He believed that only with the passing of many years would practice of the ritual dance bring about a more positive world.

Impatience, mixed with brutality and neglect from the white men overseeing the reservations, saw the Sioux turn the peaceful Ghost Dancer movement into a militant rebellion in South Dakota. In the winter of 1890, the U.S. Cavalry suppressed the Ghost Dancers in a massacre of over 150 Sioux at Wounded Knee.

Eleven centuries before the massacre at Wounded Knee, Padmasambhava, the founder of Tibetan Buddhism, foresaw the day when his people and their religion would move down the mountains of Tibet to other lands. This would take place after fairer-skinned invaders from the East – the Chinese – seized their land and destroyed their culture. Once this occurred, Padmasambhava prophesied, the Tibetan religion would spread from the East to flourish "in the land of the red man."

THE KING OF SHAMBHALA, THE HIMALAYAN AVATAR

Like a diamond glows the light on the Tower of Shambhala. He is there – Rigden-jyepo, indefatigable, ever vigilant in the cause of mankind. His eyes never close. And in his magic mirror he sees all events of earth. And the might of his thought penetrates into far-off lands. Distance does not exist for him; he can instantaneously bring assistance to worthy ones. His powerful light can destroy all darkness. His immeasurable riches are ready to aid all needy ones who offer to serve the cause of righteousness. He may even change the karma of human beings.

PROPHECY OF SHAMBHALA, AS RECOUNTED BY NICHOLAS ROERICH (1920), SHMB

The Tibetans call him Rudra Cakrin or Rigden-jyepo. The Shang Tang nomads of the frozen high desert at the roof of the world call him Gessar Khan. Farther north across the Mongolian steppes, people call him the Arghati King, the Ruler of the World. He is the Tibetan-Mongolian version of the Second Coming of Christ, and like his Christian counterpart in the Book of Revelation, he wears armor and brandishes a sword. He comes in triumph to do battle with evil and establish his kingdom upon the earth for 1,000 years.

Rudra Cakrin is the king of the mystical realm of Shambhala. He is lord over a kingdom of unbelievable spiritual and temporal riches. This Camelot of soil and spirit is not easy to find. It hides somewhere between dream and reality. Shambhala's doorway to this dimension can be found somewhere between the most remote ice-barricaded valley of the Himalayas and the most secret source of enlightenment hiding behind the eyes wide shut of a holy lama. When the world sounds the depths of its iniquity, the King of Shambhala will come forth from that dimension with his spiritual warriors from every land and wage the Asian version of Armageddon against an Asian-style Antichrist.

To many Tibetans, the Chinese Communist dictator Mao Tse-tung was the Antichrist. They believe that the Communist invasion of their land, and the devastation wrought upon their monasteries and culture by a half-century of Chinese occupation, are the final signs of tribulation before the advent of the Shambhala King as their deliverer.

Not all followers of the Shambhala prophecy interpret this coming war between good and evil as a literal military crusade. They say that King Rudra's kingdom and his person are the spiritual lion hiding under the lamb's clothing of all who have traded their innate state of enlightenment for the distractions of the ego. The kingdom of Shambhala, therefore, is a silent Shangri-la buried from our view by the snowdrifts of our endless desires and mental chatter. These are the signs of the real Antichrist.

[The lamas] are thinking that they will be able to go back. They have predicted this also. They have written down everything for when the time comes. That is why they have preserved all their occult sciences. In astral traveling, every day they are visiting Tibet. They think that after the year 2000, they will be able to return there physically. His Holiness [14th Dalai Lama] told me. The cycle will change. That is what their predictions are, but I do not know whether it will come true.

HIS HOLINESS LAMA KARMAPA (1968)

THE WHITE BURKHAN

The Messiah of Central Asian nomads will come when the people of the steppes have abandoned their ancient gods. It seems we have already entered that time. The nomads abandoned their pagan gods during the days of the atheistic Soviet Union. With the passing of the Communist dictatorship, watch for the silhouette of the White Burkhan galloping from the East across the steppes. It is said that he will come to offer the Central Asians and the entire human race a spiritual rebirth.

RIGHT **The nomadic peoples of Tibet expect a Messiah who will offer spiritual rebirth to all of humankind.**

SAOSHYANT, THE SECOND COMING OF ZOROASTER

ABOVE **This illustration is from a mystical Zoroastrian work. The Zoroastrians believe in a final battle between good and evil.**

The founding father of apocalyptic and messianic traditions in the West was Zarathustra – also known as Zoroaster (*c.* 1700 B.C.E.) – the creator of the Persian Zoroastrian faith of the eternal flame. The cornerstones of Judaism's and Christianity's end-time scenario were first recorded almost ten centuries before those visualized by the Old Testament prophets. The idea of a battle between the forces of a good God and an evil devil, leading to the climactic arrival of an all-powerful savior and a judgment day for the world, parallels Zoroastrian scripture. Some biblical scholars will go so far as to say that Jewish apocalyptic scriptures borrowed Zoroastrian prophecy. The Jewish Immanuel and Christ's Second Coming could be eschatological variations on a messiah prophecy composed much earlier than these. A far more ancient vision sees the Second Coming of Zarathustra as Saoshyant, the new Persian messiah. He appears at the onset of the Zoroastrian twelfth millennium, which in Judeo-Christian calendars is around 2000 C.E.

The Islamic religion does not subscribe to the idea of a messiah. The Holy Qur'an declares it a mortal sin to designate someone like Jesus Christ as an "equal partner with Allah." Nonetheless, the Muslims honor the Christian messiah, even though they demote him from being the one and only Messiah to simply being one of God's messengers, just like their founder, the prophet Muhammad.

Muhammad and his mullahs must have agonized over what to do with Christ's crucifixion and resurrection. Jesus can't be seen blaspheming Allah if he shows divine equality with God; if, however, he merely died on the cross, they would be blaspheming one of Allah's great prophets. A prophet of God like Christ cannot die, for then he would have failed in his mission. Apparently Allah untangled the mess with a revelation to Muhammad that someone else stood in for the Christ and died in his place on the cross. Jesus therefore did not die but disappeared from the earth when Allah lifted him into heaven. As we will see, the disappearing acts of Islamic prophets of God are a cornerstone of the appearance of a final Islamic judgment-day messenger.

MUNTAZAR, THE FINAL PROPHET OF SUNNI ISLAM

In Isfahan, the city where the faithful of Allah bow in prayer beneath the mirror glitter of the Crystal Mosque, the white horse of Muntazar the Muslim messiah is saddled and waiting. Sunnis comprise 90 percent of the Islamic faithful, and Muntazar is their final prophet, successor to Muhammad, and the al-Mahdi ("the one who is at the end of time") who will unite the races of the world.

THE 12TH IMAM, THE LAST PROPHET OF SHI'ITE ISLAM

The [12th] Iman will return at a time when a thing called an "antenna" is on the way.

ALI (*c.* 650), NAZR ULAGA

The word "antenna" was an enigma to Ali, the founder of the Shi'ite sect of Islam. It did not exist in the Persian language. Yet these metallic feelers of radio and television signals date the return of the Shi'ite final prophet in our times.

Ten percent of Muslims belong to the Shi'ite sect, who differ from their Sunni brethren on how divine messages descend from Allah to the people. While Sunnis believe divine guidance, or *sunna*, comes from the consensus of the community, the Shi'ite Muslims seek *sunna* from the revelations given to their God-inspired religious leaders, or *Imams*. The Shi'ites believe their Imams are direct descendants of Muhammad's nephew, Ali, who possessed important esoteric knowledge imparted by Muhammad before he flew body and soul into heaven. Ali was the first Imam who passed his secret knowledge to his descendants – a lineage that runs for seven Imams, or twelve, depending on which of the three subsects of the Shi'ites you speak to.

The 12th-Imam sect asserts that the last Imam is hiding somewhere, and that Allah has allowed him to wait out the centuries until the Last Judgment. He will reappear alongside Jesus, whom Allah took up to heaven 2,000 years earlier. On some not-too-distant March 21 in the new millennium, Jesus and the 12th Imam will come out of hiding and restore Israel to the Arab world, thus completing the Qu'ran prophecies. The 12th Imam, also known as the *Qa'im* ("the promised one"), will step forward and rule the earth. Shi'ite prophecy states that the Qa'im "will manifest the perfection of Moses, the splendor of Jesus, and the patience of Job." He will chastise the infidel and the blasphemer.

Some Imamites venture that this final Imam is Muhammad in disguise, who will come to "fill the earth with justice after it has been filled to the brim with tyranny." He will not return until the Islamic faithful reach a critical mass of agitation for political reform and clamor for a return of religious fundamentalism.

KHIDR, THE SUFI FINAL LAWGIVER

Khidr, the Sufi final prophet, is the mysterious guide of the Islamic spiritual underground. He is the Sufi version of the Shi'ite 12th Imam and Muntazar of the Sunnis. He is the unseen master who will reappear on March 21 of some near-future year. Khidr's motto is said to be this: "Each man is a man of bright prospects because each man has God as his ultimate flowering…. Only by living it will you know it."

RIGHT **It is believed that the pyramids carry secret messages about the coming of the Messiah.**

⊙SIRIS, THE EGYPTIAN SAVI⊙R

Occultists say that the passageways leading to the King's Chamber inside the Great Pyramid of Giza contain mathematical prophecy. Major changes in the passageways' design mark milestones in the Adamic Age (4000 B.C.E. through 2000 C.E.). Interpreters of the Pyramid Prophecy claim that the final measurement between the entrance of the chamber and the opposing wall represents the latter days before the end of the world. At that time the human race will either begin a new stage of evolution in consciousness or suffer a global breakdown. The entrance to the King's Chamber marks inch number 1,953 – the time some prophets say that the emergence or rebirth of Osiris, the Egyptian Christ, will occur. If each inch in the Pyramid Prophecy represents a year on the Judeo-Christian timeline, then Osiris was born after the year 1953 and will be preaching his mission of salvation of the earth no later than September 2001.

THE AE⊙N, THE ⊙CCULT MESSIAH

Aleister Crowley, the controversial English occult mystic and self-professed messenger of the Aeon, foresaw him as the Angel of the Last Judgment. The Aeon's chief element is the fire of purification. A reincarnation of the Egyptian god Horus, the Aeon appears after the old universe and the present civilization are destroyed. He is the incarnation of innocence and is too young and tender to establish a new universe. Symbolically speaking, that means the New Era (also known as the Aquarian Age) will be guided by a more spontaneous and unpredictable destiny.

LEFT **Aleister Crowley, English mystic and occultist, claimed to be a messenger of the Last Judgment.**

THE RETURN OF KRISHNA

I have been born many times, Arjuna, and many times hast thou been born. But I remember my past lives, and thou hast forgotten thine. Although I am unborn, everlasting, and I am the Lord of all, I come to my realm of nature and through my wondrous power I am born. When righteousness is weak and faints and unrighteousness exults in pride, then my Spirit arises on earth. For the salvation of those who are good, for the destruction of evil in men, for the fulfillment of the kingdom of righteousness, I come to this world in the ages that pass. He who knows my birth as God and who knows my sacrifice, when he leaves his mortal body, goes no more from death to death, for he in truth comes to me.

KRISHNA (*c.* 3000 B.C.E.), GITA 4:5–9

Various Hindu prophecies state that when the world is in darkness, Krishna will reincarnate again as a new avatar. The ancient Hindu *Puranas* and the *Srimad Bhagavata* state that we are living in the darkest times right now. The Hindus refer to it as *Kali-yuga*, the Age of Iron and Chaos.

RIGHT **Hindus believe that Krishna will return in judgment when the Earth's skies turn dark.**

KALKI, THE LAST AVATAR OF HINDUISM

He is the 10th and final Hindu *avatar* ("incarnation of God"), also known as Javada. He will appear from the West. The vision of a triumphant Kalki mounted upon his white horse got a full 1,000-year jump on St. John's vision, in the Book of Revelation, of the Christian messiah riding down evil on a white horse.

LEFT **A shrine to Kalki, the final Hindu incarnation of God, who will arrive from the West at the end of time.**

Many interpreters of Eastern prophecy believe the Christian redeemer called "Glorious and True" is the martial reincarnation of the middle deity in the Hindu trinity comprising Brahma the Creator, Vishnu the Preserver, and Shiva the Destroyer.

Kalki is also known as the conqueror of death, of all dualities, and of darkness and unconsciousness. The whiteness of his horse symbolizes the power of his purity, the unity of all the colors of existence.

One legend says that when Kalki returns, his horse will stamp its right foot, causing the tortoise that holds up the world to fall into the void. Only then will the gods be able to restore the world to its original purity.

MAITREYA THE BUDDHA

I am not the first Buddha [awakened one] who has come upon the Earth, nor will I be the last. In due time another Buddha will rise in the world, a Holy One, a supreme enlightened one, endowed with auspicious wisdom embracing the Universe, an incomparable leader of men, a ruler of gods and mortals. He will reveal to you the same eternal truths, which I have taught you. He will establish his Law [religion], glorious in its origins, glorious at the climax and glorious at the goal in the spirit and the letter. He will proclaim a righteous life wholly perfect and pure, such as I now proclaim. His disciples will number many thousands, while mine number many hundreds. He will be known as Maitreya.

BUDDHA GAUTAMA (c. 500 B.C.E.)

The founder of Buddhism, Gautama Siddhartha, "the Buddha," proclaimed the advent of the Buddhist mainstream messiah, Maitreya. His name either means "the world unifier" or simply "the friend." He will not be the aloof and otherworldly Lord Buddha returned, but a very human god-man who Buddha predicted would be his second coming and a greater awakener of humanity than himself.

AMIDA BUDDHA

The Mahayana Buddhist messiah. He is a great Christlike Bodhisattva, scheduled to come 25 centuries after Lord Buddha (around the year 2000). His likeness, so similar to the Zen patriarch Bodhidharma, may imply that their savior is an Indian from South Asia.

RIGHT **A Nepalese statue of Maitreya Buddha, the Buddha of the future, who will come to enlighten and bring together all humanity.**

THE JAPANESE MESSIAH

> It happened in the past and it will happen again in the future that Susano will come in earthly form and all but one country will reject him. As a gift Susano gave a charm, an omamori, to the land that did not reject him – wooden talisman with two triangles merged as one.
>
> KUKAMI MONJO
> (ANCIENT JAPANESE MANUSCRIPT)

ABOVE **Susano, the god of water, will be incarnated as a Messiah according to some Japanese sects.**

Several sects of Japanese Buddhism and Shintoism foresee a variant of the Buddhist Maitreya, who is to appear after August 8, 1988 (8/8/88). He is the incarnation of the god of water, Susano. The talisman in Kukami Monjo's vision could represent the double-triangle star symbol of South Asian Tantra schools, or even the Jewish Star of David. This would give credence to the Messiah being either a Tantric master from India or the Jewish messiah, Immanuel.

THE SPIRITUAL KING,
THE INDONESIAN MESSIAH

The 12th-century Indonesian king Dojobojo had a vision of the coming of a great "Spiritual King" from the West. This would take place after three milestones were fulfilled in the history of the Indonesian people. First Indonesia would be invaded by "white-skinned, blue-eyed, and fair-haired men from the northwest." The whites would rule with an "iron hand for 350 years." Indeed the Dutch did conquer Indonesia from the northwest and ruled for 322 years, from 1610 to 1942. Next Dojobojo saw the white men overcome by new invaders – small, "slant-eyed, yellow dwarflike men" – sailing down from the northeast. But the yellow men would only rule for a short time ("one planting of corn"). This seems to refer to the four-year occupation of the Japanese.

Finally, Dojobojo promised that Indonesians would be ruled by their own people. The messianic king would not appear until the tyranny of two Indonesian dictators had ended. This appears to be a reference to Sukarno and Suharto; the latter stepped down only recently, in 1998. The downfall of the last dictator would usher in a time of "bloodshed and troubles." This could describe the Indonesian economic crash, along with the ecological disasters and social unrest that has plagued Indonesia in the late 1990s. Dojobojo promised that these crises would be short-lived. Before long, news will be received of a "Spiritual King" from the West who will come to "unite all the world's religions" as well as its races and cultures in a "thousand-year era of peace."

THE NAZI MESSIAH

The work Christ started but could not finish, I Adolf Hitler will conclude.

ADOLF HITLER (C.1930s)

Adolf Hitler is our Savior, our Hero,
He is the noblest being in the whole wide world.
For Hitler we live, for Hitler we die,
Our Hitler is our Lord.

GERMAN CHILDREN'S SONG OF PRAISE TO ADOLF HITLER

BELOW **Adolf Hitler, the most horrific modern example of the self-proclaimed Messiah.**

The old beliefs will be brought back to honor again.
The whole secret knowledge of nature, of the divine, of
the demonic. We will wash off the Christian veneer and
bring out a religion peculiar to our race.

ADOLF HITLER

The philosopher of Nature will be terrible because he will appear
in alliance with the primitive powers of Nature, able to evoke the
demoniac energies of old German Pantheism – during which
there will awake in him that battle-madness which we find
among the ancient Teutonic races who fought neither to kill nor
to conquer, but for the very love of fighting itself. It is the fairest
merit of Christianity that it somewhat mitigated that brutal
German...joy of battle, but it could not destroy it. And should
that subduing talisman, the Cross, break, then will come crashing
and roaring forth the wild madness of the old champions, the
insane Berserker rage, of which the Northern poets say and sing.
The talisman is brittle, and the day will come when it will
pitifully break. The old stone gods will rise from the long-
forgotten ruin and rub the dust of a thousand years from their
eyes, and Thor, leaping to life with his giant hammer, will crush
the Gothic cathedrals.

HEINRICH HEINE (D. 1856)

I want to see in the eyes of youth the gleam of the beast....
And when I am no longer needed, after my
mission is accomplished, then I shall be called away.

ADOLF HITLER

Nearly a full century before Hitler's reign, when Heine penned his ominous prophecy, there were secret societies of right-wing German occultists expecting the advent of a white supremacist German messiah who would save Deutschland from the Jewish taint of their Christian messiah. Adolf Hitler (d. 1945) seized power in 1933 and for 12 years was supreme leader (Führer) of Nazi Germany. This anti-Semite who believed he was the reincarnation of the prophet Elijah unleashed the closest thing to Armageddon that humanity has yet seen.

Hitler believed that Jesus Christ was the "greatest early fighter in the battle against the world enemy, the Jews." One might think the Panzer of his line of thinking had slipped its caterpillar track, but no. The Nazi messiah who thought he was the incarnation of an Old Testament prophet reasoned that Christ was only a *mischling* (a half-Jew) and as such did not follow the Jewish religion. Thus Hitler believed that Christ, by having the Holy Spirit rather than Joseph the Jew as a father, was free of the Jewish pestilence. Thanks to the Holy Spirit and a virgin birth, even the mischling messiah could have squeaked past the Nazi racial purity test to become an SS officer.

A few days before he committed suicide, the war-worn and depressed Führer let his mind play with a vision of a future Nazi messiah, to the chaotic and muffled boombox beat of Russian artillery shells vibrating the cement walls of his bunker in Berlin. The man who had already foretold the Cold War with chilling accuracy added:

"It is all finished. National Socialism is dead and will never rise again! Perhaps, in a hundred years or so, someone might appear who would bring the idea back to life. Perhaps a similar movement might arise with the power of a religion and spread throughout the world."

ABOVE **Victims of Messianism: a group of Jewish survivors from one of the Nazi concentration camps.**

RUTH MONTGOMERY'S NEW AGE MESSIAH

The New Age movement has been around long enough to establish its own dogma of what the Messiah will be like. If various summoned entities are correct – like those spirits who guide the hand of former journalist-turned-medium Ruth Montgomery – then their revised view of the Bible's good news just gets "gooder" in the new millennium.

But first there's a catch. Before the New Age Christ comes, there will be a catastrophic shift in the Earth's rotational axis. Montgomery's spirit guides insist that this shift will happen soon. That means the earth could capsize in space anytime after we've either inharmoniously converged with 2000, or during the grand alignment of many planets around May 5, 2000.

After the tsunamis and the thousand-mile-an-hour winds subside, most of the world's continents will have suffered a huge facelift. Yet Ruth Montgomery's guides foresee the survival of enough infrastructure for our civilization to muddle on. The survivors are helped in this endeavor by a charismatic visionary who does not hold office but exerts tremendous influence on the leaders and people of the earth through his control of world media. This two-faced fellow is the dreaded Antichrist. But ultimately this Dr. Jekyll and Mr. Hitler character fails to create a global police state, and at last he is hanged by a mob.

Two years after the death of the Antichrist, Montgomery's guides believe there will come a man born from the same entity who was the Virgin Mary the last time, but this time will give birth to the spirit of the New Age Christ. Meanwhile, many souls will return to earth to pave the way for the new Messiah. Some are human souls, while others are extraterrestrials on hiatus from their alien habitats. Some are born into bodies, while others, called Walk-ins, switch souls with beings already biped-aling along in their human containers.

The New Age Christ transmigrates sometime around the 2020s through the 2050s. Everyone will recognize him, it seems, and through him God will establish his kingdom on earth. War will be forgotten and wounds healed by a patient and loving savior, and humanity will live happily and harmonically converged ever after.

THE IDIOTIC MESSIAHS

You should read some of the correspondence from my admiring readers. It seems that I am a very popular guy with a number of heavy-duty holy ones around the world.

"Dear Mr. Hogue," begins this particular brand of letter, "I have read your books and find them to be the most informed I've encountered. I especially like your discourses and examinations of who you think the next great spiritual catalyst or savior may be. However, there is this one small problem. For some reason you have overlooked me...."

And so it goes on, often for pages and pages. The miffed and overlooked messiah in question usually chases his divine drunkenness with a boilermaker of elaborate notes, diagrams, press clippings, and whatnot to break the back of my mail carrier and prove his point beyond any doubt.

Conversely, there are folks who wish to have my seal of approval to be proclaimed the Antichrist. A week rarely goes by without my usually normal and mainstream haystack of fan mail hiding a needling from some "bloody Alice" who wants me to acknowledge her as Nostradamus's *Bloody Alus*.

I receive faxes from archangels, too.

I get registered letters from reincarnated Apostles, and postdated proposals from final prophets.

You should see my letter filing system. We have every primary savior and supernormal being neatly indexed under the heading "Koo Koo Messiahs." Next in line come the archangels and lesser angels, which are divided into subfiles. For instance, I file the letter under "Cetacean" if the writer claims to channel angelic dolphins, or "Elvis Archangels" if he is a humanoid angel sending me thrilling snapshots of his costume armor and his chicken-feathered wings.

I put all the St. Johns, St. Pauls, and St. Ringos in the "Reincarnated Apostles" file. I really shouldn't tell anyone about the little black book listing the names and addresses of all the girls who believe they have had a past life piece of Aleister Crowley's oversexed oversoul. So far my file on Princess Di and Mother Teresa sightings remains almost empty.

If I didn't know there were so many messiahs, angels, aliens, channeled dolphins, and Antichrists out there rooting for me, I might not have written this book.

LEFT **Elvis lives! Contemporary stardom and the desire to confer immortality on our heroes shows that the messianic habit is hard to break.**

SIGNS OF THE END TIMES

Drought, famine, disease and war will sweep the world. People will no longer have any religion to which they can turn for solace or liberation: the doctrines of materialism will overwhelm their minds and drive them to struggle for their own selfish ends. The lust for power and wealth will prevail over teachings of compassion and truth. Nations will fight nations, and the larger will devour the smaller.

PROPHECY OF SHAMBHALA (BEF. 700 C.E.)

SIGNS OF THE END TIMES

Hear from the signs which will be at the end of this world, when the end of the world will be fulfilled before my elect come forth from the world.

Y'SHUA (BEF. 5TH CENTURY C.E.), A OF T

This earth stands assailed at present by the age of Kali, the helpmate of unrighteousness. There is no truthfulness...purity of body and mind, and compassion, nor is there generosity to the poor. The people are sick at heart and engaged only in filling their bellies. They make false statements.

THE SRIMAD BHAGAVATA (BEF. 300 C.E.)

The Age of Evil has come to the world.... Everyone steals and hoards great wealth, and sensual sin rules the day. The end of the world is at hand — yet men are hard and cruel, and listen not to the doom that is coming .... No one heeds the cries of his neighbor, or lifts a hand to save.

THE RAGNARÖK: ANCIENT NORSE PROPHECY

When a cow has all four of her legs with all hooves planted firmly on the ground, she can easily graze her fill and make milk. Take away her right front leg and she can still manage to stand, albeit with some strain, while she chews her cud. Cut a hind leg and she lurches drunkenly when lowering her muzzle to shave the grass. Cut a third leg (the remaining hind leg) and she makes a poor specimen of an upended cow.

Now you might ask, "What in the world does this cow have to do with messiahs, coming at the end of time?" A lot, if you are a Hindu who loves bovine metaphors.

The Hindus are among the most ancient time-counters in human history. They believe that history runs in cycles of great cosmic eras, or *kalpas,* each of which can be divided into four smaller eras, or *yugas.* The course of spiritual and social health of each passing yuga is comparable to the stability of a cow losing one leg at a time. In the first *Sat-yuga* (the Era of Truth), her balance of spiritual and material existence is four-square and harmonious. In the *Dwapa-yuga* (the Second Age), she is still well and able to put up a good stance, but she begins to lose balance in her spiritual and material nature. But in the Third Age, the *Tretta-yuga,* the signs of material and spiritual lameness are clearly overtaking her. At last the final and darkest era comes, where all balance is lost – the *Kali-yuga,* or the Age of Iron and Chaos. In this age the kalpa has entered its Cretaceous era, its age of decay and death. This is autumnal history entering its wintertime, before the tender spring of a new kalpa and a new Age of Truth can grow from its corruption and begin the cosmic cycle once again.

LEFT **Two cows block a busy Bombay street. Their status in Hindu culture is sacred, and they are often seen roaming cities unhindered.**

ABOVE **Deer sculpted from stone gaze at a Buddhist wheel of Dharma representing unity and the cycle of time. The wheel is symbolically pushed to begin a new era.**

The gear action of the Hindus' timekeeping is essentially the same as in other ancient clocks. Other calendars may be longer or shorter, or may run faster or slower, but whether we are talking about the Hindu yugas, or the Buddhist Wheel of Dharma (religion) needing a fresh push every 25 centuries, or even about the Christians holding their breath every millennium for an ascent into the clouds to Christ, we are talking about a cycle of entropy. The eras of earthly paradise devolve into hells on earth before returning to a new Golden Age and a new cycle of decline.

Many are the various timekeepers of the past who share a belief that the darkest eras end with the advent of spiritual catalysts who cast off the gloom and sin with their enlightenment, or renovate truth as one might push a stalled prayer wheel into renewed spinning.

There are striking degrees of consensus in the apocalyptic prophecies of Eastern, Western, and other seers that describe the present day as the spiritually corrupted end time before the advent of new John the Baptists and Baha'i Babs proclaiming their invasion of saviors for a new Golden Age.

THE KALI YUGA: AGE OF IRON AND CHAOS

Is it possible that we really are living at the end of history? What follows is just a small selection of the hundreds of presaged signs that point to our current uncontrolled population growth and consumerism, our besieged traditions, our global weather disruption, and the lack of state or religious leadership in dealing with them as the clarion calls of the end before the advent. The foreseen era is that of the Christian Tribulation, the Viking Ragnarök, the Jewish Armageddon, or whatever label a religion stamps on its white-hot chastisement branding iron, probing for the shivering loin of the yuga-cow of our time.

WEIRD CLOTHES AND LOTS OF SEX

The signs of these times are new and fantastical modes of dressing – traditional styles forgotten.

PADMASAMBHAVA (8TH CENTURY C.E.), STUPA

Chastity shall be broken with maidens, wives and widows, religious men and virgins, with more ill than I can tell of, from that which God us defend.

MERLIN (5TH CENTURY C.E.)

The learned pandits [Hindu theologians] for their part indulge in sexual commerce with their wives like buffaloes. They are expert in breeding children and are not at all clever in attaining Enlightenment…the substance and depth of things has disappeared everywhere.

THE SRIMAD BHAGAVATA (BEF. 300 C.E.)

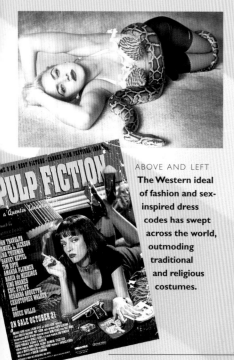

ABOVE AND LEFT
The Western ideal of fashion and sex-inspired dress codes has swept across the world, outmoding traditional and religious costumes.

Let fall the lungis, pull on your Levis. Across the world traditional attire is disappearing. Gone are the folk dresses, the veils, the sexless blue and gray Mao uniforms. Discarded saris, dhotis, and sarongs nestle in greater numbers with the mothballs in Third World closets.

The covetous and inviting curves and bulges once covered from sight by baggy Punjabi kurta pants and full-length veils and chadors now emerge in well-packed jeans. First World sloppy or sexy mores are a global craze.

The modern-day media that interconnect the world deliver a kaleidoscope of divergent and often schizophrenic messages. On the television one sees family values rub and byte together with sex and titillation. In the print media and on the Internet, those displaying erotic pictures can tape a slash as black as a Jesuit's robe over the nipples and private parts of nude lovers. On television one constantly sees those little clouds cloaked in black appear and disappear in front of a man or woman's exposed buttocks as if they are being chased and shaded from view by the ghost of an indignant nun. Either the world is suffering an unprecedented rash of sexual permissiveness, immorality, and teen pregnancy or the information age has accidentally stripped a false and enforced morality off a natural human promiscuity once kept under traditional wraps.

The prophets of earlier times must be horrified by the ragbag of skimpy things we wear today. To them it signals the plague of unwholesomeness they expect just prior to their messiah buttoning things up right.

END-TIME EMPIRES OF THE PENTAGON STAR

For five full cycles of the Dawn Star, the rule of the warring strangers will go on to greater and greater orgies of destruction.... Their path will lead to the Last Destruction. Know that the end will come in five full cycles, for five, the difference between the Earth's number and that of the Gleaming Dawn Star, is the number of these children of warfare.

THE SONG OF QUETZALCOATL (PRE-COLUMBIAN), HEW

Everything in the world will be at sixes and sevens when the superpowers of the fives dominate geopolitics – that is, if author Kristina Gale-Kumar's *(Phoenix Rising)* interpretations of the prophecies attributed to Kate-Zahl (Quetzalcoatl) are correct. The recently departed Soviet Union had a five-pointed star on its flag, the United States has fifty five-pointed stars on its flag, and the flag of China has a pentad of five-pointed stars. Even the flag of the world's first supernation, the European Union (E.U.), has a circle of twelve five-pointed stars. The five-sided U.S. Pentagon building is the nerve center of the "warring strangers" of the strongest and only surviving superpower in the world.

Beyond what Gale-Kumar proposes, I would add that many apocalyptic traditions within Judeo-Christianity believe that the penta-starred nations China and the E.U. will be at the peak of their power in the final days. China is marked down to offer a serious challenge to America as the next competing superpower, while many Christians, including even Pope John Paul II, have voiced their concern that the nations of the E.U. could become the new Roman Empire of the great beast mentioned in Bible prophecy.

"Five full cycles of the dawn star" Venus may date this prophecy for fulfillment sometime after the fifth century anniversary (1992) of white Christopher Columbus's discovery of the Americas.

Some interpreters date the fifth cycle's completion by counting from the year Hernando Cortés conquered the Aztec Indians (1521), which means the fifth cycle does not end until 2020. Many prophecy watchers believe the decade of the 2020s will see a collapse of civilization from a food and water crisis brought on by overpopulation.

ABOVE, CENTER
The pentagram – five-pointed star – is favored by a variety of powerful organizations and nations such as China and the U.S.

ABOVE **Pope John Paul II has warned against the new-born power of the E.U.**

LEFT **The E.U. flag is studded with pentagrams, a significant symbol for apocalypse watchers.**

GREED AND CONSUMPTION
ON AN UNPRECEDENTED SCALE

People in that era [Kali age] turn out to be greedy, immoral and merciless;
they freely enter into violence without cause and are unlucky and excessively covetous.

THE SRIMAD BHAGAVATA (BEF. 300 C.E.)

ABOVE **The floor of the stock exchange is a place of extreme energy dictated by powerful organizations.**

ABOVE **As modern consumers we are swamped by choice and bombarded by commercial campaigns.**

The American dream is fast becoming the world's nightmare. Since the end of the Cold War, America's politicians and businessmen have had nearly worldwide success in promoting the virtues of high-energy (and high-waste), market-driven economies. While the United States represents just 4 percent of the world's population, it uses 25 percent of the world's available energy. U.S. corporate gurus want the other 96 percent of the world's potential consumers to forget the insanity of the math and covet the good American life and live in the fast-and-fat-food like the affluent American minority.

Just how many people can live off this fragile planet with its finite resources and sustain the American waste-side market appetites? Only 2.5 billion, says the Worldwatch Institute. The world's current 6 billion people will breed an extra billion trash-makers and water polluters every 11 years for the next 50 years. Each year sees hundreds of millions of people in the Third World adopt a high-consumption American middle-class lifestyle. They abandon the frugal habits of the poorer generations before them, who were not allowed to forget that resources and energy are precious and finite. The hundreds of millions of people pedaling earth- and air-friendly bicycles on today's Third World streets will soon replace them with smog-belching cars.

To waste like Americans, many people desire to eat like Americans. They wish to adopt a diet high in animal products. The livestock for our hamburgers must devour a huge amount of valuable nutrients (in the form of grains) to produce a relatively modest yield of meat for the table. The lust for eating meaty hockey-puck patties made of ground-up cow sandwiched between ever supremely whiter-than-white buns pro-motes the degradation of global systems. This can only bring more starvation to the impoverished have-nots and more high-fat-related health problems and heart disease to the haves.

Finally, the merciless propagation of American-style consumerism to a world population expected to clear 11 billion souls by 2040 will demand that agriculture satiate its hunger *each year* with the same volume of food it took to feed all the people who devoured food from the beginning of human history to the year 2000!

RIGHT **The hamburger is an icon of fast-food and a high-speed lifestyle.**

FAMILY DISCORD

The warlike fall upon the peaceful, brothers kill brothers, and even children soil one another's blood.

FROM THE RAGNARÖK: ANCIENT NORSE PROPHECY

There are numerous quarrels between husband and wife.

THE SRIMAD BHAGAVATA (BEF. 300 C.E.)

Parents shall be hated by their children.

MERLIN (5TH CENTURY)

BELOW **Living alone has become commonplace in our society.**

All your culture is on the surface; inside there is conflict, inside there is deep hatred. More than hatred, there is frustration that, "You have deceived me, the dreams of love which you had given me have not been fulfilled. You had promised me a path covered with flowers but there are only thorns, nothing more."

Fathers are unhappy with their sons, sons are unhappy with their fathers, mothers are unhappy with their children, children are unhappy with their mothers. Nobody is happy with anybody else, because there is no love. This so-called love is attached to other motives and those motives are the basis of suffering.

[People's] ambitions will collide because nobody has come into this world to fulfill another's ambitions. Everybody has his own ambitions, his own bondages of karma. Every man has been born to be himself. If you have even the slightest expectation of somebody else it will work like a poison.

OSHO (1976), SHWR

LEFT **Pupils of Littleton High School, U.S.A., mourn the death of their peers at the hands of fellow students.**

A fire alarm rings and American elementary-school children file out into the playground. Their playmates who set off the alarm hide under trees at the edge of the playground, then pick them off with rifle fire.

In India a man brandishing a match corners his young bride – her sari reeks of kerosene. He is her husband, and because her dowry is not flush enough, there is hellfire to pay.

When I walk the streets of Seattle, one of America's most affluent cities, I often step over the prone bodies of refugees from broken homes, the young and dispossessed sleeping in the streets. So many of my women friends are single mothers. So many parents work to sustain their lifestyle at the cost of precious time with their kids. Parents work too long and too hard, children grow up alone, and grandparents they cannot afford to keep are wheeled away into old folks' homes. Perhaps the clarion call of moralists for a return to the traditional gospel of family values has become so strident and divisive these days because they sense that the nuclear family is actually in a catastrophic final nuclear meltdown.

Consider the statistics on the state of the family in the United States today (the nation all others desire to emulate), and one might conclude we have entered the "end times." In 1996, Purdue University's Center for Families issued a report revealing shocking trends. Between 1985 and 1990 (a mere five years), single-parent families rose from 22.7 percent to 25.8 percent, the birth rate of unmarried teenagers rose by 16 percent, the rate of violent deaths among 15- to 19-year-olds rose from 62.8 to 71.1 per 100,000, and the high school graduation rate dropped from 71.6 percent to 68.8 percent. Infant mortality has risen to 8.9 deaths for each 1,000 births, the highest in the industrialized world. From 1980 to 1992, child poverty rates rose by 19.7 percent and cases of child abuse and neglect tripled to 2.9 million. Preliminary statistics gathered in the years since 1990 show that the markers of family health continue to be in steady decline.

BELOW **The breakdown of the nuclear family has led to vagrancy and homelessness, a feature of modern cities across the world.**

THE END OF ETHICS AND MORAL LEADERSHIP

The Prince shall forsake men of the church, Lords shall forsake righteousness, counsel of aged men shall not be set by; religious fear shall not know which way to turn them.

MERLIN (5TH CENTURY)

The arrogant elevate profanity. The proletariat rules the kingdom; kings become paupers; the butchers and murderers become leaders of men; unscrupulous self-seekers rise to high position.

PADMASAMBHAVA (8TH CENTURY C.E.), STUPA

When things come to such a pass, justice, nobility, authority are lost; there is no longer a distinction between good and evil deeds. The masters and the disciples, the judges and the judged – all are carriers of this poisonous contagion. And, in fact, because they have lost all awareness of one another as such, they make light of others, blame others, quarrel with them – to such an extent that there is no longer a recognition of such relationships as parent and child, husband and wife, teacher and disciple, master and servant. The whole world everywhere ensnarled and entangled with all kinds of confusion continues to heap up for itself disorder and squabbling in grand scale.

TAMO-SAN (1960), LOOK

The final decade of the Second Christian Millennium has seen 68 convictions among Catholic priests in North America, costing the church's tithers in excess of $400 million in legal fees. Some 400 more such cases are still pending litigation.

In Buddhist Thailand monks ride in limousines paid for by a lucrative black market in which good luck charms are "blessed" and peddled at premium prices. A number of Buddhist monasteries have joined the drug trafficking business in Southeast Asia. The good brothers of the Dharma drop the study of self-awareness for the profitable business of making people more unconscious through narcotics.

Widespread cheating on exams reaches all the way to the hallowed institutions of the United States Air Force and Naval Academies. Television audiences no longer give good ratings to measured journalism. End time chimes in when politicians are no longer beholden to voters but only to special interests, and voters disengage from the political process, opting instead for the TV remote. It will be time for the savior to appear when issues are crowded out by scandals and the threshold of the new millennium becomes a gate: that is, a Watergate, an Iran-Contragate, a Paulagate, a Travelgate, a Chinagate, a "Lincoln Bedroom"-gate, and finally President Clinton's Zippergate.

LEFT AND RIGHT **American-style politics breeds international scandal from Nixon's involvement in the Watergate affair to Clinton's relations with Monica Lewinsky.**

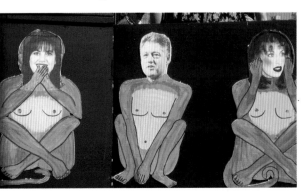

RELIGIONS ABANDONED

Drunkards preach the Path to Salvation.... Guileful impostors claim psychic powers....
False doctrines are devised from the Buddha's Word and the teachers' interpretations
become self-vindications.... Ideas are established contrary to traditions.

PADMASAMBHAVA (8TH CENTURY C.E.), STUPA

Those who present themselves as saints are constantly engaged in preaching false
doctrines. Those who have apparently renounced the world are rich in worldly
possessions, and have become family men.

THE SRIMAD BHAGAVATA (BEF. 300 C.E.)

Men of worship shall have no reverence of their inferiors.

MERLIN (5TH CENTURY)

In the coming years, great evangelical "revivals" will sweep through all countries, side
by side with Anarchy, Atheism, and Free Thought of every kind. Civilization will,
chameleon-like, change its color to suit each new wave of thought, and Chaos will
drive her chariot of destruction through fields of Peace into the avenues of War.

KEIRO (1931), CWP

Every sacred voice of the word of God will be silenced.... Such is the senility of the
world: atheism, dishonor, and disregard of noble words.

HERMES TRISMEGISTUS (2ND CENTURY C.E.), ASC 21–2

The Vatican's power fades while Voodoo becomes a world religion. Gay priests report that 40 percent of the Catholic clergy are practicing homosexuals. The Earth religions of neo-pagans are on the rise again just when the fundamentalists had thought their past inquisitions had burnt and tortured the heretics out of existence. Many religions are seeing an exodus of priests, while women around the world clamor to break out of their traditional subservient roles as second-string humans to God's creation – man – and demand ordination as priests.

Politicians promote Judeo-Christian beliefs that no longer hold the interest of their people. Faith fades as the Internet's data stream enlightens society to be more skeptical about such matters as virgin births, sons of God, salvation, and resurrection. Religions demanding obedience to God are being crowded out by those that promote personal responsibility. Hinduism falls to humanism, and the Buddhist Dharma is supplanted by doubt in these ending times.

LEFT **Roman Catholic Cardinals no longer inspire credibility or wield the power of former generations.**

HUMAN HEALTH FALTERING

The evil effects of Kali make the bodies of men get reduced in size and they will appear emaciated.... [They will be] oppressed by famine and heavy taxation.... [Their] land being divested of food, grains, and stricken with fear of droughts, people in the Kali age will ever remain disturbed in mind. Stripped of clothes and ornaments, nay even food and drink, bed and sexual happiness, they will go even without a bath and put on the appearance of a fiend [hippies and punk rockers?]. Quarreling even for a very small sum of money...having cast all goodwill to the winds, people in Kali-yuga will slay even their own family and part with their own dear life.

THE SRIMAD BHAGAVATA (BEF. 300 C.E.)

Famine, frost and hail govern many unproductive years...release[ing] diseases, horrible epidemics and plagues which spread like wildfire, striking men and cattle.

PADMASAMBHAVA (8TH CENTURY C.E.), STUPA

Already vexed by famine and heavy taxation, people will perish through drought, excessive cold, storms, scorching sunshine, heavy rain, snowfall and mutual conflict. In the age of Kali men will be tormented by hunger and thirst, sicknesses and worry.

THE SRIMAD BHAGAVATA (BEF. 300 C.E.)

New plagues will arise before the savior comes. As man bulldozes and burns the rain forests he not only destroys the places where 60 percent of all life on Earth lives, but he also exposes himself to 60 percent of all the viruses on the planet. Only in our times can Monday see you deep in a Central African jungle, and Tuesday on a plane to Paris, London, or New York. By Wednesday you may feel a flu coming on. Little do you know that you are carrying a new plague and that your sneezing and coughing have infected those on the Congo bus, the trains, the jets – and everyone you meet on a First World city street – with a new incurable organ-hemorrhaging pestilence. Ebola, AIDS, and the general sickening of humanity by chemical pollution are a hallmark of our "end" times.

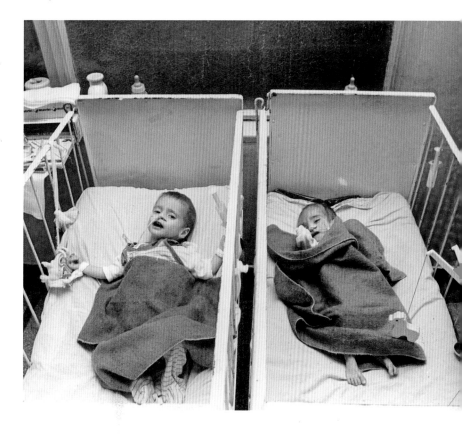

RIGHT **Victims of the deadly AIDS epidemic include tiny babies in this Romanian hospital.**

WEIRD WEATHER

When the great time will come, in which mankind will face its last, hard trial, it will be foreshadowed by violent changes in nature. The alteration between cold and heat will become more extreme. Storms will have more catastrophic results.

JOHANNES FRIEDE (D. 1257)

No rain falls in season, but out of season; the valleys are flooded.

PADMASAMBHAVA (8TH CENTURY C.E.), STUPA

The air will be diseased. Such is the senility of the world.

HERMES TRISMEGISTUS (2ND CENTURY C.E.), ASC 21–2

The decade of the 1990s has been the warmest on the planet since records began. The years 1990, 1995, 1997, and 1998 each set new all-time worldwide heat records.

The final years before the millennium have also seen a dramatic rise in severe weather conditions. The U.S. National Oceanographic and Atmospheric Administration (NOAA) predicts a new 25-year cycle of violent hurricanes. Other climate watchers believe we are in for as much as 250 years of violent weather thanks to the gradual warming of the atmosphere by air pollution.

Lethal tornadoes are on the increase in America. The warmer skies and seas that spawned the most destructive hurricane in modern memory in the fall of 1998 – Hurricane Mitch – are a precursor to storms that climatologists believe will be 50 percent more destructive during the next century than the worst storms of the 20th. Mitch's apocalyptic winds and rains killed as many as 24,000 people, left millions homeless, and destroyed the infrastructure of three Central American countries, setting Nicaragua, Belize, and Honduras back 20 years.

What would happen to the economies of the world if such storms devastated whole countries not once in a decade, but once or twice every year? Would this not be a sign that the Messiah's return was nigh?

GREAT FIRES

And the path of the winds will be confused and agitated...and all around will be noise and uproar, and everywhere there will be conflagrations...and fires will blaze on all sides.

THE MAHABHARATA
(*c.* 3000 B.C.E)

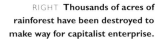

RIGHT **Thousands of acres of rainforest have been destroyed to make way for capitalist enterprise.**

In 1997 and 1998 the skies over Malaysia and Indonesia were the color of mashed mangoes. If you sucked in the air it wasn't sweet and fresh, it was two-cigarette-packs-a-day worth of yellow smoke from the slash and burn of huge forest fires raging out of control. The climatic anomaly El Niño had dried out the monsoon winds, and men set the Indonesian rain forests ablaze.

The summer of 1997 saw firestorms rage out of control across Mexico and Florida for several months. The Australian states of Victoria and New South Wales suffered some of their worst brush fires in a decade, as did the watersheds of the Spanish and French Riviera.

Satellite surveillance of the Amazon rain forest from 1997 through 1999 proved beyond doubt that the rate of rain-forest destruction is once again on the increase. Hungry fires have resumed their consumption of the rain forest with greater ferocity. In a time of global droughts caused by El Niño, Amazonian settlers have slashed and burned the rain forest with the biggest fires on record to blaze a path for hamburger ranches.

LEFT **Tornadoes sweep across the U.S. with alarming regularity destroying homes and businesses.**

EARTHQUAKES AND NATURAL DISASTERS ON THE RISE

Earthquakes bring sudden floods while fire storms and tornadoes destroy temples, stupas and cities in an instant.

PADMASAMBHAVA (8TH CENTURY C.E.), STUPA

Earthquakes will devastate greater regions.

JOHANNES FRIEDE (D. 1257)

There shall be earthquakes in diverse places, and there shall be famines and troubles.

Y'SHUA (c. 30 C.E.), MK 13:7–8

The forces of nature are growing ever more turbulent it seems. There was a marked rise in recorded earthquakes and volcanic eruptions during the 20th century, and this trend shows no sign of slacking as we enter the next millennium.

In March 1997 the state of Florida experienced its worst single tornado cluster in history. Ten twisters vacuumed up and slammed down 1,700 apartments, mobile homes, and houses, killing 42 people, and injuring several hundred more. The following month saw a monster tornado, with peak winds of 250 miles an hour, buzz-saw a mile-wide swath of near-biblical desolation across Jefferson County, Alabama.

During a normal calendar year in the Mississippi valley, January usually sees the fewest tornado events of any month; however, the first 22 days of January 1999 saw 102 twisters rake the Mississippi valley – twice as many tornadoes as there were in the last record January, more than 50 years earlier.

LEFT **Despite special reinforcements, a bridge crumbles in an earthquake in North America. Earthquakes are on the increase around the world.**

Along with increased seismic activity and killer storms, you will know it is time for the Messiah to set things straight when the world suffers unprecedented famines. The year 1998 saw 80 million new mouths to feed; 1999 will see 80 million more. You can keep adding this number of 2 percent annual growth each year *ad conceptum, ad nauseam,* for decades to come. The green revolution miraculously doubled harvests over the last 50 years, especially in the breadbasket of North America, yet it is showing signs of faltering. Global yields of the chief grains used for human consumption – wheat, corn, and rice – have leveled off since 1990, yet the population increased by nearly another billion over the following nine years. Expect it to increase by a billion people every 11 years to come.

ABOVE **Intensive agriculture tries to meet the demand of the world population, while destroying the fertility of the land that we rely on.**

RIGHT **China alone will devour the entire global food supply if output does not improve.**

The remedy put forth by experts is to farm with increasing intensity on ever more exhausted land. They propose this at a time when governments are cutting down their investments in agricultural research to give a tax break to consumers. Yields have grown an average of 1.1 percent a year since 1990, yet the food demand is over half again as large as the supply every year. What will happen 30 years hence, when all the efforts at the end of the 1990s to produce and export grains around the world will not be enough to feed China for a *single* year? Forget feeding Africa, or the billion-plus souls in India; just the Chinese alone will gobble the world's grain reserves like locusts. Are these the "famines and troubles" needed for a deliverer to return?

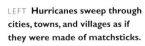

LEFT **Hurricanes sweep through cities, towns, and villages as if they were made of matchsticks.**

OCEANS WILL RISE!

And there shall be signs in the sun, and in the moon, and in the stars; and upon the earth distress of nations, with perplexity; the sea and the waves roaring.

Y'SHUA (*c.* 30 C.E.), LK 21:25

The seas will flood many lowlands. Not all of it will be the result of natural causes, but mankind will bore into the bowels of the earth and will reach into the clouds, gambling with its own existence. Before the forces of destruction will succeed in their design the universe will be thrown into disorder, and the age of iron will plunge into nothingness.

JOHANNES FRIEDE (D. 1257)

In those days the earth will not be stable, and men will not sail the sea, nor will they know the stars in heaven.

HERMES TRISMEGISTUS (2ND CENTURY C.E.), ASC 21–29

Some climatic scientists have brought forward their estimations of a potential Antarctic meltdown by a few decades. Some believe that in as little time as the next few decades the India-sized Ross Ice Shelf could slide into the southern oceans. This might bring the world's sea level up by 20 feet, flooding 70 percent of the populated areas and 90 percent of the arable land that feeds the refugees! There will certainly be distress among the nations then.

The signs in the sky are no less ominous. Airplane lights transit the stars, and the doomsday thunder of jet engines bedevils the peaceful skies. These are the sounds and images any biblical prophet could interpret as fantastic final warnings before the return of the Messiah.

LEFT **The ocean rising to flood the earth is not just a biblical myth as we face the reality of the Antarctic meltdown.**

WARS AND THE RUMOR OF WARS

And when ye shall hear of wars and rumors of wars, be ye not troubled: for such things must needs be; but the end shall not be yet. For nation shall rise against nation, and kingdom against kingdom…these are the beginnings of sorrows.

Y'SHUA (c. 30 C.E.), MK 13:7–8

Drought, famine, disease and war will sweep the world. People will no longer have any religion to which they can turn for solace or liberation: the doctrines of materialism will overwhelm their minds and drive them to struggle for their own selfish ends. The lust for power and wealth will prevail over teachings of compassion and truth. Nations will fight nations, and the larger will devour the smaller.

PROPHECY OF SHAMBHALA (BEF. 700 C.E.)

The coming of a messiah "needs" many little wars and much civil strife. Global conflicts are down since their all-time high of 52 in 1992, shortly after the end of the Cold War. Worldwatch reported as few as 27 wars on earth by 1997. However, this number could rise catastrophically in the next century if food and water industries in the next few years can no longer keep up with our numbers, and if the global economy cannot absorb the assault of more hurricanes and natural disasters caused by runaway global warming and rising oceans. World War III may be a global civil war that starts when the supersystems sustaining civilization break down, and we all have to fight for scarce resources.

The first dress rehearsal for such a breakdown may have come by the time you read this. As the calendar switches to "2000," the electronic supersystem of time-based computer chips shuts down across the world because the computers can't read the "00" when they flip over from the last midnight of the old millennium. Less technologically dependent countries may take their opportunity to wage war when the Israeli or U.S. global positioning and surveillance satellites go off-line. A computer crash in the American military lasting for hours, weeks, or even months could leave intelligence sources with nothing but rumors of a real war that China wages on Taiwan, or North Korea wages on South Korea, or Iraq wages on its neighbors.

ABOVE **The end of the second millennium threatened to bring chaos to computer systems across the globe. As the clock struck midnight, what would happen to our microchip security?**

HOLY MOTHERS TO THE RESCUE

LEFT **The Virgin Mary in standard guise from a Renaissance panel painted by Jacopp del Sellaio in 1473. Christ's mother is the go-between who defends sinful humanity against the righteous anger of her Son.**

To save souls, the Lord desires that devotion to my [the Blessed Virgin's] Immaculate Heart be established in the world. If what I tell you is done, many souls will be redeemed and there will be peace.... Otherwise, great errors will be spread through the world, giving rise to wars and persecutions against the Church; the good will suffer martyrdom and the Holy Father [the pope] will have to suffer much; different nations will be destroyed; but, in the end, my Immaculate Heart will triumph and an era of peace will be conceded to humanity.

THE PROPHECY OF FÁTIMA (JULY 13, 1917)

Mary began salvation, and by her intercession it will be finished.... An unusual chastisement of the human race will take place towards the end of the world.

BLESSED SISTER MARY OF AGREDA (1665)

Which likeness of the Savioress you see depends on where you were born. In the West the feminine archetype of salvation is an apparition of the Virgin Mary, hovering above Coptic bell towers of Egypt or plastered on burritos in Grandma's oven on Van Nuys, California. Her mild and loving form appears on almost every surface imaginable in the guise of a usually Nordic-skinned Jewish mother with a Gentile nose job.

Go East to Nepal, Sikkim, and Tibet, and your apparition of the Holy Mother is definitely not Jewish – not a virgin, either – and she's green. The goddess Tara visits the people on the roof of the world.

In the West those of the Marian cult of final visitations before the apocalypse believe she has appeared over 400 times in the 20th century alone, and the visitations are accelerating. The most significant appearance – and one of the few sanctioned by the Roman Catholic Church as authentic –

LEFT **Tibetan Buddhists worship the green goddess Tara, who is believed to have mystical associations with the earth.**

took place in 1917, in a field near Fátima, Portugal. Three shepherd children regularly prayed to an apparition no one else could see. During the last visitation, as proof that the Virgin occupied the empty space above a little bush, the three children and 80,000 people waiting in a driving rainstorm saw the sun part the clouds and turn into an orange fireball that fell and rose in the sky. Most of those present found their clothes had been blow-dried once the sun – or what some latter-day interpreters of the miracle thought was the Virgin's UFO – finished its flying show. Many of the sick and infirm among the witnesses declared they were healed.

The Virgin imparted to Lucia, the eldest of the shepherd children, a set of prophecies, some of which accurately foresaw the end of World War I, the rise of Communism in Russia, and the threat of a second world war. The Vatican leaked the last and secret prophecy in 1960. It describes a final battle of Armageddon using nuclear weapons. The Blessed Virgin warned that if people do not say their rosary and pray to her, then she can no longer stay the angry hand of the Prince of Peace. Her son Jesus will chastise sinful humanity for its errors and spiritual incorrectness with wars, earthquakes, plagues, and disasters.

In the East, Tara is a Holy Mother of all goddesses, who will reincarnate in the near future in the guise of a shrewish wife to trigger the mother of all final battles between good and evil. She will be queen of an evil one whom Tibetan prophecy calls the Great Barbarian King (the Eastern version of the Antichrist). She shows this Anti-Buddha a vision of the lavish kingdom of Shambhala in the smoke of burning incense. Tara saves the world by nourishing her husband's pride and pushing the Anti-Buddhist Barbarian potentate into a ruinous war with the king of Shambhala, the Tibetan Avatar, Rudra Cakrin.

THE FORERUNNERS

Behold, I will send you Elijah the prophet before the coming of the great and dreadful day of the Lord.

MALACHI (*c.* 500–450 B.C.E), MAL 4:5

Elias [Elijah] truly shall first come and restore all things. But I say unto you, that Elias is come already, and they knew him not, but have done unto him whatsoever they listed. Likewise shall also the Son of man suffer of them.

Y'SHUA (*c.* 30 C.E.), MT 17:11–12

And from the days of John the Baptist until now the kingdom of heaven suffereth violence, and the violent take it by force. For all the prophets and the Law prophesied until John. And if ye will receive it, this is Elias, which was for to come. He that hath ears to hear, let him hear.

Y'SHUA (*c.* 30 C.E.), MT 11:12–15

Two thousand years before Christ, the Lord God took Elijah, body and soul, into heaven on a fiery chariot. Two thousand years ago he returned – some say reincarnated – as John the Baptist. He is to return again soon. So say many Christian revisionists of the New Age Movement and their Catholic counterparts.

Catholic prophecy says Elijah (Elias) will return with Enoch, another transported elder figure from the Old Testament. Elias and Enoch are sent by God as messengers on one last call for humanity to repent before the world is overshadowed by the rule of the Antichrist, after which they will be martyred.

The 20th century's most significant American prophet, Edgar Cayce, saw the forerunner of the returning Christ as someone called John Pineal – after the gland most occultists believe is the doorway to the invisible "third eye" of psychic perception. This clairvoyant, New Age John the Baptist, along with a number of reincarnated apostles of Christ, would pave the way for his return by the year 2000.

BELOW **Christian revisionists believe that Elijah returned in the form of John the Baptist.**

ABOVE **Neo-Nazis remain certain that Adolf Hitler was the modern incarnation of Elijah.**

Catholics are not the only ones who want to see Elijah return again. Neo-Nazis say the forerunner had already returned as the stiff-arming prophet of white supremacy and anti-Semitism, Adolf Hitler. Apparently Hitler believed he was the reincarnation of this un-Aryan augurer. As the millennium approaches, the town officials of Berchtesgaden fear the neo-Nazi faithful will make a pilgrimage to the ruins of the Berghof, the former 260-acre Alpine retreat of the Führer outside of town. Teutonic fanatics could mingle with tourists and make Berchtesgaden a Hitlerian Mecca. The skinheads of tomorrow may gather and pray at the ruins for a sign that their all-white and powerful Savior will appear.

ABOVE **The white-bearded prophet Elijah shows
benevolence to a widow and her son in a painting by
Ford Madox Brown (1821–93).**

THE FINAL SIGNS

A number of prophetic traditions ask us to take careful note of a clear set of events to mark off on our end-time calendars as the final warning signs before a savior comes. For instance, Christians of every sect believe their messiah can't return unless missionaries have spread Christ's "good news" of salvation to every corner of the globe. That is why the metropolitans from sunny Greece traded their olive-tree-covered hills for snowdrifts and spread Eastern Christianity to the heathen Russians. Catholic missionaries of the Western Church came to the New World in the shadow of their rampaging Conquistadors to replace plundered gold with the good news of Christ to the conquered Native Americans and hasten the fulfillment of the final days. Indeed, Christopher Columbus delivered missionaries of Christendom to the native heathens in part because he believed he could bring the date of Christ's return a few centuries closer by making sure the New World heard the gospel.

Five hundred years later, the mission is accomplished. Essentially we are now all informed of Christ. Missionaries have talked, antennaed, and TV'd us about him until there is no eye or ear that hasn't seen or heard the news, whether we are Arctic Eskimos or ecologists watching the emperor penguins huddle together for warmth in Antarctica.

With the message sent, now comes the Christian Messiah.

What do other religious traditions say is the final sign for their messiahs?

RIGHT **Famous TV evangelists such as Billy Graham continue to spread the good news of the Messiah's return to earth.**

ABOVE **As the age of Empire flourished missionaries felt compelled to take the news of the Messiah to the new colonies.**

A KINGDOM RESTORED:
THE HOMECOMING OF THE JEWS TO ISRAEL

Jewish prophecy believes in two final steps before we see the return of the Lord of Hosts and his Messiah to rule the world in justice. The first is to reestablish the state of Israel. This happened more than a half-century before the end of the millennium, when the United Nations voted for a Jewish state in Palestine in 1948.

> And it shall come to pass in that day, that the Lord shall set his hand again the second time to recover the remnant of his people.... And he shall set up an ensign [a signal] for all the nations...the outcasts of Israel, and gather together the dispersed of Judah from the four corners of the earth.
>
> FIRST ISAIAH (783–687 B.C.E), IS 11:11–12

> Behold the man whose name is the Branch; and he shall grow up out of his place, and he shall build the temple of the Lord.... And they who are far off shall come and build in the temple of the Lord.
>
> FIRST ZECHARIAH (c. 538 B.C.E), ZECH 6:12, 15

Nineteen years after the founding of the modern state of Israel, in 1967, the sound of automatic fire and mortars reverberated off the pock-marked face of the Wailing Wall when Jewish commandos seized the old city of Jerusalem back from the Arabs during the Six Day War. With Jerusalem restored to its people, just one step remains before Immanuel, the Jewish Spiritual King, arrives. The platform of rock against which the Wailing Wall leans as the only remnant of the last Holy Temple of Judaism must see God/Yehovah's house on Earth rebuilt upon its back.

There is just one small gold cupola of a problem to surmount first. The Jews must raze Islam's third most sacred place of worship, the elegant gold-inlaid Dome of the Rock, and the adjacent al-Aqsa mosque, before the Jewish Temple can rise.

I can see grounds for Armageddon here, and so do many cabalistic rabbis and other Jewish prophecy interpreters. The Jewish mystic Shabetai Shiloh, who, it is said, accurately forecast the Yom Kippur War of 1973, declared in 1980 that the war marked the first of three rounds of fighting heralding the Messiah's arrival. The noted cabalistic seer, Chicago-based Rabbi Ariel Bar Tzadok, who appeared with me on the NBC/Learning

ABOVE **Soldiers pray before the Wailing Wall in the old city of Jerusalem at the end of the Six Day War in 1967.**

ABOVE **The dome of the rock in Jerusalem is in the way of religious fundamentalists who wish to build the Third Temple in its place.**

Channel landmark documentary on doomsday predictions, *Ancient Prophecies* (1994), related to me that his teachers and contacts to cabalistic sages in Jerusalem also see the final battle of Armageddon fought in three stages. Their interpretation says the conflicts are definitely not local in nature but global. We have already passed stages one and two, the world wars. Expect the third world war by the early 21st century.

Both Shabetai Shiloh and Rabbi Bar Tzadok's sources agree that drastic actions taken by Jerusalem will see the whole world isolate the Jewish state in the near future. Shiloh thought this would happen when Israel obliterates an Arab capital. This almost came true in 1991, when Saddam Hussein targeted Tel Aviv with Scud missiles in a desperate ploy to bring Israel into the Gulf War and break down the Arab-Western coalition. American pressure barely stayed the hand of Israeli nuclear retaliation on Baghdad.

Rabbi Bar Tzadok and his sources in Jerusalem foresee a time in the not-too-distant future when passions and expectations in Israel for the coming of the Messiah will bring about the current secular government's overthrow by right-wing religious fundamentalists. Bar Tzadok's sources in Jerusalem predicted this event as early as 2005 or 2006. I would add that once this takes place it is highly likely that the new government would make its move to raze the Dome of the Rock and begin construction of the Third Temple. Perhaps the future fundamentalist Israeli government would threaten nuclear retaliation on its Arab neighbors if they went to war to stop the destruction of the Dome of the Rock and al-Aqsa. Such actions and threats would isolate Israel from the world, and probably even from its chief ally, America.

Rabbi Bar Tzadok says, "The end times are *now*. We're living in them.... The enemies of Israel will attack Israel, during the night, with a major chemical and biological attack, and the number of casualties will be tremendous. And it is said Israel will respond strategically with nuclear weapons, beginning World War III."

Any chemical weapons attack on the small Jewish state could trigger a nuclear counterstrike from Israel's not-so-secret arsenal of at least 200 nuclear weapons. They would obliterate every Arab and Iranian army, air base, missile site, city, capital, and camel in the Middle East. Thus the atomic slingshot of the people of David could fulfill the prophecies of Isaiah, Ezekiel, Daniel, and Zechariah that foresaw Israel's enemies turned to dust from fires in the sky.

Bar Tzadok told me that the war would become the second holocaust for Jews living in Israel. The survivors would be scattered again in a second Diaspora. Jerusalem and the new Temple would escape destruction, and the Jewish people would eventually return, led by Immanuel the Messiah. I would add that Jerusalem's survival is ensured because of its special place in the hearts (and the religious bigotry) of its Arab and Jewish Semite combatants. Both see it as "their" holy city. Who would dare destroy it?

Rabbi Bar Tzadok predicts that in this war America will not abandon Israel, and for its troubles will suffer a nuclear attack from an Arab source. I would guess the target would be the skyscrapers of New York, which often come up in the prophecies of Nostradamus as the place of "hollow mountains" destroyed by a "great and scattered flame." New York is also the center of America's largest Jewish community.

Back in 1997, a quiet ceremony held on a corner of the temple mount in Jerusalem may have set in motion tomorrow's terrible events. A small group of Jewish fundamentalists laid the cornerstone here for their future Temple. That event begins a 30-year prophetic gauntlet where two messianic traditions clash for survival. The Jews will either level the Dome of the Rock so Immanuel can appear and preach in a new Temple constructed in its place, and thus return the Arabs to righteousness; or Muslims will save the Dome from destruction so their 12th Imam can convert the Jews to their righteous faith.

RIGHT **New York's Jewish community would be a likely target of Arab factions.**

"UNGULATIONS" OF THE ADVENT

If Israelis must build a Third Temple before the Jewish Messiah comes, then something must be born that hasn't been seen mooing since 70 C.E. – a heifer with a flawless red coat. Before Jewish priests can enter the Holy Temple's inner sanctum they must mix the ashes of a pure red heifer, ritually slaughtered in her third year of life, with water and use them to purify God's newly constructed guesthouse on Earth.

In the same year the cornerstone of the new Temple was laid, many Jewish scholars announced the birth of little Melody, the first pure red heifer in 1,930 years. Fundamentalists see her arrival as a portent from God that construction of the Temple should begin at once, because the Messiah Immanuel will appear at the new millennium. Some extremists considered celebrating Melody's birth with the detonation of the Islamic Dome on the Temple Mount.

Before masonry flew, Jewish rabbis threw in some doubts about Melody's purity. Her local rabbi, Rabbi Shmaria Shore, believes Melody isn't quite kosher. She has a pair of white hairs in her tail, white whiskers in her snout, and eyelashes that are red only on one end. "If I really thought she was [pure red], I'd send her away to an undisclosed location," says the rabbi.

Melody will be of burnt-offering age by the new millennium, but her minor impurities will probably win her a longer life as chief breeding stock for another generation of red heifers. In the meantime a group of rabbis is searching out families of *cohanim* (the priestly caste) who will hand over their babies for a childhood and youth of isolation and purification that will make them kosher keepers of the next pure red heifer, if and when she appears. Rabbi David Yosef Alboim, the leader of the movement of Orthodox Jews to rebuild the Temple, knows that this final prophecy can't be fulfilled unless there exist ritually pure priests.

Today all Jews are considered unclean because they have handled the dead and have trod upon the earth where the dead are buried. Therefore the rabbi is enlisting expectant mothers who are ready to give up their male babies to the mission in order to create a class of pure priests. Some say that these children are already being isolated and trained, and that their rabbis prevent their feet from touching the soil. They must live and walk their days on floors and ramps above the unclean earth so that they can be ready to build the inner sanc-

tum of God's House on Earth when the Temple in Jerusalem is rebuilt.

Four years prior to the cohanim celebrating the advent of a red cow in Israel, Sioux shamans corralled and coddled a baby white buffalo born in 1994. Floyd Hand, the revered Ogala Lakota medicine man, believed this white she-calf was the fulfillment of Sioux prophecy. They had been awaiting the birth of a white buffalo they call "White Buffalo Woman." Her appearance would be a last sign before the buffalo herds would rise as if from the dead and fill the American plains. Afterward, the spiritually and physically starved Sioux would return to the sacred hunt as in olden times.

In 1994 the birth of the calf named "Miracle" made her corral in Janesville, Wisconsin, a mecca for over 32,000 pilgrims. They generally beheld her white furry suckling self with the reverence one sees from Catholic Marian cultists praying at Fátima, Portugal, and Lourdes, France. Geneticists say that such a birth is one in a million, but the pilgrimage began to lose steam after a few months, when the little buffalo's white hide began its natural transformation to the dingy reddish brown of a normal buffalo.

RIGHT **Cultists pray at a shrine in Fátima, Portugal, visited in 1917 by an apparition of Mary.**

A KINGDOM DESTROYED: THE TIBETAN APOCALYPSE

War will burst like a hurricane over Tibet and China and the inhumanity of that calamity will triple the weight of darkness, and famine and disease will usher all living beings into an abominable hell.... The [Chinese] armies will dart from valley to valley like incinerating lightning and then invade and conquer Western Tibet.... One-half of the Tibetan people will be slain while the temples are devastated, the images desecrated, the Sacred Scriptures trampled in the dust and the monks and priests murdered. The ruined villages will become desolate, for the survivors of this holocaust will escape to Sikkim, Bhutan, Nepal and India as refugees and to the Secret Valleys of the Himalayas. Those who remain, tied by avarice to land and wealth, will be massacred with their cattle by the barbarian iconoclasts.

PADMASAMBHAVA
(8TH CENTURY C.E.), STUPA

LEFT **The Chinese army remains a threatening presence in Tibet.**

RIGHT **Tibet's spiritual head, the 14th Dalai Lama, has had to witness the loss of around one million lives and gradual erosion of his people's culture.**

For the final days, prophets foresee the restoration of one theocratic kingdom (Israel) and the destruction of another. Two years after the restoration of Israel in 1948, the Tibetan Apocalypse began in 1950. The Chinese Communist army invaded the western frontiers of Tibet and over the coming decades razed thousands of temples and defiled holy relics and Scriptures. The 14th Dalai Lama estimates that over one million Tibetans have perished. The near-annihilation of the Tibetan culture in its own homeland is the final warning before the appearance of Rudra Cakrin, the Shambhala king.

FIVE SIGNS OF THE ADVENT OF THE 12th IMAM (AL-QA'IM)

ABOVE **Mecca, considered the holiest city of Islam, is prophesied to be the site of an apocalyptic assassination before the return of the al-Qa'im.**

Islam also has its final warnings. The Shi'ite interpreters may shuffle the sequence, but they agree that in the same near-future year five incidents will take place before the al-Qa'im comes out of hiding. In the first two incidents, two liberators will arise. The first, al-Yamani, will rise up and conquer the Abbasid regime from the east; the second, al-Sufyani, will conquer the Abbasid regime from the west.

Political hopes drive the fulfillment of these first two signs. Shi'ite sects did suffer under the Abbasid caliphs who reigned from 750 to 1258 C.E., but the armies of al-Yamani and al-Sufyani never appeared to take the Abbasid capital of Baghdad. This deed was left to the infidel Mongol hordes who in 1258 rode down from the "northwest" and the east to torch the Abbasid capital of Baghdad and slay nearly all of its inhabitants.

This therefore leaves the last three signs as possible future final warnings heralding the imminent arrival of the 12th Imam. Sign number three will be the assassination of a much-revered and pure soul living in Mecca. This will happen, it is said, just 15 days before the al-Qa'im makes his reappearance. Sign number four will come as a deafening, thunderous outcry falling from the sky in the morning in the name of the al-Qa'im. And the fifth and final sign will see the disappearance of an entire army. As they march on Mecca the advancing troops will sink out of sight and vanish into the sand.

"WHEN THE COMET WILL PASS"

Shi'ite seers proclaim that the 12th Imam "will appear again like a shooting star in the dark night." Will this be literal or metaphorical? Prophets of all traditions consider comets transiting the skies as portents of change, both divinely auspicious and dire. One of the best-known bearded star sightings came from the amply bearded 16th-century prophet-doctor Nostradamus. A number of his four-line prophetic quatrains speak of a great comet appearing just before the end of the current millennium, around the time that Western Europe will experience a total solar eclipse. (Indeed, a great solar eclipse did darken much of Europe just four months before the new millennium, on August 11, 1999.) It marks the onset of a 30-year period of global upheaval.

Upon these final warnings Nostradamus has written:

**The great star will blaze for seven days.
The cloud will cause two suns to appear:
the great dog will howl all night, when the
great pontiff will change lands. (C2 Q41)**

The collision of 21 fragments of the comet Shoemaker-Levi with Jupiter took place over a seven-day period in July 1994. The peak viewing time for the passing of the comet Hale-Bopp lasted seven days in spring 1997. Look for the evacuation of a future pope from Rome if the well-known double flash of a nuclear detonation targets the city of the Seven Hills.

**After a great misery for mankind an even
greater approaches. The great motor of the
centuries is renewed: It will rain blood,
milk, famine, iron and pestilence. In the
sky will be seen a fire, dragging a
trail of sparks. (C2 Q46)**

The first "great misery" for mankind was World War II. The next could be World War III, slated for a time when the "great motor of the centuries" is renewed – at the millennium. The references to blood in the prophecies of Nostradamus may hint at future blood plagues, like Ebola or a new virulent form of AIDS,

or even the significant outbreak of blood diseases like hepatitis B and C, which are currently responsible for killing three times as many people each year as AIDS. A global famine as a final warning before the redeemer comes is a common vision of Nostradamus. The fire "dragging a trail of sparks" could be a double pun for the fiery trail of either a great comet seen just prior to World War III, or it may describe the flight of a missile. So far, the passing of Hale-Bopp in the spring of 1997 is the closest cosmic omen to pass near the time of the millennium, when the "motor of the centuries is renewed."

**Mabus will soon die, then will come a
horrible undoing of people and animals.
At once one will see vengeance [from] 100
powers. Thirst, famine, when the comet
will pass. (C2 Q62)**

After a comet has passed at the end of the current millennium Nostradamus foresees a terrorist Antichrist figure from the Middle East (Mabus) who (he states in other visions) will wage a 27-year war starting perhaps as soon as July 1999. As the cabalists have said, the chemical or nuclear extermination of just one of the region's capitals would result – as Nostradamus implies – in the sudden exposure of the Holy Land's ancient vengeances in a region-wide orgy or, as the prophet calls it, "great destruction of people and animals."

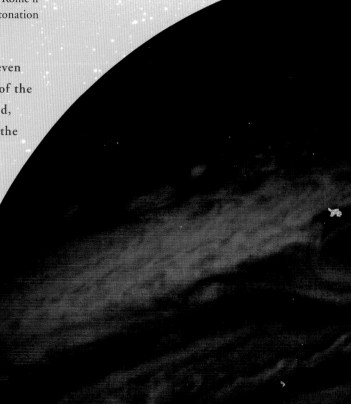

COBWEBS AND HOUSES IN THE SKY

ABOVE **An airplane leaves a spidery trail in the sky – a fulfillment of Hopi prophecies?**

The Hopi Indians of the American Southwest give us a very clear and un-esoteric account of the final steps the white man will take before he completely destroys civilization.

According to Hopi prophecy, when the final days have arrived, we will see the once-clear blue skies covered with "cobwebs." To see the fulfillment of this prophecy one only has to look up in the air into any late-20th-century sky crisscrossed with vapor trails from numerous jets to see that we are living in those final days.

The last Hopi warning states that we will know the end is near when the white man builds a "permanent teepee" in the sky. Could this prediction perhaps be a reference to the International Space Station Alpha? The first segments are already floating in space in 1999, and the deadline for final completion is now 2006.

ABOVE **A series of airplane contrails create a striking pattern that presages the cobweb of the end times.**

LEFT **Astral collisions, such as that of the Shoemaker-Levi comet with Jupiter, are recorded in apocalyptic texts.**

COUΠTERFEIT CHRISTS

Many will say to me on that day [Judgement Day],
"Lord, Lord, did we not prophesy in your name,
and drive out demons and perform many miracles?"
Then I will tell them plainly, "I never knew you.
Away from me, you evildoers!"

Y'SHUA (30–33 C.E.), MT 7:21–22

COUNTERFEIT CHRISTS

Take heed that no man deceive you. For many shall come in my name, saying, I am Christ; and shall deceive many.

Y'SHUA (*c.* 30 C.E.), MT 24: 4–5

And then shall many be offended, and shall betray one another, and shall hate one another. And many false prophets shall rise, and shall deceive many. And because iniquity shall abound, the love of many shall wax cold. But he that shall endure unto the end, the same shall be saved.

Y'SHUA (*c.* 30 C.E.), MT 24:10–13

Then if man says to you, Lo, here is Christ; or lo, he is there; believe him not: for false Christs and false prophets shall rise, and shall [show] signs and wonders, to seduce, if it were possible, even the elect [God's chosen]. But take ye heed: behold, I have foretold you all things.

Y'SHUA (*c.* 30 C.E.), MK 13:21–23

The False Messiah will rise up, with the word "Unbeliever" [Kafir] written between his eyes…and…Jesus will descend from Heaven and slay him.

AHMAD IBN HANBAL
(9TH CENTURY C.E.)

LEFT **Kitschy images of Christ abound in modern society, especially around Christmas time, and may amount to blasphemy according to some strict doctrines.**

MY MESSIAH MUST BE YOUR ANTICHRIST

ABOVE **Christ stands at the entrance to Hell
in this painting by Duccio di Buoninsegna.
So who is he welcoming in?**

It has to be so. How else can you view my savior? I got it from divine sources that your messiah is my antichrist. Don't ask me for proof. You'll just have to accept it on faith, because I won't argue the point with you.

That's how we play the in-Jesus'-name-calling game, is it not? If there must be a final battle between good and evil, then someone else's right messiah has to be less right than mine, because there's no way we can be good sports about this end-time game. After all, everybody knows there's no next time after the terminus of time. This is a game we play for keeps. I have to make sure that your behind – and not mine – is behind Satan. And let it be your behind that dips into the lake of fire for eternity.

What a web my theology weaves when it says other saviors deceive! My theology has essentially the same arguments to support my messiah's efficacy over your theology, but you know how it goes. It is not the arguments that matter, no matter how compelling they may be. What matters is who is making the argument. If it isn't my religious teaching, then all that your teachings say is a lie, no matter what you say.

Nevertheless I'll be kind and nod my head as you press your argument about your deliverer. I will look at you with those baby-blue iron-curtain eyes. My windows to the soul will draw shut their dogmatic curtains behind my glassy-eyed windowpane. Through the film of these curtains I still safely look back at your lost soul.

All protests of true believers aside, an open-eyed review of messianic prophecy – stripped of its taken-for-granted stances on who is a counterfeit or a true messiah – will reveal many intriguing similarities.

Take, for example, the following quotes without their bylines. Can you tell who is "false" and who is "true" without the proper signposts to direct your opinions?

He that curseth father or mother, let him die the death. (1)

It's not fair to demand more of a man than he can give. (2)

I will kill her children with death! (3)

Now, he who destroys life is himself risking death. (4)

What comes naturally to mankind is the sense of eternity and that sense is at the bottom of every man. (5)

My soul is exceedingly sorrowful. (6)

The soul and the mind migrate, just as the body returns to nature. Thus life is eternally reborn from life....The soul is unplumbable. (7)

Do not let too much sorrow break your heart. Keep the whole world always in your farsighted eyes. (8)

All my life I have endured the pain of poverty and suffered many disappointments and heartaches common to mankind. For that reason I try to make others happy and secure. (9)

It's a mistake to think that man should be guided by his greed. (10)

O faithless and perverse generation, how long shall I be with you, and suffer you? (11)

Man, alone amongst the living creatures, tries to deny the laws of nature. (12)

Soldiers from heaven fight the corrupt and evil. (13)

There is no greater good for a warrior than to fight in a righteous war. (14)

How sweet will be the victory of the wretched [the poor and disenfranchised], and how great! How beautiful their dawn, when it comes forth and shines without requesting permission – how magnificent will the sun be on the day of the wretched ones, when it dazzles the world. (15)

I shall rule them with a rod of iron! (16)

As long as man controls man, the difficulties and problems of the world as it is now witnessed...are going to remain. (17)

Prepare for war with peace in thy soul. (18)

Those who do not remember the past are condemned to repeat it. (19)

The truly strange thing in your lives is that you not only fail, but fail to learn your lesson.... No matter how much your beliefs betray you, this is never accepted by you. (20)

Do unto others as you would have them do unto you. (21)

But what can be said about love that hasn't been said already? One thing only, the simple but universal rule: Love is a Clothes Line. Yes, it's true, and on it hang all the other emotions – hence the expression "putting yourself on the line"! So go ahead – fall in love! It's the bravest thing you can do – especially if it's raining! (22)

You can't believe in what you don't understand. (23)

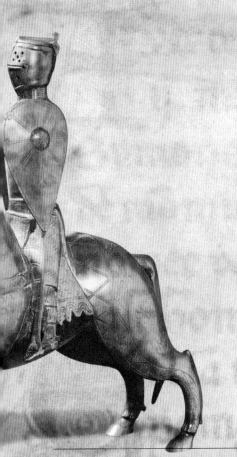

(1) Y'shua (c. 30 C.E.), MK 7:10
(2) Adolf Hitler (1941), SCRTC
(3) Y'shua (c. 30 C.E.), RV 2:23
(4) Adolf Hitler (1941), SCRTC
(5) Adolf Hitler (1941), SCRTC
(6) Y'shua (c. 30 C.E.), MT 26:38
(7) Adolf Hitler (1941), SCRTC
(8) Mao Tse-tung (1949)
(9) Reverend Jim Jones (1978)
(10) Adolf Hitler (1941), SCRTC
(11) Y'shua (c. 30 C.E.), MT 17:17
(12) Adolf Hitler (1941), SCRTC
(13) Mao Tse-tung (1930)
(14) Krishna (c. 3000 b.c.e), GITA 2:31
(15) Muammar Qaddafi (c. 1996)
(16) Y'shua (c. 30 C.E.), RV 2:27
(17) David Koresh (c. 1992)
(18) Krishna (c. 3000 b.c.e) GITA
(19) Reverend Jim Jones (1978)
(20) Muammar Qaddafi (c. 1996)
(21) Buddha Gautama (c. 500)
(22) Max Headroom (c. 1987)
(23) David Koresh (c. 1993)

THE ANTICHRIST IS A NERD

And they worshipped the beast, saying, "Who is like unto the beast? Who is able to make war with him?" And there was given unto him a mouth speaking great things and blasphemies.... And it was given unto him to make war with the saints, and to overcome them: and power was given him over all kindreds, and tongues and nations. And all that dwell upon the earth shall worship him.

ST. JOHN OF PATMOS (81–96 C.E.), RV 13:4–5, 7–8

The Antichrist will become world ruler in the sense that he will handle the guidelines and direct those who will carry out his orders. Rather than elective, these offices will be appointive, and within the network will be spies who probe into the personal lives of people during that...era.... His managerial powers at first will seem God-sent, but as he becomes more ambitious still, he will demand worshipful obedience, and in pretending to be the Christ will offend those who realize that he is satanic in his ambitions.

SPIRIT GUIDES OF RUTH MONTGOMERY (1979), AMG

If there is an antichrist coming he won't lead an army of denizens from hell to fight the Viking knights of Valhalla. He won't be a multihorned, multiheaded beast. He will be the head of a multinational corporation. If there is a false prophet coming, he won't commit maniacal murder, he will commit "media merger." He will slay individuality by conquering communication. He will buy up all the avenues for free ideas on byte, on wire, and on the satellite dish. He will be a greater master of the information gate than any nerd or genius ever was. He will filter your ideas through his monopoly, his software, his entertainment censors.

The popular interpretations of antichrists cooked up in millennia past fit the expectations of times that are long dead. They looked like Roman emperors and Mongol potentates. They bore the number "666." That number has nothing to do with you, me, or the bar code on your packet of frozen chicken cacciatore. The number 666 is the numerical representation of the Hebrew letters that spell out the name of a man who lived 19 centuries ago. The author of the Book of Revelation was certain that, in his lifetime, this man would rise after receiving a mortal head wound and fight a final battle with the returned Christ. St. John of Patmos's Antichrist was Nero, the pyromaniac emperor who burned down Rome.

The Antichrist is not Nostradamus's foretold *Napaulon Roy* (Napoleon) or that Austrian kid *Hister* growing up as Hitler on the River Danube. Maybe he's not even *Mabus*, that last man of evil Nostradamus expects will appear in 1999 in the Middle East. The Antichrist I envision doesn't lead terrorists from the Middle East or armies from Communist China. He doesn't have a stable of 200 million horsemen. He's not so medieval as to be seeking land, natural resources, or money. Perhaps he's not even going to be a terrorist, as this John Hogue fellow has so often spouted about on TV and radio. Nor is he going to be a pope, a president of a nation or supernation, or leader of a biblically regurgitated Roman Empire. He's not going to run the U.N. or the E.U. or the U.A.R.

He's a creature of ones and zeros. He's binary. He will sell you his computer, his software, his virtual reality implants. He is the one shaping your thoughts. He's entertaining you. He won't be one who's interested in controlling the bomb and all the bullets. He aims to control the real currency of the new millennium, INFORMATION. He subverts you from within your perceptions by controlling how you are in-formed.

He is the messiah of media. He is Cyber-Christ. Byte Buddha. A Megabyte Muhammad. He will be the dictator of what you will see, how you will live, work, think. He will not attack with Scud missiles; on the contrary, he'll launch sorties of electrons and light waves. He'll change your thinking bit by byte of data.

The man of perdition is not some Sunday school rehash of what people 20 centuries ago thought was evil. I sometimes wonder if the Christian broadcasting networks are already under the Antichrist's spell as they describe a coming bad guy who would better delude simple Roman peasants, not modern people, with his dictatorial ways, his sleight-of-hand miracles, and his play-act messianism. What do you think happens to people who imitate Christ in the long hair and robes on New York streets? The straitjacket is their destiny, not the rulership of the world.

A few shared prophecies try to see the real future man beyond the biblical anachronisms and point to a figure who doesn't hold office but controls the direction of the most important currencies of the future, such as information. He has a better chance of being an ad man than a military man, a corporate emperor than the ruler of a political empire. He will be the one who wires you to your computer games.

My vision of the Antichrist isn't pretty. He isn't charismatic. He stinks as an orator. He's someone with broken glasses taped together for the umpteenth time. But he will have a genius for creating new media technology and monopolizing it. My vision of the Antichrist is someone who works in the shadows. He knows how to manipulate data, media, and people on a level far ahead of even our times. He will gobble up media and sports franchises in a way that would make some media moguls as green as Australian sheep dip with envy because he will do it without leaving any dirty, inky footprints on contracts, and without throwing his ego around.

In my opinion, Ruth Montgomery's guides have gotten it all wrong. The Antichrist won't be some clean-cut, attractive, respectable fellow who gets the girls squealing over his piety and speeches. He won't pose as the savior of the world – he'll package the way you see and think about saviors of the world on your web TV. He won't speak to you, he'll change the way you speak. He won't give you any new ideas. He'll warp your ideas through subliminal conditioning. His is the dictatorship of the dumb-down. And he'll do it not by openly thwarting your good deeds, but by reconditioning you to see his idea of good deeds. He covets world domination covertly. He's a creature from the X-file-minded, and within a few decades he'll be coming to the media outlet, think pad, and entertainment station nearest you.

LEFT **The modern stereotype of the computer nerd may be the next antichrist; the nerd will use media channels to spread his propaganda.**

CHRIST, THE FALSE PROPHET OF THE CHRISTIANS

A rabbi once confided to me, "You Christians are still waiting for your Antichrist. We have already been suffering from ours for two thousand years."

Jewish interpretations of the *Nevi'im* (which includes the books of prophets from what Christians call the Old Testament) expose many of the flaws in the Christian belief that Christ's first coming was authentic. Could it be that Daniel, Ezekiel, Zechariah, and other Jewish prophets recognized Christ as the false prophet? Did they warn that this Jewish heretic would establish a worldwide Gentile-oriented faith that combined pagan ideas with Jewish mysticism? And finally, is the faith of the Christian cross the same world-dominating faith forewarned in the Nevi'im as the persecutor of the Jews until the real Messiah, Immanuel, returns sometime in the 21st century?

JESUS DIDN'T BECOME A KING, NOR WAS ISRAEL IN DESOLATION

> Hear ye, O house of David.... the Lord himself shall give you a sign; Behold, a virgin [meaning in Hebrew, a pure and innocent woman of marriageable age] shall conceive, and bear a son, and shall call his name Immanuel. Curds and honey shall he eat, that he may know to refuse the evil and choose the good. For before the child shall know to refuse the evil, and choose the good, the land that thou abhorrest shall be forsaken of both her kings. The Lord shall bring upon thee, and upon thy people, and upon thy father's house, days that have not come, from the day that Ephraim departed from Judah.
>
> FIRST ISAIAH (783–687 B.C.E), IS 7:13–17

Though descended from the line of David, Christ did not become king of Israel as Isaiah 7:13–17 implies. Isaiah's abhorred kingdoms of Aram and Israel are long gone by the time of Christ; however, Isaiah expects Immanuel will be born to a future Jewish realm in grave distress, its spiritual survival at stake. The allusion to curds and honey connotes the modest repast eaten during times of acute famine and desolation.

At the time of the birth of Christ Rome subjugated Palestine, but it also tolerated Jewish law and religious rites and relied on Jewish administration. The Jewish people certainly chafed under the rule of Rome, but Palestine was definitely not in desolation or suffering great famines or religious and cultural annihilation – at least not until three decades after Christ was crucified.

However, Jewish mystics believe the prophesied desolation is yet to come. Rabbi Ariel Bar Tzadok conveyed the time window of 2005 through the 2060s as the time cabalists in Jerusalem calculate the arrival of Immanuel, the Messiah. He will come at a time when the Jewish people in Israel suffer a second holocaust from a chemical and biological attack by its Arab neighbors. The first Isaiah's passage quoted above could describe such a coming desolation. Moreover, it may foresee what life could be like later in the 21st century when water runs out in the Middle East and global warming vexes the area with droughts and extreme weather, causing a time of curds-and-honey famine.

LEFT **Jewish mystics debunk the heroism of Christ's suffering and dismiss him as a false prophet.**

THE DAY OF THE LORD'S JUDGMENT DID NOT IMMEDIATELY FOLLOW THE ADVENT OF JESUS

And it will come to pass in that day, that the Lord shall hiss for the fly that is in the uttermost part of the rivers of Egypt, and for the bee that is in the land of Assyria. And they shall come and rest...in the holes of rocks, and upon all thorns and upon all bushes. In the same day shall the Lord shave with a razor that is hired, namely, by them beyond the river, by the king of Assyria, the head, and the hair of the feet [euphemism for "pubic hair"], and it shall also consume the beard.... And it shall come to pass in that day, that every place shall be, where there were a thousand vines at a thousand silverlings, it shall even be for briers and thorns. With arrows and with bows shall men come thither; because all the land shall become briers and thorns.

FIRST ISAIAH (783–687 B.C.E), IS 7:18–20, 23–24

When Christ walked the earth there was no record of a plague of bees and flies covering Egypt and the lands formerly called Assyria. None of their citizens were buzz-cut pate to pubes to toes by God's terrible bold swift razor. This might better describe the ordeal of Jews during modern times, during the Nazi Holocaust. The land of Christ's time was not a place of briers and thorns, nor did invaders menace Palestine's frontiers. In short, Judgment Day was postponed.

These dire predictions might better describe the Holy Land in the 2020s when water runs out and the wineries and crops are reclaimed by the desert and its thirsty flies. All of this is likely if the weather patterns expected from global warming desiccate the Near East far beyond its already fragile water sustainability. Israel currently obtains 40 percent of its water supply from the Palestinian West Bank, and it is now drawing more water away from neighboring Jordan, Lebanon, and Syria with a plan to dam the headwaters of the River Jordan. Turkey is a few years away from completing its ambitious multidam project, which Iraq and Syria fear will dry out the River Euphrates. Even the Jewish Christian seer St. John of Patmos predicts that Armageddon and the final judgment will take place when the Euphrates dries out (see RV 16:12).

RIGHT **Life on the banks of the river Euphrates will be severely disrupted if Turkey's complex multidam development goes ahead.**

JESUS DID NOT GATHER THE SCATTERED PEOPLE, MOUNT THE DAVIDIC THRONE, AND RESTORE ISRAEL

The people that walked in darkness have seen a great light: they that dwell in the land of the shadow of death, upon them hath the light shined…. For thou hast broken the yoke of his burden, and the staff of his shoulder, the rod of his oppressor…. For unto us a child is born, unto us a son is given: and the government shall be upon his shoulder: and his name shall be called Wonderful, Counselor, The mighty God, The everlasting Father, The Prince of Peace. On the increase of his government and peace there shall be no end, upon the throne of David, and upon his kingdom, to order it, and to establish it with judgment and with justice from henceforth even for ever. The zeal of the Lord of Hosts will perform this.

FIRST ISAIAH (783–687 B.C.E), IS 9:2, 4, 6–7

And he shall set up an ensign for the nations, and shall assemble the outcasts of Israel, and gather together the dispersed of Judah from the four corners of the earth.

FIRST ISAIAH (783–687 B.C.E), IS 11:12

The orthodox Jewish interpretation of the Nevi'im – the words of the prophets – is unequivocal. According to the Scriptures, the Messiah must gather together the scattered people of Israel. He will then sit upon the throne of David and establish David's sovereignty. He will not contradict the laws of Moses but restore them, not only for the Jews but as the code of law for all people of the world. The Messiah then will reign over the world and see to it that the Jewish people flourish and that righteousness triumphs in the human and even the animal kingdoms.

Now, none of this happened when Jesus Christ walked the earth. Contrary to the prophecies, Jesus was a reformer. He came to revise the laws of Moses, not to uphold their traditional interpretation. He didn't triumph over the enemies of Israel – a Roman ordered his crucifixion after Jerusalem's Jewish citizens voted for it en masse. Rather than reassemble the people of Israel, Christ would die on the cross decades before Roman legions devastated Palestine and scattered the Jewish people in the Diaspora. No wonder, say Jewish critics, that Christians promote the idea of a Second Coming. Christ needs a second chance to fulfill key signs given in Scripture of Immanuel's coming.

LEFT **This modern depiction of Christ on the cross by Paul Gaugin breaks from the tradition of representing heroic suffering; Gaugin's Christ looks utterly defeated. Did this man really save the world?**

JESUS WAS DEFINITELY NOT A DIVINE WARRIOR IN HIS FIRST COMING

I will tread them in my anger, and trample them in my fury; and their blood shall be sprinkled upon my garments, and I will stain all my raiment.

THIRD ISAIAH (4TH CENTURY B.C.E), IS 63:3

Chapter 63 of Isaiah promotes God himself with muscles rippling and his robe stained in the winepress of the blood of Israel's enemies. The above passage and other militaristic references in these King James translations of the Nevi'im have influenced Jews and Christians alike to view the return of their Messiah as a warrior, not a lover.

One could even interpret Christ's famous peeve "Father, why hast thou foresaken me?!" yelled on the cross at God, as a sign that even Jesus expected the Lord of Hosts to descend from the clouds with hosts of angels to free his son from the cross and clothe him in royal finery and armor to kick some Roman butt.

It didn't happen. What's a Jewish apostle of this Christ who knows his Scripture to do? Well, first Christian theologians had to rationalize that Christ cannot fail prophecy, so they pushed his appearance as an all-conquering divine warrior ahead into the future. Otherwise how can Christ, hanging there so miserably on the cross, be seen as the theocratic warrior-king and Alexander the Great of the all-conquering Jews?

CHRIST'S BIG BOO-BOO

Immediately after the tribulation of those days shall the sun be darkened, and the moon shall not give her light, and the stars shall fall from heaven.... And then shall appear the sign of the Son of man in heaven [Christ]...coming from the clouds...with power and great glory...[gathering] together his elect from the four winds.... Verily I say unto you, this generation shall not pass, till all these things are fulfilled. Heaven and Earth shall pass away but my words shall not pass away.

Y'SHUA (*c.* 30 C.E.), MT 24:29–35

Jewish rabbis can shake a forelock at flaws of eschatology in the Christian testament itself. Thanks to the transcriptions of Matthew 24:34, Mark 13:30, and Luke 21:32, Christ seems to be hammering a crucifix nail into his own foot on dating his immediate return and the end of the world. Christians retort that their savior was only talking about the destruction of Herod's Temple, which took place in 70 C.E. when the Romans destroyed Jerusalem. Nevertheless, this sidesteps all the clear references that paint a picture of history coming to an end with the return of Christ. So far, Christ's return is off by 20 centuries and counting.

I had a vision in a dream that the heavens opened and that a radiance became visible like a big square, in which a figure of light, like the image of the founder of the Christian religion, appeared as if poised for a flight to earth. All on earth prostrated themselves before him. But I remained standing upright and, still dreaming, meditated on the meaning of this dream image, and I interpreted it to mean that a time will come when the Christian religion will strive with all its power to achieve dominion over the whole planet in all four directions, and even if everybody else bows down before its power, I will stand upright and defy it – and I awoke with the exclamation: "Hear O Israel: the Lord our God is One Eternal Being." I had the feeling of a martyr who is firmly determined to give his life for his religious conviction.

RABBI HILE WECHSLER (*c.* 1859), EWM

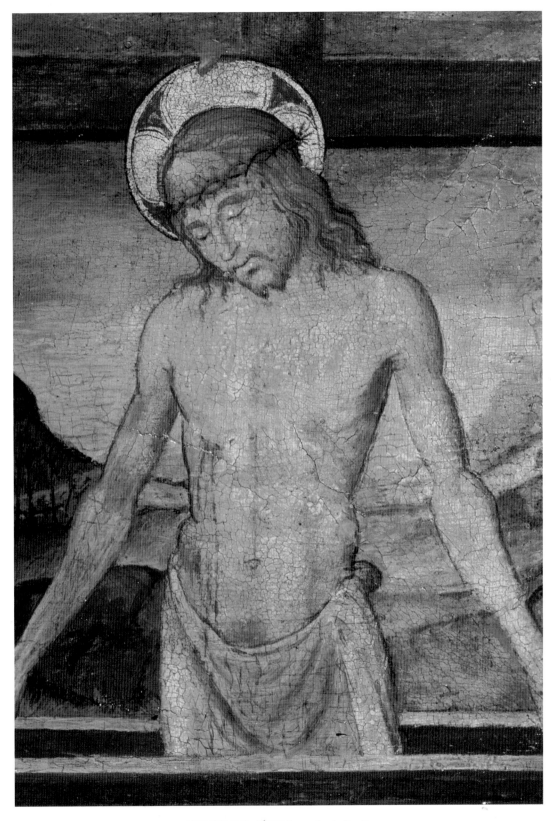

OPPOSITE AND ABOVE **According to the New
Testament, Christ's resurrection, which has caught
the imagination of generations of artists, was
destined to bring about the end of the world.**

IMMANUEL, THE FALSE PROPHET OF THE JEWS

Christian interpreters believe they can glean visions from the Old Testament to construct a compelling prophetic argument that proves the Jews missed their Messiah and worse. They counter that there are a number of specific details about the life of the true Messiah that Jesus Christ did fulfill.

BORN IN BETHLEHEM

But thou, Bethlehem Ephratah, though thou be little among thousands of Judah, yet out of thee shall he come forth unto me that is to be the ruler in Israel: whose goings forth have been from of old, from everlasting.

MICAH (*c.* 721 B.C.E), MIC 5:2

ABOVE **The story of Christ's birth is well known, yet the debate concerning the exact location of this event is still heated.**

member of the fourteenth generation directly descended from the bloodline of King (Messiah) David. Mary was the wife of Joseph (if not of the baby's father, the Holy Ghost), and because Christ would be born in Bethlehem, the city of David, Christians believe he could stake his claim as Messiah.

BELOW **This 16th-century painting tells the story of Christ bringing sight to the blind, a miracle retold in the New Testament.**

Jewish seers say the Messiah should come from an unknown place. Historical flaws in the Christian Christmas tale ironically support their view. New revelations in archaeology cast doubt on whether Jesus could call the town of Nazareth home, because it didn't exist before the end of the first century C.E. The story goes that Joseph and his new and divinely impregnated bride, Mary, left Nazareth, in Galilee, to be counted in Bethlehem in the Roman census of Emperor Augustus because the Imperium demanded that all subjects of Rome be counted in their home village or town. Bethlehem in Ephrathah was also the birthplace of Israel's greatest ruler, David. The apostle Matthew uses Ruth 4:18-22 to cite Joseph, the husband of Mary, as a

PRECEDED BY A FORERUNNER

Behold, I will send my messenger, and
he shall prepare the way before me:
and the Lord whom ye seek, shall
suddenly come to his temple, even the
messenger of the covenant, whom ye
delight in: behold, he shall come,
saith the Lord of hosts.

MALACHI (*c.* 500–450 B.C.E), MAL 3:1

One Jewish interpretation says the messenger is the
Messiah, and the one coming afterward to rule
the world is the Lord of Hosts himself. Christians use
this and a number of other passages as proof that John
the Baptist was the preordained forerunner who would
preach and pave the way for the first coming of Christ.

RIGHT **Breughel depicts John the Baptist
preparing the path for Christ, but some
still argue that Christ is merely a
precursor to the real Messiah.**

HE COMES AS A SAVIOR, MIRACLE WORKER, AND HEALER

Your God will come with vengeance…he will
come and save you. Then the eyes of the
blind shall be opened, and the ears of the
deaf shall be unstopped. Then shall the lame
man leap as a [deer], and the tongue of the
dumb sing: for in the wilderness shall
waters break out, and streams in the desert.

FIRST ISAIAH (783–687 B.C.E), IS 35:4–6

Jews say God comes to heal the sick, and perform
miracles; Christians say it is the Son of God.
Although the Bahá'í prophet, 'Abdu'l-Bahá, would say
producing water in a desert is metaphorical for Jesus
producing the water of love and compassion to those
thirsty ones in the desert of sinfulness, many Christian
fundamentalists believe this passage foresaw Jesus performing miracles and producing water in the desert to
quench the thirst of the crowds that would come to see
him speak.

HE GOES INTO JERUSALEM ON A DONKEY

Rejoice greatly, O daughter of Zion; shout, O daughter of Jerusalem: behold, thy King cometh unto thee: he is just and having salvation; lowly, and riding upon an ass, and upon a colt the foal of an ass.

SECOND ZECHARIAH (*c.* 160 B.C.E), ZEC 9:9

Jesus entered Jerusalem on an ass. There were so many Messiah claimants riding in on asses during those days that there must have been a run on palm fronds and donkey rentals. By the time of Jesus there was a popular belief that the Old Testament prophets had slotted their time for the coming of the Messiah. Historical references survive showing a number of people claiming to be the savior and trying to fulfill the foreseen acts of the coming Messiah, like palm frond waving and donkey riding into the Holy City. As there can be only one true claimant, the Christians argue that theirs was the one, because his actions to fulfill what was written eventually led to the spread of his message across the whole world.

BETRAYED BY THE COIN

Yea, mine own familiar friend, in whom I trusted, which did eat of my bread, hath lifted up his heel against me.

PSALM 41:9

And I said unto them, "If he think good, give me my price; and if not forbear." So they weighed for my price thirty pieces of silver.

SECOND ZECHARIAH (*c.* 160 B.C.E), ZEC 11:12

Thirty pieces of silver was the going price for purchasing a slave and handing over a savior to enemies. A friend and intimate disciple of Jesus, Judas Iscariot, handed him over to his enemies in the Sanhedrin (the Jewish religious governing body) and the Romans for a bag of thirty pieces of silver.

TORTURED AND WHIPPED

But he was wounded for our transgressions, he was bruised for our iniquities: the chastisement of our peace was upon him; and with his stripes we are healed.

SECOND ISAIAH
(4TH CENTURY B.C.E), IS 53:5

His back would bear the bloody stripes of a whipping. Christ would be mocked, beaten, and die a martyr for the sins of humanity.

RIGHT **Jesus fulfilled prophecy by suffering humiliation and torture inflicted by his captors.**

THEN A CRUCIFIXION – NOT A CRUCE-"FICTION"

> For dogs have encompassed me: the assembly of the wicked have enclosed me; they pierced my hands and my feet. I may tell all my bones: they look and stare upon me. They part my garments among them, and cast lots upon my vesture.
>
> PSALM 22:16–18

> And they [believing Israelites] shall look upon me [the Messiah] whom they have pierced and they shall mourn for him, as one mourneth for his only son.
>
> SECOND ZECHARIAH (*c.* 160 B.C.E), ZEC 12:10

Many Christians see this passage as fulfilled by the passion of Christ on the cross. The people mourning over him are his disciples. Anti-Semitic Christians use passages such as this as prophetic justification for the punishment and retribution doled out to the Jewish people over the last 2,000 years, claiming that they failed to recognize their Messiah and then murdered him.

RESURRECTION FROM THE DEAD...

> Therefore my heart is glad, and my glory rejoiceth: my flesh also shall rest in hope...and at my right hand there are pleasures for evermore.
>
> PSALM 16:9–11

Christians take this to mean the physical and spiritual victory of Christ over death. On the third morning after he was laid to rest, it is said that the guards, having fallen asleep before the tomb, woke up to find the stone covering the tomb's entrance silently rolled aside, letting the reanimated occupant walk away.

...BECOMES A CATALYST FOR A WORLDWIDE RELIGIOUS MOVEMENT

> Yea, many people and strong nations shall come to seek the Lord of hosts in Jerusalem, and to pray before the Lord.
>
> FIRST ZECHARIAH (*c.* 538 B.C.E), ZEC 8:22

Rather than take the Orthodox Jewish view that many nations would worship the Messiah after his future return, Christians feel that Christ has already fulfilled this prophecy before his Second Coming. Whereas Jews have felt oppressed and persecuted by Christian domination of the world's religious scene for the last 20 centuries, Christians see the spread of the "good news" of Christ to the farthest corners of the planet as fulfillment of this prophecy.

His return did not happen as soon as he promised in the New Testament (within the same generation), but then Christians can also cite Christ's statement, recorded in Matthew, Mark, and Luke, when in so many words he said that no one (not even he) can be certain when God decides it is time. If he appeared to miss a number of important prophetic steps in his first coming, the holes can be filled when he returns the next time in glory.

WHO IS IMITATING IMMANUEL?

Bible scholar Hal Lindsey rekindled Christian end-time interpretations of Scripture in the 1970s with books like *The Late, Great Planet Earth*. Since that time most evangelical Christians have taken Lindsey's lead and characterize the Messiah expected by Jews in the 21st century to be the False Prophet who will deceive Israel before the real Jesus returns. Some call Lindsey's spin divinely inspired. Others disagree – and some Jewish scholars of prophecy have confided to me that they consider it a form of prescient anti-Semitism.

Lindsey has spent decades fine-tuning his vision, and would deny being anti-Jewish. However, it is my contention that no one who believes Christ is the promised Messiah can avoid the darker implications of their belief. For it must follow that the Jews, as God's chosen people, have to believe that they committed a grievous error by rejecting Christ – an error that leaves them open to divine punishment of the worst sort.

ABOVE **Jews in Germany were recognized by the Star of David forced upon them by the anti-Semitic regime.**

If this is so, what is the next logical step? *How* does God punish the wayward? Wars, pestilence, and bad weather have always been part of God's arsenal in the biblical tradition. How have the Jews *in fact* been punished? By centuries of persecution, culminating in Hitler's "final solution."

This line of beliefs leads to a logical conclusion most Christians shy away from: if God is punishing the Jews, then those millions of Christians who either looked the other way or actively took part in the Holocaust – running the trains, pulling the levers in the gas chambers, and performing a litany of other inhuman acts against Jews – were only acting as helpers in God's divine chastisement.

ABOVE **Hitler's persecution of German Jews continues to defy human understanding.**

Christians have killed each other in huge numbers over whose sect of Christianity is *the* true and correct one. Yet each of these warring sects – at least in their most doctrinaire expressions – believes that once this (apparently divinely sanctioned) persecution of the Jews is ended, Christ will come to deliver those same chosen people and restore them to glory – alongside the Christians, of course, who got it right in the first place.

Conversely, Orthodox Jewish interpreters of the Bible say the real Immanuel will deliver them despite 2,000 years of world domination by a deceived religious cult. This cult, they contend, grew out of a failed Jewish

reform movement and survived by spreading itself beyond Palestine and adopting heathen and Gentile ideas. Where Christians like Lindsey promote the idea of the rise of a second Roman Empire in Europe under a tyrant Antichrist, Orthodox Jews say the empire of Daniel's multihorned "Beast" has been around for two millennia, and has been the prime source of their persecution and near-annihilation.

Is the punishment from God? Yes, say many Jewish mystics, but not for missing Christ. The Diaspora, like the Babylonian captivity before it, is part divine punishment and part atonement for the fact that God's chosen people strayed from the Torah. Perhaps God used the false prophet of the cross to convert their first oppressors, Imperial Rome, and then sustain the persecution through European empires and kingdoms to this day. These anti-Jewish nations were often at war with each other, yet they had one uniting bond – their hatred of the people their priests told them killed their Messiah. Sixteen centuries of official papal policy condemning Jews as "subhumans," only "good for slavery," saw them crowded into ghettos, their clothes branded with yellow Stars of David, their children abducted and forcibly baptized as Christians. Religiously sanctioned hatred created a climate in Europe that finally saw Jewish bodies incinerated in concentration camps.

At least the wholesale butchering of six million Jews by the Nazis has impelled Christians to shrink away from their old ways. Perhaps the willingness to make ghettos will never return. Anti-Semitism will find itself forced into finding more civilized and subtle guises.

But maybe Hal Lindsey is right, and the Jews are awaiting a false prophet. If so, what are the signs?

The wilderness and the solitary place shall be glad for thee; and the desert shall rejoice, and blossom as the rose. It shall blossom abundantly, and rejoice even with joy and singing: the glory of Lebanon shall be given unto it the excellency of Carmel and Sharon. They shall see the glory of the Lord and the excellency of our God.

FIRST ISAIAH (783–687 B.C.E), IS 35:1–2

Hal Lindsey believes that this passage foretells the restoration of the kingdom of Israel to Palestine. You would know the final times of the *false* prophet, and Christ's return, had come when the Jews returned to Israel and applied revolutionary agricultural techniques to transform desert lands into a green oasis. The land of Israel has undergone a transformation into a green oasis since the state's creation in 1948.

And he shall confirm the covenant with many for one week: and in the midst of the week he shall cause the sacrifice and the oblation to cease, and for the overspreading of abominations he shall make it desolate, even until the consummation, and that determined shall be poured upon the desolate.

DANIEL (c. 6TH TO 4TH CENTURY B.C.E), DAN 9:27

ABOVE **The formerly arid Jordan valley has been transformed into productive agricultural land since the foundation of the state of Israel.**

Lindsey believes this augurs a deal to be closed in the near future between a false prophet arising in Israel and some future European leader. The European Union leader will guarantee Israel's military and political protection and "Temple rights" in Jerusalem's old city (which I imagine means their right to rebuild the Temple over the Dome of the Rock), if Israel will, as Lindsey says in *The Late, Great Planet Earth,* "sign the treaty and worship the false Jewish prophet as the Messiah and the Antichrist as God Himself." I imagine

Lindsey sees this European leader as the Antichrist; however, I think this prophecy is vague and open to whatever one's religious limitations want to read into it.

Lindsey soldiers on, unraveling the double-talk of St. John in the next passage about "the beast(s)."

And I beheld another beast coming up out of the earth; and he had two horns like a lamb, and he spake as a dragon. And he exerciseth all the power of the first beast before him, and causeth the earth and them which dwell therein to worship the first beast, whose deadly wound was healed. And he doeth great wonders, so that he maketh fire come down from heaven on the earth in the sight of men. And deceiveth them that dwell on the earth by the means of those miracles which he had power to do in the sight of the beast; saying to them that dwell on the earth, that they should make an image to the beast, which had the wound by a sword, and did live.

And he had power to give life unto the image of the beast, that the image of the beast should both speak, and cause that as many as would not worship the image of the beast should be killed. And he causeth all, both small and great, rich and poor, free and bond, to receive a mark in their right hand, or in their foreheads: And that no man might buy or sell, save he that had the mark or the name of the beast, or the number of his name.

Here is wisdom. Let him that hath understanding count the number of the beast: for it is the number of a man; and his number is six hundred threescore and six [666].

ST. JOHN OF PATMOS
(81–96 C.E.), RV 13:11–18

LEFT **St. John of Patmos had a vision of a hybrid beast that bore the mark "666"; he predicted that this beast would be widely worshiped and that the mark would be received by followers. This has led to the modern interpretation of a false Messiah bearing the same mark.**

Lindsey believes this psychedelic bad trip of biblical eschatology is a profile of the false Jewish prophet who will do miracles and masquerade as the Messiah. Lindsey's idea of a cosmically inspired con man exploiting the Israeli people is not completely without merit. There are religious zealots in and outside of Israel intent on triggering a fundamentalist revolution to overthrow the secular Israeli government sometime in the near future.

My anonymous sources in Israel tell me the move toward this goal began with the assassination of the moderate prime minister Yitzhak Rabin by a fundamentalist zealot during Rabin's reelection campaign in 1995. Accusations fly that the right-wing-dominated Interior Ministry then helped Netanyahu squeak past Rabin's successor, Peres, in the polls by giving party members fake identity cards so they could vote more than once. Netanyahu won the election by a mere 15,000 votes.

Even if this accusation is false, the country *is* moving steadily to the right, thanks to the Interior Ministry granting thousands of generally right-wing European Jewish immigrants permission to settle in Israel. The religious right in the Interior Ministry encourages those settlers to have as many children as possible by offering generous welfare payments – a family with ten children, for example, could receive a hefty check equaling U.S. $2,500 a month. In a decade or so, and with a population sympathetic to extreme fundamentalism, Israel could have its own "Ayatollah"-style dictator.

In such a future Hal Lindsey's interpretations above seems to be more than plausible. A right-wing government welcomes the second beast – a false "Lamb of God," the counterfeit Jewish prophet. He gives Israel's allegiance to the first beast – the Antichrist – who leads the European Union of tomorrow. Subsequently this Antichrist will miraculously recover from a head wound received in an assassination attempt, "proving" he is Christ returned. Then everyone will get his number tattooed – some interpreters say electronically – on their foreheads and right hands. Without the mark you won't be able to buy or sell a thing, receive your social security check, or log on to America On-Line.

ABOVE **Yitzhak Rabin's assassination has been seen as the beginning of a process by which a false Messiah will be placed at the head of the Israeli government.**

Thus does the number 666 bring another Bible interpreter under its intoxicating and devilish spell. Hal Lindsey promotes a future timeline that actual history has disconnected for nearly 2,000 years. As I stated earlier, the number 666 stands for the Hebrew letters that spell out the name of the Roman Emperor Nero, a man St. John of Patmos expected would suffer a serious head wound and then revive. In fact Nero never suffered any such head wound, and he has been very dead now for over 19 centuries. Lindsey, like his predecessor John of Patmos, is biased toward seeing an apocalypse in the near future, and it seems both visionaries are willing to twist Scripture's arm until it submits in print, if not in reality.

RIGHTEOUS WRONGS

Woe to every sinful liar, who heareth the verses of God recited to him, and then, as though he heard them not, persisteth in proud disdain!...There is a shameful chastisement coming for them.

MUHAMMAD (c. 620–630), QUR 45:6, 8

Who is a liar but he that denieth that Jesus is the Christ? He is Antichrist, that denieth the father and the Son.

JOHN THE ELDER
(c. 1ST CENTURY C.E.), 1 JN 2:22

There is no God but God, and Muhammad is his prophet!

FROM THE SHAHADAH
(TESTIMONY OF ISLAMIC FAITH)

We are of God: he that knoweth God heareth us; he that is not of God heareth not us.

JOHN THE ELDER
(c. 1ST CENTURY C.E.), 1 JN 4:6

[The Jews] both killed the Lord Jesus, and their own prophets, and have persecuted us [Christians]; [they] please not God, and are contrary to all men. Forbidding us to speak to the Gentiles that they might be saved... for the wrath is come upon them to the uttermost [measure].

SAUL OF TARSUS (51 C.E.), 1 THES 2:15–16

No baptism, no mixed marriage will protect us against the omnipotent hatred of Jews. Under this extreme pressure, when there is no escape at all, in the last days, then Israel will return to the Lord his God.

RABBI HILE WECHSLER (c. 1873), EWM

And this shall be the plague wherewith the Lord will smite all the people that have fought against Jerusalem [i.e., against the Jews, perhaps Christians included]: Their flesh shall consume away while they stand upon their feet and their eyes shall consume away in their holes and their tongue shall consume away in their mouths.

FIRST ZECHARIAH (c. 538 B.C.E), ZEC 14:12

He will root out false doctrines and destroy the rule of Muhammadism. [God's] dominion will extend from the East to the West. All nations will adore God their Lord according to Catholic teaching.

THE VENERABLE BARTHOLOMAEUS
VON HOLTZHAUSER (1658)

Vishnu will return...as [Kalki] the last Avatar, amid fire and flames...he will travel across the globe...butchering the sinful with his sword.... He will overthrow [the religion and political power of] the Mleccas [Western foreigners, i.e., Muslims and Christian Europeans].

THE SRIMAD BHAGAVATA (c. 1500 B.C.E)

And ye shall be hated of all men for
my name's sake: but [the Christian] that
shall endure unto the end, shall be saved.

Y'SHUA (*c.* 30 C.E.), MK 13:13

In the final days...many men will doubt whether
the Catholic faith is the true and only saving one
and whether the Jews are perhaps correct when
they still expect the Messiah.

ST. METHODIUS (385 C.E.)

Almost all unbelievers and the Jews will be
converted and there will be one law, one
[Catholic] faith, one baptism, one life.

JOHN OF VATIGUERRO (13TH CENTURY)

And it shall come to pass that every one that
[survives] of all the nations which came against
Jerusalem [and the Jews] shall even go up from
year to year to worship the King, the Lord of
hosts and keep the feast of the tabernacles....

SECOND ZECHARIAH (*c.* 160 B.C.E), ZEC 14:16

The [12th] Imam will bring Israel
back [to Islam].... All nations will
be converted [to Islam].

ALI (*c.* 650), NAZR ULAGA

Thou shall love and worship
no other Gods but me!

ATTRIBUTED TO YAHWEH, THE JEWISH GOD

And to you who are troubled rest with us, when the Lord Jesus shall be revealed from heaven with his mighty angels, in flaming fire taking vengeance on them that know not God, and they obey not the gospel of our Lord Jesus Christ. [They] shall be punished with everlasting destruction from the presence of the Lord, and from the glory of his power.

SAUL OF TARSUS (*c.* 51 C.E.), 2 THES 1:7–9

Before the Second Coming of Christ, [the Blessed Virgin] Mary…will extend the reign of Christ over the heathens and the Mohammedans.

BLESSED SISTER MARY OF AGREDA (1665)

I am the *only* begotten Son of God.

(ATTRIBUTED TO CHRIST)

I am the *last* Prophet of God.

(ATTRIBUTED TO MUHAMMAD)

I came to save the world.

(ATTRIBUTED TO HITLER)

Someone messianic may be coming, but he is lost in all the finger-pointing and prejudice.

It seems to me that God's chosen can never escape the chain their comparison forges with the "unchosen." If there were no judgment of others as lower, then those feeling righteously higher would have no raison d'être. People would just be people. Religion would just be "religiousness." To be special, to be forgiven, you have to make others "unspecial" and keep them "unforgiven."

Does righteousness need divisions to survive?

To me the famous statement "Judge not lest ye be judged" can be taken in a new way. To judge or compare yourself with another must put you in a division: it must chain rightness to wrongness, otherwise how can judgment exist? The one who judges must draw psychic and emotional borders and barbwire them shut with definitions.

Yet every religion preaches that we should not judge others. Why? Perhaps because there is a lot of judging going on.

Each religion covers the ugly face of its judgments with the masks of love, compassion, and forgiveness. Certainly there has been a lot of persecution, torture, and war down through history coming from the same hands that press together in prayer.

Perhaps judgment has made a false prophet out of everyone's messiah.

Whenever discord prevails instead of unity, wherever hatred and antagonism take the place of love and spiritual fellowship, Antichrist reigns instead of Christ.

'ABDU'L-BAHÁ (1912), PRM

Only people condemn who have some part in what they are condemning.

OSHO (1976), SHWR

The Advent

A great teacher with olive skin and bearded will come from the direction of the rising sun, flying in a huge canoe with massive wings a few centuries after the coming of the white brother.

QUETZALCOATL (*c.* PRE-COLUMBIAN)

THE ADVENT

Behold, I come quickly: and my reward is with me, to give every man according as his work shall be. I am the Alpha and Omega, the beginning and the end, the first and the last.

Y'SHUA AS CHANNELED BY JOHN OF PATMOS (81–96 C.E.), RV 22:12–13

Where do we look on the day of reckoning, the advent of the Messiah? East of Eden? West of Java? Look! Up in the sky!

Is it a bird symbol? Is it a flying canoe plane? No! It's the Savior flying down from the clouds.

If he shows me his mysterious seal or offers me his stone tablet calling card, will I recognize the right sign from the wrong? Will it be his face smiling on the mala bead necklace?

Will he speak in Hebrew, or thee-and-thou me with archaic King James jabber?

Just what does a messiah wear on his coming-out day? A robe made of the light of his beatitude? A Corpus Christi? No corpse? Does his bloody wine and bready flesh dissolve in everyone's body?

What color is the skin of my messiah?

I hope it's my skin color, or I'll be as blue as Khrist – I mean Chrisna – with consternation.

ABOVE **Popular perceptions of the second coming envisage Christ descending from Heaven.**

SALVATION RIDES A WHITE HORSE

THE WESTERN MESSIAH

And I saw heaven opened, and behold a white horse; and he that sat upon him was called FAITHFUL AND TRUE, and in righteousness he doth judge and make war. His eyes were as a flame of fire, and on his head were many crowns; and he had a name written, that no man knew, but he himself. And he was clothed with a vesture dipped in blood: and his name is called THE WORD OF GOD. And the armies which were in heaven followed him upon white horses, clothed in fine linen, white and clean. And out of his mouth goeth a sharp sword, that with it he should smite the nations: and he shall rule them with a rod of iron: and he treadeth the winepress of fierceness and wrath of Almighty God. And he hath on his vesture and on his thigh a name written, KING OF KINGS, AND LORD OF LORDS.

And I saw the beast, and the kings of the Earth, and their armies gathered together to make war against him that sat on the horse, and against his army. And the Beast was taken, and with him the false prophet that wrought miracles before him....These both were cast alive into a lake of fire burning with brimstone.... And the remnant were slain with the sword of him that sat upon the horse, which sword proceeded out of his mouth: and all the [birds] were filled with their flesh.

ST. JOHN OF PATMOS (81–96 C.E.) RV 19:11–16, 19–21

ABOVE **Vishnu is pictured in this 18th-century panel at the center of his incarnations as ten avatars. In his final incarnation he is predicted to return amid flames riding a white stallion who will bear him across the globe as he vanquishes wrong and restores righteousness.**

THE EASTERN AVATAR

Vishnu will return as Kalki, upon a white horse, as the last Avatara, amid fire and flames.

HINDU PURANAS (*c.* 900 C.E.)

When the Kali age...is well-nigh past, the Lord will appear in His divine form consisting of Sattva [purity] alone for the protection of virtue.

Lord Vishnu adorned of the whole animate and inanimate creation, and the Soul of the universe, appears in this world of matter for protecting the virtue of the righteous and wiping out the entire stock of their Karma and thereby liberating them. The Lord will appear under the name of Kalki...riding a fleet horse...and capable of subduing the wicked. The Lord of the universe wielding...divine powers and possessed of endless virtues and matchless splendor, he will traverse the globe on that swift horse and exterminate with his sword the robbers [those whose minds are devoted to iniquity] by the tens of millions.

THE SRIMAD BHAGAVATA (*c.* 1500 B.C.E.)

He will, then, reestablish righteousness upon Earth; and the minds of those who live at the end of the Kali age shall be awakened, and shall be as translucent as crystal.

VISHNU PURANA (*c.* 900 C.E.) VIS-P IV: 24, 26–27

Whether you live in the East or the West, salvation comes riding to your rescue on a white horse. St. John paints a symbolic picture that most Christian interpreters take for granted as the militant return of Jesus Christ come to judge the wicked at the end of history, but it could just as well be a Hindu avatar galloping to our rescue. The Hindu scriptures give their own prophetic legend of the latter-day Messiah as Kalki riding down illusion upon Revelation's white horse.

Hindu scriptures tell us that each great cycle of time can expect ten avatars (incarnations of the god Vishnu) to visit the earth and give the evolution of human consciousness a loving nudge – or a kick – in the backside.

The first divine incarnation of Vishnu on earth was a fish. This is an interesting parallel to the view held by science that mankind's oldest land ancestor was some eccentric fish who one day flopped out of the waves and forever remained a fish out of water, bringing vertebrate life to the continents. This corporeal manifestation of the God Vishnu, the preserver of the world, incarnated once again as a tortoise. In other words, the next leap in evolution was from fish to reptilian dinosaurs. The later epochs received their savior in the guise of a boar (perhaps representing evolution's next leap of consciousness to mammals), a man-lion, and a dwarf (perhaps one of our diminutive and hairy cave-dwelling ancestors).

Then enlightenment's messenger evolved into something more primate in appearance, like Parashurama the demon-killer, who wielded an ax. Then came Lord Rama – hero of the epic poem *The Ramayana*. After Rama the Vishnu oversoul incarnated as Lord Krishna, the blue-skinned God-man of mischief and cosmic play.

If we correlate Hindu timings with those of the less mythical but archeologically tested computations of the West, we might discover that, since the time of Rama, avatars have incarnated roughly once every 25 centuries or so. This takes in Lord Buddha, living around 500 b.c.e, as the most recent avatar. Twenty-five centuries forward deposits us in our own time, which should see the appearance of the final avatar, who some interpreters believe will draw the gunmetal gray days of the Kali yuga to a dramatic close. The Hindu Puranas caution us to be aware that this incarnation will not come as a playful flute player and heartthrob of twelve thousand gopis, like Krishna, or sit and contemplate Nirvana's navel like Buddha Gautama. The tenth avatar will be the supergod Vishnu himself as the apocalyptic equestrian, Kalki (meaning "conqueror of time"), astride a white stallion, coming to ride down illusion (and those attached to their illusions) and then take whatever remains of humanity on to a higher stage of spiritual evolution.

THE MAN FROM THE EAST

Long awaited he will never return. He will appear in Asia [and be] at home in Europe. One who is issued from great Hermes, and over all the Kings of the East will he grow.

NOSTRADAMUS (1555), 10 Q75

He will reappear from the East [East of Iran, that is — possibly India].

ALI (*c.* 650), NAZR ULAGA

And, behold, the glory of the God of Israel came from the way of the East: and his voice was like a noise of many waters: and the earth shined with his glory.

EZEKIEL (593–571 B.C.E), EZ 43:2

From the Black Sea, and great Tartary, there will be a king who will come to see France. [He] will penetrate through Russia and Armenia, and into Byzantium [Istanbul] where he will leave his bloody rod.

NOSTRADAMUS (1555), 5 Q54

For as the lightning cometh out of the East, and shineth ever unto the West; so shall also the coming of the Son of man be.

Y'SHUA (*c.* 30 C.E.), MT 24:27

The man from the East will come out of his seat, passing across the Apennines to see France. He will fly through the sky, the rains and the snows, and strike everyone with his rod.

NOSTRADAMUS (1555), 2 Q29

I see barbed wire fences in Mongolia and far into Russia [bringing to mind the Communist era]. After that a man will appear in the East with a face like carved stone. The hilt of his sword he always has in his hands. A body like polished marble.

MADAME SYLVIA (1931)

A great teacher with olive skin and bearded will come from the direction of the rising sun, flying in a huge canoe with massive wings a few centuries after the coming of the white brother.

QUETZALCOATL (*c.* PRE-COLUMBIAN)

I am forever looking and praying eastward to the rising Sun for my true white brother to come and purify the Hopi. My father, Yukiuma, used to tell me that I would be the one to take over as leader at this time, because I belong to the Sun Clan, the father of all the people on the Earth. I was told that I must not give in, because I am the first. The Sun is the father of all living things from the first creation. And if I am done, the Sun Clan, then there will be no living thing left on the Earth. So I have stood fast. I hope you will understand what I am trying to tell you.

DAN KATCHONGVA, HOPI ELDER (1972),
FROM *THE BEGINNING OF LIFE TO THE DAY OF PURIFICATION*

And the [American Indians] had a prophecy from the old days: that a man from the East, with his followers wearing red clothes, would come to this land and free them from slavery imposed on them by the invaders. By coincidence, my people were wearing red clothes; by coincidence, I was coming from the East. And red Indians started coming, saying that "We have been waiting – because this prophecy we have heard for generations." These were the fears the [U.S.] government would never talk about. I could have provoked the red Indians against the whole American government, I could have created a revolution – this was their fear. They wanted to destroy me and the commune as quickly as possible.

OSHO (1986), BYND

On the day the authentic Messiah arrives, don't be caught straining your eyes westward. A preponderance of visions transcending the doctrinal boundaries of many a religion hint that the next great deliverer of humanity will come from the East. Tibetan legends speak of the spiritual efforts of adepts hidden deep in the Himalayas. These masters use their occult and meditative skills to induce the incarnation of a great Eastern soul into the body of a Westerner, so that he will appear as a spiritual conqueror to destroy centuries-old ignorance.

Until the day he transmigrates into a Western body, no savior will have much success in dissolving the snares of the West. Some on the fringe of Hindu messianic tradition believe that even if the deliverer is physically born in the West, he will nonetheless be an Easterner in spirit. The followers of the American mystic Franklin Jones (1939–), currently addressed by the Sanskrit name Adi Da, believe that he is the reincarnation of Hindu Swami Vivekananda (d. 1902), who was a pivotal mystic messenger from the East bringing Vedantic Hindu ideas to the Western world. The followers of Adi Da/Vivekananda add the role of Kalki to his current incarnation as the tenth Hindu avatar.

Theosophy – an amalgamation of Eastern traditions into a new religion founded at the end of the 19th century by the Russian mystic Helena Petrovna Blavatsky – declared that one of its most important goals was to prepare a human vehicle for the spirit of Maitreya (the Second Coming of Buddha). The early-20th-century Theosophist leaders, Annie Besant and C. W. Leadbeater, sought South Asian as well as Western children as Maitreya's targets for transmigration. Leadbeater looked for children whose auras were pure enough for their bodies to undergo the occult conditioning needed to ready them for the descent of the Buddhist Messiah.

All spiritual changeling, breeding, and transmigrating aside, it must be stressed that most of the followers of more mainstream Buddhist and Hindu traditions set their third eyes on their own homegrown, Eastern-born gurus as prime kandidates for Kalki. Even visionaries

ABOVE **Leading British Theosophist, Annie Besant. Her cult believed that Buddha would return to save the West.**

ABOVE **The Russian Helena Petrovna Blavatksy founded the 19th-century religion Theosophy that sought to facilitate the return of Buddha to earth.**

with a distinctly Western bias, like the 16th-century seer Michel Nostradamus and the 19th-century Russian novelist and Christian mystic Leo Tolstoy, look beyond the Christ to the approach of an Asian world avatar.

Nostradamus is quite specific that this man would come from the East and bring a Hermetic-style religion to the West. The nondual aspects of Hermetic philosophy make it one of the Occident's most Asian-sympathetic mysteries. Nostradamus's sources for Hermetic teachings are Near Eastern neo-Platonist writers of Byzantium and Syria. He describes this man from the East flying in some aircraft before he strikes everyone with his "rod." In this case the "rod of iron," usually held like a weapon of retribution against sinners by biblical versions of the Messiah, finds a more compassionate Hermetic definition as the caduceus "rod" of a Hermetic master. He strikes human beings with his awareness-stick.

ABOVE **Although a Christian mystic Tolstoy believed in the return of an Asian avatar.**

Russian Empire, the Armenian-Greek mystic, G. I. Gurdjieff (1866?–1949). Around 1900, Gurdjieff was traveling to Tibet. He had already finished two decades of trekking through much of Central Asia, the Middle East, India, and Mongolia in search of mystery schools and enlightenment.

Gurdjieff's mystical awakening came several years after Tolstoy wrote his prophecy. He resurfaced in Moscow in 1912 to begin gathering such disciples as P. D. Ouspensky and other Russian occultists and intelligentsia. By 1925 Gurdjieff had come from the East, by way of Turkey (or "Byzantium," as Nostradamus called it), to "see France." He established his mystery school for what he called the harmonious development of man at the Château Prieuré near Avon, outside Paris. There he introduced Western people to a new teaching combining the spiritual sciences of Eastern Orthodox Christianity, Sufism, and Asian religions.

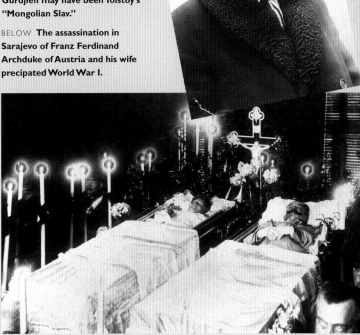

RIGHT **The religious reformer G. I. Gurdjieff may have been Tolstoy's "Mongolian Slav."**

BELOW **The assassination in Sarajevo of Franz Ferdinand Archduke of Austria and his wife precipitated World War I.**

Leo Tolstoy (1828-1910) was no mean prophet, even though he is better known as the creator of the novels *War and Peace* and *Anna Karenina*. In his essay *Christianity and Patriotism* (1894), and later in *Bethink Yourselves!* (1904), he foresaw the weapons and horrors of modern warfare and the rapacious greed of modern consumerism as it wantonly devoured the human spirit along with the world's natural resources. Tolstoy accurately dated a new world war spreading from the Balkans, which he said would "develop into a destructive calamity in 1913."

"In that year," adds Tolstoy, "I see Europe in flames and bleeding. I hear lamentations on huge battlefields." In 1913 war did erupt in the Balkans, and the assassination of Austrian Archduke Franz Ferdinand the following year brought on the First World War. Europe bled for four years, with over 10 million dead choking the trenches cut across muddy battlefields hundreds of miles long.

Tolstoy believed that sometime after this war – around the year 1925 – a religious reformer would appear from Central Asia. He would come out of the East during a time of moral and spiritual decay. Perhaps this is a prophecy for the Roaring Twenties, the amoral decade when America and Western Europe knew loose women, cabarets, and gangsters. Tolstoy's reformer, whom he calls the "Mongolian Slav," would then "clear the world of the relics of monotheism and lay the cornerstone of the temple of pantheism. God, soul, spirit, and immortality will be molten in the new furnace, and I see the peaceful beginning of an ethical era."

Tolstoy sensed that this man was already walking the earth at the time he recorded this prophecy, around 1900. He saw him as a man of action who at the time was not aware of his superior power. Tolstoy's prophecy may have foretold the coming of a fellow citizen of the

ABOVE **The West has gradually been introduced to Asian religions over the last four centuries. Krishna is now worshiped across the world.**

Gurdjieff was one of many mystics from the East drawn to spread their message even farther westward, to America. In 1924 he made the first of nine trips to America, intent on seeding his brand of spiritual "study groups" there.

There are prophecies from India and Tibet that describe America as the cradle of the new religions of the coming two thousand years of the Aquarian Age. To many, the idea of a filthy-rich, materialistic, and self-centered America becoming the home of the next avatar seems far-fetched. Yet Hindu and Buddhist scholars remind us that the last great father of a new world religion, Siddhartha Gautama (the Buddha), lived at a time when the not-yet-overpopulated Indian civilization was a great center of wealth and culture.

Indeed, it may be true that only those cultures that achieve many of their worldly dreams can experience how it must feel to be the dog who caught the car. (The next time a canine chases your wheels, slow down and stop your car and you'll see what I mean.) Many of the greatest founders of Eastern religions, such as Krishna and Mahavira, were satiated yet frustrated rich princes suffering an existential crisis. Buddha was the Howard Hughes of his time. He had it all – women, money, and a garage of chariots at his disposal. And if even a dog has Buddha-nature, then it is not disrespectful to say that Prince Gautama was just another dog who finally caught a carful of life's seemingly unattainable desires. Once attained, he dropped them all, escaped to the forest, and began a new religion renouncing the Indian

dream. Perhaps Maitreya, Buddha's successor, will be a modern man of comparable stature. Even a billionaire prince of cyberspace might stop chasing the American dream and all of its illusions once they were caught.

While Asian prophecies point to America as their savior's final destination, a whole welcoming crowd of Native American prophecies point to the East as their deliverer's launching pad. North and South American Indians have been waiting for their Asian Indian savior for over a thousand years. More than five hundred tribes share a like number of prophecies describing the man from the East. Since space here is limited, I will distill them down to the following shared details.

The man who will restore the law and religion of the Native American comes from the eastern horizon. He is olive-skinned and is often described as either wearing a white robe and having a long white beard, or wearing a red robe and hat. His people dress in red cloaks and caps and arrive with this man in a big "flying canoe."

The Hopi say the religious leader they call the "True White Brother" will send two helpers before he arrives. They carry three secret symbols: a swastika, a cross, and a sign of the sun. (Before Adolf Hitler raped the occult significance of the swastika, this ancient sun symbol was first the sign of the South Asian Jain religion, and later was adopted as a sign of the Hindus and Buddhists.) The Hopi also say the savior's "red-capped and cloaked" people will come in great numbers to the American West, but eventually they will vanish from sight.

The last 30 years of the 20th century have seen the Native American tribes of the western United States mark the passing of two spiritual leaders and two waves of their red-cloaked followers from the East. If one of these is not the awaited True White Brother, then perhaps they are his helpers or forerunners.

ABOVE **Odilon Redon gives his own impression
of Buddha in this early 20th-century painting.
Westerners have increasingly turned to Buddhist
philosophy and practices.**

Tibetan lamas dressed in maroon cloaks and caps began sending their ambassadors to America during the latter days of the 20th century. They did this because of the fulfillment of all three precursory signs in Padmasambhava's 1,200-year-old prophecy, which are said to pave the way for Buddhism's transplantation to America. The prophecy, authored by the founder of Tibetan Lamaism, says, "When the iron bird flies [airplanes] and the horse runs on wheels [cars], the Tibetan people will be scattered like ants across the face of the Earth, and the Dharma will come to the land of the red men."

In 1976, Gomang Hhensur Rinpoche, a high lama in the exiled Tibetan community, met with a Hopi elder, Grandfather David Monongye, in a sacred kiva in the Hopi village of Hotevilla on Third Mesa in Arizona. In his book *The Return of Pahana,* Robert Boissière, a French author and long-time friend of the Hopi Nation, says the meetings between the two attempted to evaluate whether Hopi and Tibetan prophecies shared the same vision. The Hopi wondered if the coming of the red-robed Tibetan monks to America was a sign that Pahana, the Great White Brother, was at hand. The Tibetans wondered if this indeed was the time in history when the seed of Eastern religion would fly westward to the land of the red man, as Padmasambhava had foreseen.

In 1950, invading Chinese soldiers started crushing the mother flower of Tibetan Buddhism underfoot; their campaign to systematically dynamite monasteries and obliterate Tibetan culture was well advanced by the 1970s. The Tibetans of this time flew in metal planes and rode around in wheeled cars, and the Chinese had effectively scattered the lamas and Rinpoches and over a million Tibetan refugees like ants across the world. By the mid-1970s, many a Tibetan monk of Buddhist Dharma was placing a sandaled foot upon hot tarmac and car pedal in the land of the red man.

ABOVE **The 14th Dalai Lama presides among the bright robes of his priests. Their color was determined by their founder.**

After the encounter of Rinpoche and the Hopi elder, Grandfather David Monongye sent a message of welcome to the Dalai Lama and the Tibetans acknowledging the spiritual connection of the two peoples. Since that day many more meetings have taken place between the two groups, culminating in the 14th Dalai Lama himself paying a visit to the Hopi elders on their reservation in 1991.

In 1984, nearly a decade after Grandfather David met his first candidates for the red-cap-and-cloak tribe, he entertained a red-clothed man and woman who were emissaries from another tribe coming from the East. Swami Sudhiro, in whose veins runs the blood of two aboriginal races, Native American and tribal Filipino, was a long-time and beloved friend of Grandfather David. Sudhiro's woman companion, whose name was Ma Waduda, was part

ABOVE **Tibetan monks in ceremonial dress blow trumpets as part of spiritual ritual.**

Cherokee Indian and was a noted psychic and therapist. Both were disciples of the Jain-born Asian Indian mystic, Bhagwan Shree Rajneesh (currently called Osho), who had come to the West a few years earlier to take up residence in a remote part of former Indian land in eastern Oregon. Eventually thousands of his red-clad followers gathered around him to build a commune city called Rajneeshpuram on the 64,000-acre spread called Rancho Rajneesh.

Waduda – who is currently a faculty member at the Osho Academy in Sedona, Arizona – related to me that Grandfather David welcomed both of them to stay as guests in his house. At that time he was recovering from an injury to his eyes.

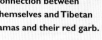

LEFT **Hopi Indians have acknowledged a spiritual connection between themselves and Tibetan lamas and their red garb.**

"He began by explaining to us that he had an accident chopping firewood," she said. "He had hurt his eye and was not able to read any longer.

"He had just received some mail. And he asked us would we read some letters to him. He sat down with us on a bench and put his arms around both of us, one on each side. And we read his letters to him. One was a personal letter from a friend – the kind of letter that just says we love you and hope you're doing well. And the other letter was from the United Nations. It was a letter thanking Grandfather David for coming to the United Nations and presenting the Hopi vision for preventing the ending of the world.

"We gave Grandfather David…an Osho book and he was very delighted to receive it. We told him about Rajneeshpuram and people all wearing red and he was very thrilled to hear this. We told him that [Rajneeshpuram] was a place where all races and all nationalities were meeting together."

Grandfather David replied that he had tried the same experiment on the reservation. He wanted to bring together many races and nationalities, but the U.S. government prevented the Hopi Nation from creating this little global village where people from all over the world could live together in harmony.

"That is why Grandfather David was so thrilled that we were managing something similar," said Waduda. She then added, in a voice warm with the sweet memory of the old man's kind presence, "He was tremendously loving to us. And tremendously grateful and very encouraging. And very joyful."

That night Sudhiro and Waduda stayed in Flagstaff. Neither of them could fall asleep. They were so filled with blissful memories of the old Indian, and the ordinary yet extraordinary lightness of his presence, that Waduda says they stayed awake giggling until five o'clock the following morning.

"We realized many, many things," Waduda reflected later. "One of them was that, first of all, going to see Grandfather David was quite a mysterious thing. He was revered among his people in the same way that Osho was with all of his disciples, and for someone to just walk up to, let's say, Osho's house and just have an interview with him …. Well! That would have been quite an honor. So we realized that we had been honored greatly. It was a tremendous thing to be able to read this letter from the United Nations acknowledging Grandfather David, and to recognize… the significance and the importance of that man within the Hopi tribes and even within the United States and within the world."

Before they left his home, Waduda and Sudiro invited Grandfather David to come visit Rajneeshpuram. They told him that they were inviting many Native American Indians to move to Rajneeshpuram and live with them, and asked if he would grant his blessings, which he gladly did. Grandfather David requested that they only gather Indians living off the reservation, because he said it was necessary for Indians living on the reservations to stay where they were in order to prevent the foretold end of the world, known in Hopi prophecy as the Great Purification.

ABOVE **The Indian mystic Osho (Bhagwan Shree Rajneesh) seated with followers at his feet.**

ABOVE **Osho inspired the migration of thousands from the East to the U.S.**

Grandfather David never got a chance to visit Rajneeshpuram, because in the following year it was destroyed and the red-clad followers had (reminiscent of the Hopi prophecies) scattered to the four corners of the world and gone "underground."

By 1985 other Hopi elders were aware of Osho. Some of them cautiously admitted that his followers – who at the time were flying in by the tens of thousands (mostly by jet, from the East) to meditate with their teacher – seemed to fulfill many of the Hopi prophecies. Even the shadow of controversy surrounding their free-style religion and free-living ways fulfilled predictions that the red-capped, red-cloaked "tribe" would fashion a religion that was unique in the world – one that rebelled against the fear-mongering and dogmatically life-negating ways of the status-quo religions. Hopi prophecy-watchers knew that the established religions, especially those of the whites, would violently oppose the red tribe's stay in America. Indeed, the mainstream religions in America branded the Rajneeshees a cult, and Osho was especially frightening to the right-wing Christian elements in President Reagan's cabinet. Osho's ruthlessly playful observations of American politicians, along with his scathing criticism of the treatment of Native Americans, had the Reagan administration worried that he might take on the mantle of the promised red Indian savior.

Osho dismissed the idea, but he did challenge the white people to ask permission to stay on the Native Americans' continent. "All of us who are only guests here should ask the red Indians for their forgiveness," said Osho. "We all should leave at once for our homelands if they tell us to go."

By late 1985 the Reagan administration found a way to deport Osho and, without their master present, his followers disbanded their commune in Oregon. After 1986, the Rajneeshee tribe abandoned their distinctive fiery scarlet clothing and seemed to disperse from sight.

Other Native American tribes were sensitive to the prophetic significance of the red Rajneeshees. Shortly after Osho was deported from the U.S. in late 1985, Good Horse Nation (Oyaté Sunkawakan), a Visayan medicine man, pipe carrier, and sun dancer of the Lakota Teton Sioux, related to Osho's disciples in their commune newspaper that their spiritual community in eastern Oregon was a sanctuary of peace and hope for all people seeking a spiritual life. He had been drawn to visit the commune after a vision quest, in which he been given a revelation of a man in a red blanket, who had come from the East. Good Horse Nation said it was no accident that Grandfather (Osho) and his friends had come to this land.

"Great Spirit moves all things," said Good Horse. "Slowly, I came to understand that [Osho's] dream was the same as the vision sent by the man in the red blanket. We had both been directed to the same place, to bring together a spiritual family of all nations, to purify and prepare to walk into the new world. As I saw this, I was grateful to the Great Spirit. I was filled with amazement and joy that [Osho] and his friends had come…to clear the way."

When asked how he would feel if the Oregon commune was destroyed by the U.S. government – as later happened – he replied, "There would be emptiness, a void, a sense of sadness. I would miss the friends I have come to know, respect, and love."

LEFT **The US government feared Osho would take up the cause of the Native Americans, and he was deported in 1985.**

BELOW **The red robes of the Rajneeshees, Osho's followers, were imbued with prophetic significance by Native American tribes.**

MAITREYA THE TRANSMIGRANT

No master of Wisdom from the East will himself appear or send anyone to Europe or America…[at least] until the year 1975.

He will appear as Maitreya Buddha the last of the Avatars and Buddhas, in the seventh Race. Only it is not in the Kali Yuga, our present terrifically materialistic age of Darkness, the "Black Age," that a new Savior of Humanity can ever appear.

H. P. BLAVATSKY (1888), SCDOC

The year 1986 is the year beginning the age of Maitreya who will at that time appear in the world. It says the end of the world or "night" of the world will end ten years later [1996].

MEICHI NOZAMA (1989), CHANNELING MEISHU SAMA

When Buddha Gautama peacefully lay down and died, the tearful though grateful monks in the assembly believed he was free from the misery of ever being born again to suffer another spin on the wheel of life. Nevertheless, before their fully awakened guru split the lightning bolt of his awareness and dissolved into Nirvana's all-and-nothingness, he had promised his return some 25 centuries hence as Maitreya, "the Friend."

Their pundit of paradox had left them to preen their brains with one of Buddhism's first koans: How can a man who has fully awakened and has therefore dissolved all his karmas, attachments, his physical body, and all six remaining astral bodies come back to the hell-life of earthly existence?

Answer: He does, and he doesn't, at the same time.

Before you slap me with that one hand clapping, let me explain. According to Buddhist esoteric understanding, we all have seven bodies. The first is physical; the rest contain the vibrations of our more etheric, subtle, psychological, psychic, and spiritual realities. Once a human being awakens to the seventh body, he or she cannot be reborn. The "soul" of Buddha is not coming back, period. Yet he promised his return.

Perhaps there was a way Buddha could preserve his emotions, experiences, and memories before he blissfully dissolved into the cosmic body of the universe. Buddhist occultists believe that after Buddha attained full awareness up to his fifth body and beyond, he could resolve to preserve his second, third, and fourth bodies. In other words, a master of deep compassion can preserve the vibrations of these bodies in inner space or the astral dimensions. The second, or etheric, body preserves all the emotional experiences of his past lives; the third, or astral, body contains a record of his past karmas and life lessons; and the fourth, or mental, body is a kind of thought-form library containing all the achievements of Buddha's mind.

Before Buddha attained to the seventh body and evaporated, he had fashioned his own time capsule, so to speak, which floats through spaces unknown to the average semiconscious human minds. The will of his intent to preserve these bodies before his death gives these thought waves a life span of their own. For 25 centuries they have wandered the invisible hallways of the inner world in search of an appropriate body and soul who is pure enough to receive them. And time is running out.

If Maitreya would not take birth, these bodies would not be able to hold on any longer, they would disperse. Now their momentum is about to end. Someone should now be ready to absorb these three bodies. Whoever absorbs these will, in a way, cause the rebirth of Buddha. The soul of Buddha will not come back, but the soul of the individual will take on the bodies of Buddha and work accordingly. That person will at once involve himself in the mission of Buddha.

OSHO (1970), MYST

SAVIORS FOR THE BIRDS...

Almost the entire world will be undone and desolate [from the Apocalypse].
Before these events [take place] many rare birds will cry in the air,
"Now! Now!" and sometime later will vanish.

NOSTRADAMUS (1557), EPISTLE TO HENRY II

By God! This bird of Heaven, now dwelling upon the dust, can, besides these
melodies, utter a myriad of songs, and is able, apart from these utterances, to unfold
innumerable mysteries.... Let the future disclose the hour when the Brides of inner
meaning will, as decreed by the Will of God, hasten forth, unveiled, out of their
mystic mansions, and manifest themselves in the ancient realm of beings.

BAHÁ'U'LLÁH (1858), IQN

I want therefore to set man free, rejoicing as the bird in the clear sky,
unburdened, independent, ecstatic, in that freedom.

J. KRISHNAMURTI (1929), FROM THE MANIFESTO: *TRUTH IS A PATHLESS LAND*

The voice of the unusual bird is heard.

NOSTRADAMUS (1555), 2 Q75

The next commonly held Advent-day prophecy sees our savior(s) descending from the clouds like strange birds, or cloaked in the feathered promises of bird symbols. Whether they take the hint from Nostradamus or not, a number of new religious movements use birds as their symbol. For example, Osho's red-clothed tribe, in their Oregon commune city, flew a flag displaying two birds in a green circle, a white seagull guiding a red seagull. Later, after Osho died, his disciples changed the symbol on their flags to a swan. Now they display the great white bird breaking free of the avatar's silver mystic egg to soar in the blue endless eternity of space.

Even less contemporary messianic movements have waxed avian in their descriptions of their deliverers. For instance, a birdlike serpent symbol depicts Quetzalcoatl, the savior of the Native Americans. The strange bird need not only be a symbol. Swami Yogananda (d. 1952), one of the most successful messengers of Eastern religion to galvanize the West, added the prefix "Paramhansa" (meaning "Great, Incomparable Swan") to his name. The

"strange" birds of Nostradamus could represent the strangeness of such visionaries who challenge our ideas. They circle and descend to the depths of our confusion to alert us to the warm updrafts of a message that will take us to higher flights of religious understanding. If we do not hear their call, will they pass us by?

RIGHT **Quetzalcoatl, the Aztec god, is shown as a plumed serpent. A birdlike god appears in many religions.**

... COMING FROM THE CLOUDS

Look, if it isn't Superman, or a bird, or a plane (plain astral or otherwise), whatever "it" or "he" is, "it" or "she" will come descending from the clouds to save the world just when we've nearly nixed it. I only hope that, given some of the similarities to heavenly sightings like the Virgin Mary or UFO contacts, some extraterrestrial race isn't exploiting the myths and desires of apocalyptic prophecy to trick us into welcoming their unholy invasion with open arms.

The Indians don't have messiahs.... But if the time comes when the big destruction starts, towards the end, there will be one. He's just a kid, a young kid, who will come in the clouds. A voice will be with him, a strong voice who will talk.

GRANDFATHER SEMU HUARTE (1985), CHUMASH NATION

I saw the night visions, and, behold, one like the Son of man came with the clouds of heaven.

DANIEL (c. 6TH TO 4TH CENTURY B.C.E), DN 7:13

What can [we] expect but that God should come down to them in the shadows of clouds?

MUHAMMAD (c. 620–630), QUR 2:210

Behold, He cometh with clouds; and every eye shall see Him.

ST. JOHN OF PATMOS (81–96 C.E.), RV 1:7

And these [changes] will begin in those periods in '58 to '98,
when these will be proclaimed as periods when His Light will
be seen again in the clouds.

EDGAR CAYCE (1934), NO 3976–15

[Kalki] shall descend upon the Earth.

VISHNU PURANA (*c.* 300–1000), VIS-P 4

A WISH LIST OF WOES BEFORE "HE" RETURNS

Before Gabriel blows his horn for the hecatomb holidays, he has a little list. Here is doomsday at a glance. These are the various "punishments" the major religions (who on other occasions preach that God is love) expect their version of God to send to this planet before the advent of their savior.

You ought to see the Sun turn black as sackcloth made of goat's hair and the sky will roll up like a scroll. The Moon will turn blood red and the stars will fall out of the sky like ripe figs.

> WISH LIST OF ST. JOHN OF PATMOS (81–96 C.E.), RV 6:12–17

Before "He" comes the skies, soils, waters and all other elements of the world should be desolate. You should see no more birds in the skies. No animals on land will remain alive – no fish in the sea either. Men will be silenced forever. They will never sail the seas again and before Christ can return the world should groan with the gore of many wars. All men should hate, gnash their teeth and be fearful. Everyone should be starving, plague-ridden and wish to die but God makes certain that they cannot find release from death, let alone take a sleep break. Plead as they like, God should be deaf to their prayers until Christ returns.

> WISH LIST OF THE SIBYLLINE ORACLES (c. 3RD CENTURY C.E.)

Kill off one-third, or better, two-thirds of humanity.

> WISH LIST OF JAPANESE PROPHETS (c. 19TH AND 20TH CENTURIES)

The weather before "He" comes should see blood-soaked fire mix with the ice water of hailstones raking and braising the world, turning all foliage to cinders. A great meteor should slam into the sea turning it into blood, sinking a third of mankind's merchant marine fleets, and Christ absolutely cannot return until a third of the fish and marine mammals have died. Then Wormwood the star must crash into the dry lands and poison a third of the rivers, lakes and springs and a myriad of people must gag and die on their newly poisoned drinking waters. Christ can't come back until God whacks off a third of the sun, the moon and the stars in the sky and daylight is diminished by one-third.

> ADDITIONS TO THE WISH LIST OF ST. JOHN OF PATMOS (81–96 C.E.), RV 8:7–12

Jerusalem and Israel must nearly be destroyed in a second holocaust before the Lord comes to the rescue.

> WISH LIST OF SECOND ZECHARIAH (c. 160 B.C.E), CHAPTERS 12–14, CH. 12:8–9

The Jews MUST be destroyed to save the world from evil.

> WISH LIST OF HITLER, THE NAZI MESSIAH

Four Horsemen should invade the world, spreading famine, pestilence, war and death. Hideous, helicopter-like scorpions should spray and sting everyone with a plague that causes unbearable torment without the release of death, and this should make the victims hate God more when they should praise him.

> FURTHER ADDITIONS TO THE WISH LIST OF ST. JOHN OF PATMOS (81–96 C.E.), RV 9:1–11

The white man's technology is only good for raping the earth, air, and oceans and decimating the native peoples. Thus the world's energy should increase 35 percent, driving most white people insane. Afterward they will drop dead from their own fears.

> WISH LIST OF VARIOUS NATIVE PROPHETS OF THE FOURTH WORLD CULTURES

Religion has to almost be a dead man walking and talking on doomsday's Death Row before a new Buddha can come.

> WISH LIST OF VARIOUS BUDDHIST PROPHETS

The ungodly people should have stamped out the virtues of widow burning. The subhuman sudras [known in Hinduism as untouchables] should be running and ruining the Earth and its religions before Kalki can restore the Hindu master race and the holy custom of widow burning can begin again.

> WISH LIST OF VARIOUS HINDU PROPHETS

Before "He" comes there should be a great killing of people by wars and plagues. Make no bones about it, He will only come to redeem the world when grass fills the streets of the cities and out of a million houses only one house will be lighted.

> WISH LIST OF GURU NANAK, FOUNDER OF THE SIKH RELIGION

Allah can only come to set things straight when the heavens eject a palpable smoke down upon the globe to enshroud humanity with torment.

> WISH LIST OF MUHAMMAD (c. 620–630) QUR'AN

And last but not least, God should take revenge on everyone who doesn't believe in *our* Savior.

> A FINAL WISH SHARED BY THE RELIGIOUS WISH-MAKERS OF NEARLY EVERY RELIGION

FROM PROPHEGANDA TO ARMAGEDDONOMICS

You know that the dark age is like a dagger,
which kings handle like butchers. Justice has taken
wing and flown away. The darkness of lies obscures
even the light of the moon, which cannot be seen....
Humanity groans under the dread dominion
of self-centeredness.... The people in their
unconsciousness are without power. They too are
eager to usurp what others have. Priests have forgotten
their craft. They dance, wear masks, beat drums
and adorn their bodies. They shout aloud, indulge
in battle songs, and uphold war.

GURU NANAK (1521)

FROM PROPHEGANDA TO ARMAGEDDONOMICS

The *Wall Street Journal* reporter leaned in with added interest as he listened to the most powerful man on earth – the fellow with his hand over the button that could launch 50,000 nukes – change the subject of their interview from economy and politics to doomsday. Ronald Reagan, the president of the United States, his eyes brightening, confessed that just that morning he had spoken with some of the leaders of the American Christian fundamentalist movement about biblical Armageddon. He admitted that they believe Scripture sees the world on the brink of a nuclear war.

"I don't know whether you know," said the president excitedly, "but a great many theologians over a number of years…have been struck with the fact that in recent years, as in no other time in history, most of these prophecies have been coming together."

Reverend Pat Robertson – even if he wasn't one of the Christian leaders consulting with President Reagan before his meeting with the *Wall Street Journal* reporter – was among Reagan's better-known religious and apocalyptic counselors. Reverend Robertson made his own bid for the presidency in 1988. He lost in the primaries, but the final decade of the second Christian millennium has seen him use his formidable financial, political, and media clout as the founder of the Christian Coalition to gather apocalyptically sympathetic and passionate Christian citizens in a crusade to bring America back to the Bible in the new millennium. He urges American Christians to elect "anybody to any office at any level"– so that upstanding and eschatologically correct fundamentalist candidates will fill the school boards, dominate the 50 state legislatures, take control of city councilships, mayoral and state government offices, all the way up the political Jacob's ladder to the Capitol Building and the White House of the United States. Robertson firmly believes that if it was God's will that he should not be president, then the millennial president should be someone equally convinced that the end times are at hand.

As Robertson sees it, a genuinely Christian future president would understand that a document as marvelous as the Constitution of the United States should not be left in the hands of "non-Christian people." If these last days of the 20th century do seem to be the final days – as the founder of the Christian Coalition tirelessly proclaims over his worldwide media empire of radio and TV shows – then the American people must elect a righteous Christian to guide America through the foreordained tribulation that sees a third of the world's waters, a third of its land, a third of its oceans, and at least a third of its people burned to cinders.

A number of messianic traditions (especially those that currently hold the most weapons of mass destruction) believe that their savior cannot return until humanity destroys the world. The selling of this interpretation of prophecy I call *propheganda* – the art of promulgating a global catastrophe as a prerequisite for the appearance of the savior. Propheganda first persuades people that they live in a bad world, not worth saving. Over time an antilife interpretation of visions takes hold over a culture. People are persuaded to believe that the end of the world is inevitable, so they subconsciously start working toward it. They use the world's resources as if there's no tomorrow, because deep down they've been conditioned by their religions to really believe in no tomorrow.

The business of that civilization, persuaded to believe in an eventual end of the world and physically working itself up for a global disaster, I call the economics of Armageddon, or *Armageddonomics.*

LEFT **Armageddon and the final retribution are reinterpreted by each generation. Contemporary beliefs consider nuclear holocaust as an inevitable stage in the advent of a second Messiah.**

The religions are effective prophegandists because they, more than anyone, believe in their own interpretation of the future. They can't see, nor indeed do they want to see, how they are self-fulfilling their own prophecies. The priests indoctrinate every new generation to promote their doomsday program. For thousands of years people listen to the priests prophegating a view that the world is mortal, an evil place, a thing fated for destruction. Slowly, inexorably, they hypnotize people to be afraid, to think small and shrink their creativity to fit the confines of a world-negative attitude. If you drum this idea into their heads long enough, people will eventually start to see themselves as meek and mild sheep needing a shepherd. You then help them create the economics to fulfill that desperate need.

The stock market and the prophecy market share a number of similarities. They both require the creative use of information and faith. One has to be a bit of a prophet to be a successful stockbroker. A stockbroker peers into the crystal ball-like glass of his or her computer screen to divine the numbers, and conjure the right financial fortune to tell. At a certain point hard data aren't enough – the broker must specu-

ABOVE **Evil need only sit back and watch during World War I in this satirical image. Will this kind of passivity toward ending warfare lead to the final days of Armageddon?**

late on the future. Or, putting it another way, he must gamble. When gambling on his hunch he has to sound so entirely convincing that potential shareholders lay down enough of their hard-earned capital to make even the broker's most subjective guess as good as God's will.

Stockbrokers have been known sometimes to jump out of windows. Can the prophecy market also crash? Just what stock should we put into visions of Armageddon? Could it be that religion has speculated on valueless shares in doomsday visions, inflating their value? Are we really heading for the apocalypse in the early 21st century, or have our doom-dealers advertised the product too long and too convincingly and made us buy into it with blind faith? What if we have accidentally (or maybe purposely) gambled with our future stock for 2,000 years, and thus worked toward a breakdown of the planet's ecosystem and civilization solely because we subconsciously trusted the omen of global destruction to be a sign that our deliverer is at hand? I'd say the odds are at least fifty-fifty that sometime after we've suffered Armageddon, we will be standing in the ruins of our world waiting for someone who isn't coming.

Religion is the greatest instrument for the order of the world and the tranquillity of all existent beings. The weakening of the pillars of religion has encouraged the ignorant and rendered them audacious and arrogant. Truly I say, whatever lowers the lofty station of religion will increase heedlessness in the wicked, and finally result in anarchy.

BAHÁ'U'LLÁH (D. 1892), *WORDS OF PARADISE*

BRAINWASHED TO MAKE DOOMSDAY HAPPEN

When one provokes in a child a fear of the dark, one awakens in him a feeling of atavistic dread. Thus this child will be ruled all his life by this dread, whereas another child, who has been intelligently brought up, will be free of it.

ADOLF HITLER (1941), SCRTC

The hidden mind is far more potent than the superficial mind, however well educated and capable of adjustment; and it is not something very mysterious. The hidden or unconscious mind is the repository of racial memories. Religion, superstition, symbol, peculiar traditions of a particular race, the influence of literature both sacred and profane, or aspirations, frustrations, mannerisms, and varieties of food – all these are rooted in the unconscious. The open and secret desires with their motivations, hopes and fears, their sorrows and pleasures, and the beliefs which are sustained through the urge for security translating itself in various ways – these things also are contained in the hidden mind, which not only has this extraordinary capacity to hold the residual past, but also the capacity to influence the future. Intimations of all this are given to the superficial mind through dreams and in various other ways when it is not wholly occupied with everyday events.

J. KRISHNAMURTI (1963), LIAH

When the apocalyptic traditions of the world's religions threaten doomsday for all of us if we do not return to their idea of the true faith, I wonder if their prophetic literature isn't just another version of a ransom note? To fashion a ransom note you first cut words and letters out of different newspapers and magazines. Then you glue the cuttings together on a piece of paper so the misshapen lines of Frankenstein-monster letters do not reveal the author's sources. In this way theologians of religions can turn their prophecies into a ransom doomsday note cut and pasted with holy texts ripped out of context and stitched together into a frightful new body of thinking.

The danger is always there that theologians of any religion purporting to speak for the departed messiah often cram scripture into their own prejudices, hopes, and fears. They rifle through the notes left behind by the first disciples of ascended masters and glue together bits and pieces of their sayings in a new arrangement. Their handle on the future often reflects the limitations of their own day. Moreover, when these expectations

don't pan out, rather than admit to the mistake – something that would threaten an interpreter's credibility when divining the next "signs" – the prescient among the priesthood retreat to the comfy quilt of soft and fluffy esoterica. For instance, when St. John of Patmos clearly meant Emperor Nero as the Beast of "666," those already persuaded by his interpretation had to rationalize the fact that his prophecy tripped over reality. The facts had to be bent to fit the vision. They reasoned that there must be another Nero coming. There must be a second Rome rising in our future. Yesterday they believed that Nazi-dominated Europe was the new Rome and Hitler the new Nero. Today they reason that Nero and Rome will rise anew as the European Union!

What will St. John junkies of theology think of in the next millennium?

If reality trips them up again, perhaps the prophecy peddled at the dawn of the fourth millennium (in 3000 C.E.) will have the preachers in space colonies of that day beaming up the idea that the president of Earth's Federation of Planets is the "new Nero of a new Rome." And so prophegandizing goes....

The religions generally preach love and forgiveness, yet they also try to convert their followers to the idea that the world – worldliness as such – has polluted human beings with sin and evil. Those who preach life eternal find it necessary to preach antilife on earth. For

ABOVE **A soldier defends himself leaving the confessional abandoned in this image of war in the Middle East.**

instance, the Judeo-Christian and Islamic traditions see the world and man as cursed by original sin. The rabbi, priest, and mullah share the view that someday God and his savior will have to set the world right for a thousand years and then destroy it. On that second judgment day the world's people will go to the highest court to be judged and either they will dwell with God in heaven or burn with Satan in hell forever.

In Eastern religions such as Hinduism and Buddhism, the lines between good and evil are a little less black-and-white, but they still view the "world" as bad. It is false, illusory – it is *maya*. You reincarnate life after miserable life, stuck in maya's muddy rut as you wander through cycles of short golden and long dark ages. The East says the world is hell, and if a chance reincarnation doesn't see you blessed by an avatar, or you don't attain liberation from this world by becoming enlightened yourself, then you can spend an eternity in the cycle of life's (and death's) soap opera.

In either case, East or West, the religions share a negative perception of the world. It is a way station. Either you transcend this world through final enlightenment, or it is a "temptation" ground for judging who goes to heaven and hell. Most of the mainstream messianic religions (especially those which include the nations that do the most polluting and arms dealing) do not value the world as an end in itself, a place where paradise is on earth rather than beyond the earth.

Maybe the priests are right. The world does seem most of the time to be a place of sadness, fear, and violence, from animal eating animal to man murdering man. On the other hand, the priests could be fundamentally wrong. Perhaps the human race is stuck in a prehistoric habit of indulging the traumas that originated when animals ruled the world and man was but a naked heretic monkey fighting for survival.

BELOW **Emperor Nero is at the center of a dispute in this Renaissance fresco. Nero has been identified as the first Beast of "666."**

LEFT **Eve tempts Adam beneath the tree of knowledge. This act of female temptation has fueled sexist propaganda for four millennia.**

short lives, which often ended between the jaws of a violent death. Perhaps it is only ancient traumas that make us vulnerable to the belief that the negative in life is stronger.

These bits of racial fossil memories, buried in the black tar pits of our collective unconscious, could make us more subconsciously malleable to anyone who knows how to manipulate them – such as someone we consider to be a religious authority who is promoting the economics of end-time negativity.

We become what we believe, and we are taught to believe what we're told. We take for granted that the world is a sinful and fundamentally bad place that we must endure until kingdom come. It is this ancient mindset that puts up so much subconscious resistance against any effort to improve life on earth.

Consider the way the world resists the betterment of more than half the human race. All mainstream religions view women as second to man – even subhuman. She is earthly, she is sex, she is the doorway to original sin. She is a valuable commodity, like the furniture, the horse, and the house; she is a blessing if she creates boy-children, a curse if she gives birth to more girls. Before the more aggressive male theologians used their extra muscle power to overthrow the matriarchal earth religions, women enjoyed equality and were praised for the things male priests of the militant God-father religions would later condemn. In the new doctrine, the macho priests made sex – the doorway to life on earth – evil. Thanks to the new myth of Eve tempting Adam with a sin-filled apple, women are thought to pay more attention to Satan than to God.

Male priests turn the title "witch" (which means "wise woman") into the wart- and hooked-nosed harpy in black robes, stealing children's souls. When our macho religions indoctrinate us from a tender age with such

Later on the "monkey" fashioned tools and fashioned a veneer of civilization over a dark continent of primal fears. To a certain extent the early hunter-gatherers upheld the law of the group over the independence and spontaneity of the individual to better survive in a hostile world. The civilized societies that came afterward continued the tradition with various degrees of repression of individuals. They did not generally program people to be spontaneous thinkers and fearless individualists because that would have made them much too hard to control.

Civilized yet more aggressive leaders, like their primitive ancestors, saw that fear was a power they could use over the group. If terrifying predators no longer threatened people, then let the leaders of society teach them to fear God. Teach them to be afraid of life and of death. The cave people feared the godlike ice-age lions and bears and lived in fear for most of their usually powerful cultural suggestions, is it any wonder that women are blind-sided by feelings of insecurity when they struggle to claim their equality as human beings? Even today most of the world still keeps women down, and even women in the so-called developed and civilized nations suffer inequality and are paid less for doing the same jobs as men.

The institution of inequality is most blatant in the leadership of the world's mainstream religions. Protestant sects have the occasional woman reverend, but rarely if ever do you see a woman as chief reverend. No woman can be a Catholic priest, let alone a pope. The Catholic nuns have essentially no power. All their religious requests must first be sanctioned by the celibate male priesthood. Don't expect a woman chief rabbi, a *popessa,* or a matronly mullah any time in the near future. Women can immaculately conceive messiahs in the Mesoamerican, Zoroastrian, and Christian religions, but God forbid that some house-frau becomes Sheesus the Christess!

Now, putting the ancestors of sinful Eve aside for the moment, let's get back to "mother" earth. When so many powerful religions view the world for millennia as a bad place, could it be possible that an antilife prejudice could work itself into the collective perceptions of humanity over the centuries? With time, could the religious teachers of the world's sins establish a dogma that overlooks the many positive and life-affirming statements of their religious founders?

Take for instance the statements of Jesus. If I was inclined to seek out what he said about the future, and if I was more open to that future being a negative one, just what would my eye catch when roving through the Judeo-Christian scriptures? Might I pluck a pious piece of this and a sacred smidgen of that out of their original context and make him accidentally say something he never intended to say? Now, what if I were a more charismatic speaker than the average theologian or apostle, and could persuade others to take my cut-and-pasted epistle as Christ's true ransom note – one where your salvation

ABOVE **Only in the late 20th century have women gained entry to the Christian church as spiritual leaders.**

LEFT **Early cultures deified the mother and associated her with the earth.**

was held hostage until you repented? What if I could silence skepticism by saying that Christ's words were symbolic rather than literal, and that there are many prophetic meanings hidden in the many mansions of his testimony? I'd need certitude, of course – an unshakable faith in my own prophaganda. I must be my first convert! My belief in my own interpretation of prophecy must be greater than that of anyone I'm trying to indoctrinate. Once I've locked away my own doubts in the dungeon of the subconscious and thrown away the key, the force of my certainty – supported by the fact that I'm talking about distant events that will only take place far beyond my own lifetime – makes my interpretation endure.

I might establish a new interpretation of my religion's apocalyptic prophecy, one that would in time become the traditional one. I might even be able to change your perception of what *apocalypse* means. Where once you knew it to mean "enlightenment," give me a few thousand years and many generations of priests adding their support to my interpretations, and the word apocalypse could become synonymous with doom, gloom, and punishment. As evidence of my gift of prophegation, I leave behind a new dogma that future generations will follow, a dogma that says the world will end – must end – before our savior can return.

Step one to fulfilling doomsday requires that my prophaganda persuade you that my interpretation of scripture will happen.

Step two, Armageddonomics, requires that I persuade you to *make* my prophecy happen.

Can I do that?

Let me tell you a story based on a true event.

Dawn broke, and the professor stretched and yawned with satisfaction. He'd had a good rest and felt cool and refreshed, ready for the responsibilities of the new day. He cheerfully showered and dressed. He went downstairs, whistling a tune as he plopped down onto his favorite chair for breakfast. Looking up from his sunny-sided eggs, he detected a clouded and concerned look on his wife's face.

"Are you feeling all right, honey?" asked the wife.

"Yes, indeed, I feel great – had such a good rest last night."

"Oh, that's good to hear," said the wife, not too convincingly, "because you don't look well."

"What do you mean? I feel well, and the man I saw in the mirror just a minute ago when I was shaving looked as fit as a fiddle."

"If you say so," she smiled.

After a hearty breakfast, the professor kissed his wife, and with a briefcase swinging lightly in his hand he went marching out the door. He was on his way to the university, eager to wage yet another day of intellectual battle with grungy graduate students as their professor of logic and philosophy. But before he left his own lawn the gardener flagged him down and said, "How are you today, sir? Didn't you have a good sleep?"

The gardener's tone was poking a rake at his brilliant mood, and the professor was forced to stop and look at the source of irritation.

"Why do you ask – do I look sleepless to you?"

"Well, sir, you're looking a bit peaked today. I was wondering if you might have that flu bug that's goin' around."

The professor felt a tickle momentarily pricking at his throat. He flushed it away with a swallow and said, "I feel fine, quite fine, thank you."

Along the boulevard leading to the university, the greengrocer called out, "Good morning, perfesser, are you all right?"

The professor stopped, clenched his briefcase, and stiffened his back.

"I'm fine. Gooood! What of it?"

There was an uncomfortable pause.

"I'm sorry I snapped at you," said the professor a little sheepishly, "but that's the third time this morning that someone's asked if I was feeling okay. It's odd, because I feel okay – at least I *think* I'm all right. Do you see something the matter with me?"

"Well," said the grocer, "when I saw you coming down the street you seemed to be dragging yourself along, and I thought maybe you have that flu everybody's talking about."

The grocer became more excitable, as he was wont to do. "You know, you should take care of yourself. I hear

that this flu's first symptom is a heightened sense of well-being, then the victim gets dreadfully ill. By the time he has a fever it may be too late.

"Really?" said the professor, with fear actually draining his face of color.

The grocer felt a little guilty. "Well, perhaps I have overstated things," he said. Then he shook that idea off and added ominously, "Maybe you should go home and rest."

The professor thanked the grocer and soldiered on to the university, a little more watchful than before, but still perplexed at how healthy he felt this morning, despite all contrary views.

A few hours later, the professor's wife saw him trudging across the lawn carrying his briefcase as if it was a sack of dead puppies.

"I'm sick," he rasped, with vocal cords sandpapered raw by a sore throat. "Everyone, even my graduate students, even you, saw that I was sick. Then the dean of the university came into my class, grabbed my hand, and told me I should cancel my classes and go straight to bed."

"Oh, I see," said his wife.

The professor thought he saw her stifling a giggle. It must be the fever making me see things, he reasoned.

His deduction was confirmed when his wife suddenly looked surprised after she pulled the thermometer from his mouth.

LEFT **How often is illness psychological? The power of suggestion is a tool at work in apocalyptic prophecy.**

"You do have a temperature, honey! Off to bed."

Hours later, toward dusk, the man, swaddled in his bedclothes, saw his wife usher in the dean of the university, the grocer, and the gardener. The professor was grateful they were thoughtful enough to check on him; however, he sensed something a little odd about their frowns of concern. Their lips stretched like balloon skins that could burst at any moment in an explosion of happy-gas laughter.

Oh, but I'm just delirious, and burning up with fever, the professor thought.

"Honey, do you know what day this is?" asked his wife.

A whisper passed through his whitening lips. "Of course...the first of April."

"April Fool!" yelled everyone around his bed.

The professor gazed in disbelief at all the laughing people.

His wife giggled. "You of all people, being such a prankster at heart, can appreciate a great practical joke."

The sick scholar of logic was speechless – only the phlegm wanted to gurgle a reply.

The dean of the university stepped forward. "Don't you remember the dare you made the other night?" he said. "Last Tuesday in my office you claimed that no one could make you believe what you didn't want to believe. Well, with April Fools' Day coming up, I thought I'd conspire with your wife and acquaintances

– the students, too – and put your declaration to the test. I told all of these people to say you were sick."

"And I'd say we did a really good job," chirped the wife, "because this morning you looked so rested and well I was worried our little practical joke would fail."

"But I wasn't feeling well this morning!" gasped the man. "You all were right...I was really coming down with that dangerous flu. Look at me. (*Gaak...sputter!*) Listen to me. The thermometer says... (*hack! splutter!*) fever. I feel like I'm at death's door!"

They all laughed even harder.

For the rest of that evening the professor defended his sickness, and no matter how much his wife and the others explained that there wasn't a flu – that it all was a joke and his symptoms were psychosomatic – it only made him protest more stubbornly that he was ill.

His logician's reasoning found a way to climb out of the nasal gunk and bleat again and again, "There is no way a man can get the flu unless there really is a flu. Look at the thermometer, look at my coughing...."

That night the professor grew even more exasperated and defiantly ill. He told his wife to sleep in the guest room so he could better recover. The following morning she checked on him – and found that he had died during the night.

If I can get enough people to say you're sick, it is more than likely that you will get sick. If I can get enough religious leaders down through history to say over and over again that you'll suffer a near or complete destruction of this beautiful planet before your messiah can come, perhaps you will believe this too. Perhaps I can even hypnotize you to make it happen without your knowing it. Then when you see the "signs" you're expecting begin to fall into place around you, this will only reinforce my autosuggestion that doomsday and the messiah are coming.

The clergy of every significant religion may have used their interpretation of apocalyptic prophecy as a tool of mass hypnosis. For thousands of years they have instilled in the human psyche the suggestion that a large percentage of the world's precious heritage of flora and fauna, plus a large portion of the human race itself, must be slaughtered and poisoned before salvation can be a possibility.

The hypnotic suggestion seems to be working.

Religions have waged a masterfully perverse conspiracy against life on the planet. Be fruitful and multiply, says the Bible, with no counterbalancing proviso for the eventual excess such a commandment would create. People have become more and more fruitful, until all our resources have nearly run out, and the world is about to break down.

Maybe that is just what the purveyor of this commandment wanted.

You cannot have Armageddon and Judgment Day without the command to be fruitful and multiply. They are two sides of the same life-hating idea. Create more people to be saved or damned in the final judgment. Perhaps that is the unconscious motivation behind priests and popes being against contraception. Killing the unborn is one thing, but what is even more essential is that you don't curtail overpopulation – if you do, the global disasters cannot come. God forbid that you should control your numbers, clean up your pollution, make life on earth better – why should the Messiah come down to save you if you've saved yourselves?

ABOVE **Apocalyptic philosophies encourage everyone to take a piece of the pie before doomsday.**

One could argue that anything that promotes health and the enrichment of life is an impediment to a doomsday dogma. Improve the quality of life, end poverty and famine, make life on earth fulfilling for all who dwell here, and you will not help bring on the great death of a third of humanity, as foreseen and promoted in texts from the Book of Revelation to the Qu'ran. If we made the world pleasant, and if we never allowed our numbers to exceed the available resources so that all people could enjoy health and happiness, who would listen to a few religious crackpots raving about eternal doom?

Don't set the world straight. It's bad for business; it's bad for the economics of Armageddon. You need to keep your consumers afraid of damnation while you keep them greedy for salvation. You persuade them to say "no" more than "yes" to life on earth. Your customers have to buy your pulpit-pitched product of fright, and your psychic goods of doomsday means must justify salvation's ends. You have to occupy them with ample offerings of genius-envy and instill in them a love of the postponement of happiness. Your constant canonical commercial advertises earthly suffering as a virtue. Goodness without sin has no context. Therefore you must keep pushing an addiction to the newest fashion of sinning to abandon while you keep them clamoring for an antidote. Feed their fast-food falls into sin with one hand while you heal them with ant-ichrist-acid pills of piety with the other. Finally, after you have thoroughly frightened and confused them, and they turn to you for serious counseling, that's the moment you inject their souls with ever more powerful drugs of hope for an off-world salvation, everlasting.

Some might say that propheganda only catches people brainwashed by religion, and that secular minds are free of such claptrap. I would argue that religious programming has influenced even the most righteously secularized among us. For instance, take the atheist. Without theists – without a God – how can he uphold a belief that there is no God? A nonreligious person is a prisoner of context as much as those who defend the faith. Even the staunchest materialist and spiritually skeptical broker on Wall Street has to play by the rules of what is essentially a Christian Puritan work ethic (in other words, pure workaholism) to be a success. When the early Puritan settlers of America deemed just about every worldly pleasure sinful except making a profit, they helped make the United States a great Armageddonomic powerhouse. Puritan propheganda made today's reigning superpower the preeminent culprit of per-capita energy consumption and waste among earth's nations. A country with 4 percent of the world population has a worldwide environmental impact amounting to 4 billion people. Its 270 million consumers produce more garbage than all the people in China and India together – 2.3 billion people! Moreover, America is promoting its successful crusade to spread its waste-aholic, Puritan-aholic consumption and business practices to places like China and India.

Messianic theology says be fruitful and exploit the wicked world. Yet it is subconsciously resistant to preserving the health and ecology of the planet. Take the story about the late James Watt, the first secretary of the interior in the Reagan administration during the 1980s. He caught heat from ecologists and naturalists for opening the United States' forestry lands for economic development. When cornered on the subject, Watt, a devout fundamentalist Christian, said something to the effect that concern over how business buzz-cuts the forests was irrelevant because he believed the end of the world and Christ's return were nigh. It has a certain logic. If religion programs you to believe that history is about to end, what's the point of trying to save the whales and the rain forests?

Messianic theology resists peace on earth. Take the Middle East – a calling-down-the-fires ground for such doomsday-dedicated messiahs as Christ, Osiris of Egypt, Saoshyant of Persia, Immanuel of Israel, and the final Muslim messengers such as the 7th and 12th Imams of Shi'ite Islam, Khdir of the Sufis, Muntazar, and a half-dozen al-Madhis of Sunni Islam. Please don't make lasting peace there – heaven forbid! There has to be a climate of fear and enmity, otherwise how can you get people to fight the battle Jews and Muslims *must* wage over the Temple Mount in Jerusalem in order to fulfill their final prophecies?

BELOW **Mass consumption and waste impact upon the environment and create pre-apocalyptic scenes as this.**

If you are a Christian and you want to fulfill Armageddon prophecy and see your messiah return, then return the Jewish people to their homeland and keep them under siege by 150 million angry Arabs. Create a "super-Waco" compound called "Israel" and surround it with Arab tanks and regional ballistic missiles. Snipe it with Katyusha rockets. Plant bombs in Israel's buses. Let hate fester. Condition people there to expect a final war by arming them to fight rehearsals for it in 1948, 1956, 1967, during Yom Kippur in 1973, and at Beirut in 1982. Let the Gulf War of 1991 be a dress rehearsal for the biologically tipped warheads to be dropped on Tel Aviv from Iraq sometime between now and the 2020s. To expedite Armageddon in the Middle East, a long line of Christian presidents of the United States and Christian prime ministers of European states must make sure they promote a one-sided policy where the Arabs need only to hint at building an atomic bomb before the righteous Christian leaders are ready to unleash a Desert Storm of missiles and bomb them back to the Stone Age.

Uneven-handedness is programmed into Western world leaders by propheganda. You can see it when they look the other way every time Arabs complain that Israel has stockpiled over 200 atomic bombs and has a large arsenal of chemical and biological weapons of mass destruction. The Christian leaders are persuaded by 2,000 years of conditioning to close their ears to these complaints while giving Israel enough Armageddonomic support to wipe out all of its neighbors in the near future.

ABOVE **The 1991 Gulf War brought further tragedy to Israel when scud missiles were mistakenly dropped over Tel Aviv.**

Perhaps peace in the Holy Land remains elusive because a long line of American presidents, such as the Catholic-conditioned Ronald Reagan, the Episcopalian George Bush, and the Baptist Bill Clinton cannot shake off their unconscious indoctrination that a showdown between Arabs and Jews must come. Even a dedicated peace-broker and moderate Southern Baptist like Clinton, who generally angers right-wing Christians of the apocalypse such as Reverend Robertson, cannot and does not deny the scriptures of their common faith which say there must be a final battle over Israel. Maybe he and other peacemakers are programmed to sabotage their own efforts and surrender to their weaknesses so they can be compromised, even scandalized. In the final reckoning, how can a messiah come if the Jewish, Muslim, and Christian world leaders demilitarize the Middle East? If someone persuades the Israelis to dismantle their atomic bombs, how can Israel fulfill the interpretations of Isaiah and Ezekiel that see their enemies burned to dust from a fire coming from the skies?

Back in the 1980s President Reagan, who excitedly admitted his belief in being a president at the threshold of the final days, also on several occasions used his doomsday-inspired anti-Soviet rhetoric to call the atheist U.S.S.R. an "evil empire." Soviet reports released after the Cold War reveal that after Reagan's speech Soviet Premier Andropov concluded that the American president was a Christian fanatic hell-bent on launching a nuclear attack on Russia. The rattling of Reagan's righteous saber so disturbed Andropov that he set in motion plans to change four decades of Soviet nuclear defensive policy and consider plans for a preemptive offensive strike. By late 1984 one of Andropov's chief aides, Mikhail Gorbachev, had convinced him not to launch a thermonuclear war. Later, as the new and final Soviet premier, the avowed Communist-atheist Gorbachev was the first to promote to the God-fearing Reagan the option of complete nuclear disarmament – an idea that could really pull the missile cone teeth out of Armageddon's maw.

It is easy to condemn the occasional crackpot cultist, the Christian reverend, the Ayatollah who loses it and does something crazy in the name of fulfilling apocalyptic prophecy. It is bad enough that one madman, the Christian Reverend Jim Jones, can prevail upon 900 of his American followers to commit suicide in a warped resurrection scheme at their isolated Jonestown commune in Guyana. David Koresh's obsession with the Seven Seals of Revelation may have caused the death of four federal agents, the wounding of a dozen more, and the immolation of 76 out of 83 Christians near Waco, Texas. The wrongful death of any individual in the name of Jesus, the

ABOVE **President Reagan did little to improve relations with the U.S.S.R. and Premier Andropov was dissuaded from attack by Gorbachev.**

RIGHT AND BELOW **Jim Jones orchestrated mass suicide and David Koresh precipitated the deaths of 76 followers in the Waco tragedy.**

Shambhala king, the Hindu Kalki, or whatever savior one is waiting for is terrible, but far greater messianic mischief can come from a president in the Oval Office, with his finger on the button of thermonuclear war – one who believes his Bible says the end times are around the corner. Are there Judeo-Christian and Islamic fundamentalist leaders coming in our near future who might subconsciously act out doomsday?

Rather than a false prophet coming to threaten the world, the greatest danger may arise from a false interpretation of scriptures that destroys the world.

ABOVE **Arab prisoners of war suffer in Jenin – an area known as the triangle of terror.**

Very often the accredited [mainstream] religions have opposed progress and sided with the forces of obscurity and oppression.

P. B. SAINT HILAIRE, *THE HUMAN CYCLE*

Religion, in the true sense of the word, does not bring about separation, does it? But what happens when you are a Moslem and I am a Christian, or when I believe in something and you do not believe in it? Our beliefs separate us; therefore our beliefs have nothing to do with religion. Whether we believe in God or do not believe in God has very little significance, because what we believe or disbelieve is determined by our conditioning, is it not? The society around us, the culture in which we are brought up, imprints upon the mind certain beliefs, fears and superstitions which we call religion; but they have nothing to do with religion. The fact that you believe in one way and I in another largely depends on where we happen to have been born, whether in England, in India, in Russia or America. So belief is not religion, it is only the result of our conditioning.

J. KRISHNAMURTI (1963), LIAH

HIS TERRIBLE SWIFT SWORD

From the East to the Middle East to the West there exist cells of psychotic cult leaders and their followers who think God, Jesus, Allah, or Kalki are telling them to hasten the advent by triggering the apocalypse through terrorist action. In 1995, Shoko Ashahara's Japanese doomsday cult, Aum Shinrikyo, tried to engineer the end times by releasing Sarin gas simultaneously in five Tokyo subway stations, killing 11 people and injuring several thousand. In January 1999, the Israeli police deported a dozen members of the Concerned Christians group when they uncovered their conspiracy to start a gun battle in Jerusalem to hasten the arrival of Jesus on New Year's Eve, 1999. Meanwhile in America the FBI waits for a war of domestic terrorism involving more aggressive fundamentalist white supremacist factions in the tradition of Christian Identity, or a Phinehas Priesthood who might make use of anything from C-4 plastic explosives to stolen weapons of mass destruction to derail what they view as Satan's U.S. federal government.

ABOVE **A statue of Kalki is worshiped in the Thugee temple, Bhagwan.**

All the present governments, religions and all moneyed monopolies are to be overthrown and go out of existence....

The increase in unrest in society is an unmistakable sign foreshadowing what is to come to the great masses of people in a short time.

[Note that Newbrough thought this would happen in 1947. He may be off by 50 to 100 years (1997–2047).]

Various combinations of capital and labor are signs of increasing weakness. Extremes so opposite must culminate in destruction....To prevent the coming calamity many combinations will be resorted to. Our present form of so-called Christian religion will overrun America, tear down the American flag, and trample it underfoot. In Europe the disaster will be even more terrible. Capital will back up the church in persecution, general anarchy will follow and hundreds of thousands of people will be killed. In China and India so terrible will be the fall that words cannot describe it. All nations will be demolished and all the earth be thrown open to all people to go and come as they please.

JOHN BALLOU NEWBROUGH (1889)

> You know that the dark age is like a dagger, which kings handle like butchers. Justice has taken wing and flown away. The darkness of lies obscures even the light of the moon, which cannot be seen.... Humanity groans under the dread dominion of self-centeredness.... The people in their unconsciousness are without power. They too are eager to usurp what others have. Priests have forgotten their craft. They dance, wear masks, beat drums and adorn their bodies. They shout aloud, indulge in battle songs, and uphold war.
>
> GURU NANAK (1521)

> False deceivers approach, spreading reports on Earth.... Then indeed a confusion among holy men.
>
> CHRISTIAN SIBYLLINES (2ND CENTURY C.E.), CHRISTIAN APOCRYPHA

> Righteous conduct, the path of Yoga and austerities have vanished under its influence.... In this era righteous men remain dejected and the unrighteous feel elated indeed....
>
> THE SRIMAD BHAGAVATA (BEF. 300 C.E.)

One hundred thirty-plus years ago, my American forebears engaged in a bloody civil war. The victors of that conflict later became identified with a battle ditty that both sides sang as they marched into the fog of war. They call this inspiring and blood-stirring song *The Battle Hymn of the Republic*. It opens with the words: "Mine eyes have seen the glory of the coming of the Lord;/He is trampling out the vintage where the grapes of wrath are stored;/He hath loosed the fateful lightning of his terrible swift sword,/His truth is marching on./Glory! Glory! Hallelujah!...etc."

Today this quasi-patriotic and religious war song has become a favorite battle hymn of many right-wing militias in America. These groups include in their numbers many a man of single-pointed righteousness who has bought the visions of Christian end-time propheganda hook, line, and sink-a-bullet in the magazine of their AK-47, ready for Armageddon.

I have seen documentary footage of such men, armed to the teeth in full military gear, but they belong to no standing army. They run, bent forward, automatic rifles blazing, charging through obstacle course pathways stung by the muddy ejecta of live ammunition. I've seen movies of men creeping and crouching like wild beasts on the hunt bearing the mark of the Christian cross on their military parkas as they rehearsed throwing grenades into the houses of full-sized mockups of towns built far from civilization in the American wilderness. They believe the end is coming. Soon! And they don't want to go like lambs to the lion's lunchtime as the first Christians did a few millennia ago. They believe the

devil is afoot, giving civil rights to niggers, beaners, faggots, heebs, and whining broads, and the devil is uniting the world through that new commie conspiracy called the United Nations.

New nazis for Jesus believe the devil is out to extinguish the white race – Christ's only true representatives on earth – unless they act. It is only a matter of time before a handful of the most emotionally isolated paranoids among their number hear voices saying they should become messianic terrorists and pave the way for Christ's return with car bombs blazing. Soon their eyes will see the C-4 blow a pathway for their Lord. They will steal the bio-weapons where such grapes of wrath are stored. They'll unleash atomic lightning on the sinful they abhor. Their truth is marching on!

The new millennium begins with a "gory, gory" Hallelujah!

RIGHT **American Nazis led by George Lincoln Rockwell spread anti-Semitic messages.**

THE GREAT
ESCAPE

You know angels don't really have wings.
It's really…it's a, it's a spaceship….
It's a vehicle, I mean, and it travels by light,
the refraction of light.

DAVID KORESH (1993)

THE GREAT ESCAPE

Behold, I will show you mystery; we shall not all sleep, but we shall be changed.

SAUL OF TARSUS (48–50 C.E.), 1 COR 15:51

The gods will come from Ganden Paradise and take those people back with them.

THUBTEN NORBU, BROTHER OF THE 14TH DALAI LAMA (*c.* 1980)

But in those days, after that tribulation, the sun shall be darkened, and the moon shall not give her light, and the stars of heaven shall fall, and the powers that are in heaven shall be shaken. And then shall you see the Son of man coming in the clouds with great power and glory. And then shall he send his angels, and shall gather together his elect from the four winds, from the uttermost part of the Earth to the uttermost part of Heaven.

Y'SHUA (*c.* 30 C.E.), MK 13:24–27

For this we say unto you by the word of the Lord, that we which are alive and remain unto the coming of the Lord shall not prevent them which [have already died]. For the Lord himself shall descend from heaven with a shout, with the voice of the archangel, and with the trumpet of God: and the dead in Christ shall rise first: Then we which are alive and remain shall be caught up together with them in the clouds, to meet the Lord in the air.

SAUL OF TARSUS (51 C.E.), 1 THES 4:15–17

While we were yet sinners, Christ died for us. Much more then, being now justified by his blood, we [Christians] shall be saved from wrath through him.

SAUL OF TARSUS (48–50 C.E.), ROM 5:8-9

If you believe in the right messiah, will he take you away from the tribulations to come? Will you disappear from the earth and be placed on a cloud until it's safe to descend to a new earth and start a new age of peace? Well, if you hearken beyond your own particular Rapture rap music, it might surprise you to find members of other religions jostling for space on your cloud.

For thousands of years religions have preached that this world is something to transcend. These religions have encouraged seekers of God to withdraw – some say escape – from this world and its abiding sinfulness.

Now, for many devoutly religious people perched on the threshold of the millennium, escape to the monastery or to a cave in the Himalayas isn't far enough. A significant number declare they will literally escape from the world, body and soul.

UFO cults like Heaven's Gate share many common views with the mainstream Christian Broadcasting Network about a divine rescue. When people pray for salvation by aliens, or avatars, and they stretch the Bible and other scriptures to their interpretive limits to find a Rapture exit route, are they essentially expressing a desire to put off responsibility for what we have all made of our world? Are the prophecies of terrestrial escape symptomatic of a humanity suffering from Peter Pan syndrome?

Any nonsense which can give you a feeling of belonging, which can give you a feeling that you know what reality is, will be picked up and the human mind will become tethered to it.

OSHO (1971), GATE

SAVED BY A UFO

I was taken up past Orion.... I went up and found that God was actually [the creator of] an ancient civilization that was before the world.

DAVID KORESH (1993)

The Katarians came from Sirius.... Impossible to say now how many [human beings] will be taken off Earth before the shift [of the Earth's poles], as it depends in large measure on the willingness of those there to leave the Earth and go into orbit, and also on how many at that time will deserve rescue. The Kantarians will be helping with the alerts and assisting in rescue to some extent, although the Ashtar Command will be in charge of the actual rescue mission.

SPIRIT GUIDES OF RUTH MONTGOMERY (1985), ALNS

You know angels don't really have wings.
It's really...it's a, it's a spaceship.... It's a vehicle,
I mean, and it travels by light, the refraction of light.

DAVID KORESH (1993)

Then they will put on the garment of eternal life: the garment from the cloud of light which has never been seen in this world; for this cloud comes down from the upper kingdom of the heavens by the power of my Father, and will invest with its glory every spirit that has believed in me.... Then they will be carried off in a cloud of light into the air...into the heavens and remain in the light and honor of my Father. Then there will be great joy for them in the presence of my Father and in the presence of the holy angels.

Y'SHUA (BEF. 5TH CENTURY C.E.), AOFT

I think that there are still some among you who retain hope with the Earth.... I do not think that the entire family of mankind could possibly move to another planet if it should at all be technically possible. You have no right to sacrifice the majority only for the uncertain possibility of migration by a small number of you.... You had better restore the most part of your attention to the Earth though you may share a bit of interest to the outer space.... Unless something is done here and now to save the very stage of your drama, your dreams of discoveries, inventions, etc. would inevitably end with the last curtain fall.

TAMO-SAN (1957), MOOR

DESTINATION: THE PEARLY GATES OR HEAVEN'S GATE?

"Welcome to *Beyond Human,* last call…."

With these words, the leader of a modern Rapture cult began videotaping his final message to the world. Herf Applewhite, known as "Do" by his faithful followers, was the castrated gatekeeper to the quasi-New Age UFO-cum-Christian resurrection religion known as Heaven's Gate.

With eyes bright and glistening, Applewhite regarded the camera with a mixture of world-weariness, relief, and more than a little insanity. "Do" explained that the experiment was over. He and his followers had learned their lessons and lived long enough in the sex-obsessed and sinful containers of their bodies. It was now time to hitch their souls to the bearded star. By 1997, Herf was Hale-bent to bee-Bopp with the UFO Star Trekkers he believed were hovering in a mother ship behind the comet Hale-Bopp.

In the 19th century those who believed in physical resurrection kept their special white ascension robes packed away in the attic while they waited for their own bright-eyed Adventist preachers to announce the final day. In the 20th century, the 40 bright-eyed space cadets of Heaven's Gate stored their purple triangular shrouds and brand-new black Nike tennis shoes for the ascent to glory into the Milky Way's star clouds. The Heaven's Gate "adventists," being progressive, used technology to force their ascent into UFO paradise. They toasted eternity with a carefully poisoned vodka-and-applesauce cocktail.

Applewhite and his followers relied mostly on Christian apocalyptic interpretations and turned it into a Star Wars, sci fi faith of their own. Perhaps their cocktails for death and resurrection were inspired by the final act of a Christian reverend nearly 20 years before, who in 1978 took his apocalyptic sect not to a passing comet in space, but deep into the rain forests of Guyana to establish an agrarian Christian commune known as the People's Temple.

The people of Jonestown had escaped the world to prepare themselves for God and the end of the world. Their leader, Reverend Jim Jones, rehearsed their final departure several times by having the 900 men, women, and children go through a ritual called "white night." The true believers would line up to drink vats full of Kool-Aid, or parents would squirt the substance into the mouths of their children with a syringe. Reverend Jones said he did this to test their faith in the apocalyptic sect. For rehearsals, the Kool-Aid tubs lacked one important ingredient – cyanide.

Reverend Jones issued real poison on their collective ascension day, which finally came on November 17, 1978, after armed members of the Jonestown commune ambushed U.S. Congressman Leo Ryan and his aides and several journalists who had come to Jonestown on a fact-finding mission. After spending the day at Jonestown, Ryan, three journalists, and three defectors from the People's Temple were killed while standing on a dirt landing strip in the jungle waiting to board a plane back home. When Reverend Jones heard of this attack, he persuaded his entire following to commit mass suicide.

BELOW **Thousands believe that a UFO hovered behind the Hale-Bopp comet, shown here above New Jersey.**

RIGHT **In November 1978, 900 men, women and children committed suicide under the guidance of their apocalyptic cult leader Jim Jones.**

Some might take me to task for calling a man like Reverend Jim Jones a Christian. Unfortunately it is a fact that mainstream Christians would prefer to forget. Before Jones got too caught up in his own interpretations of apocalyptic deliverance, he was a well-respected Christian leader in Indianapolis and the San Francisco Bay area. He dined with noted Christian leaders like Rosalynn Carter, the wife of U.S. President Jimmy Carter, and flew with Vice President Walter Mondale on his private jet. The mayor of Indianapolis appointed Reverend Jones the first full-time director of a human rights commission because of his selfless service to the poor and needy and his efforts to bring civil rights to African-Americans.

Some might say that Jones was a good Christian gone bad, and that Herf Applewhite (another black-sheep Christian) had cut and pasted a doctrine of UFO

deliverance out of a few misunderstood passages in the New Testament. These are the same passages that hundreds of millions of "normal" or "good" Christians – mostly Evangelical, Pentecostal, and Baptist – believe describe a physical as well as spiritual deliverance from the earth, popularly called "the Rapture," for chosen lovers of Christ. There are prominent Christian leaders – some of them, like Pat Robertson and Jerry Falwell, religious advisors to past presidents of the United States – who, like Hal Lindsey, promote an imminent Rapture in which people will one day mysteriously vanish in the twinkling of an eye. The number of those chosen can be as few as 144,000 or as many as several million men, women, and children. They will ascend through the clouds to dwell with Jesus Christ in the sky for at least seven years. During that time those believers and non-believers left behind are to endure what Lindsey calls the Tribulation – a time of cataclysms, the rule of a false Jewish prophet, and world domination by a suave Hitlerian Antichrist using the European Union as his new Roman Empire. The Tribulation nearly destroys the world when it ends in a final battle of Armageddon fought by China, Russia, and the Arabs against Israel.

Now, I'm not talking about "kooks" here. I've heard this story come out of the mouths of well-adjusted and self-proclaimed "good Christian" family members, working partners, and generally even-tempered and seemingly sane people who pay their taxes, try to raise their families in the best way they can, and go to church every Sunday. I've heard people whom I had up to that moment considered "normal" look me in the eye and say sincerely that Jesus will take them up into the clouds at the appointed time to dwell with him there until the smoke of Armageddon clears and the Antichrist is slain – after which they'll get the "all clear" from Christ and descend in unison from the clouds to establish a new world under his direct control for 1,000 years.

When I ask these people if they see any parallels between their Rapture beliefs and those of the Millerites more than a century and a half earlier, typically they either sidestep or flatly deny the similarities. William Miller, the founder and prophet of the Second Adventist movement, declared that Christ would return and the world would end sometime between March 21, 1843, and March 21, 1844. During those 12 months between the equinoxes, true-believing farmers abandoned their fields, businessmen gave away their fortunes, and thousands of Adventists dutifully slipped on their white ascension robes and spent the night waiting on the rooftops properly attired for their launch into the clouds. They kept the faith and stood on the roofs even after March 21, 1844 passed, and each newly appointed time calculated by Miller proved to be a bust. After 1844 drew to a close, it was clear that Miller's Great Advent became his great disappointment – businesses and fields were ruined, and a few believers even committed suicide. Miller died in 1849, but his movement spawned a number of today's apocalyptic sects, from the "respectable" Seventh-day Adventists to the "fringe" Branch Davidians.

A popular hybrid Rapture eschatology awaits those who attend "psychic" churches and dip their souls into the cheesy fondue pot of Christian, Eastern, and native religious ideas. This new transmutation either puts Christ in a flying saucer teleporting people into space, or it hides behind a popular vision that we have cosmic space brothers. Incorrectly described in our sacred literature as angels, they are in fact spiritually advanced astronauts always watching our progress and ready to take a chosen few of us onto their vast fleet of flying saucers the day the world is about to end.

Hal Lindsey's "mainstream" fundamentalist Christian apocalyptic stance puts a different spin on "extraterrestrials" and UFOs. To Lindsey they don't come from another planet, but instead are deceptions of Satan. He says false signs in the sky are leading the world astray in the final days. In other words, as I understand Lindsey, those doe-eyed aliens are devils, and their abduction of men and women to perform operations or to have sex are a modern version of medieval incubi and succubi of sexually obsessed slumberers.

Jewish theologians are not so dismissive of extraterrestrial life. They cite Ezekiel's famous prophetic dream as the descent of a flying wheel of fire occupied by alien beings from another dimension or world. The Jewish mystics speak of the Merkabah, angelic beings from the skies who ride God's heavenly fleet of 60,000 or more "flying chariots."

The Gnostic wing of early Christianity (deemed heretical by mainstream Christianity) tried but failed to bring the idea of Merkabah into Christian doctrine. The Gnostic *Apocalypse of Thomas* quotes Jesus describing the appearance of an angel of great power who will lead a fleet of angels sitting on "chariots of clouds, rejoicing and flying around in the air under Heaven." Christ says these angels will then deliver the elect who believed in him, and they "will rejoice that the destruction of the world has come."

BELOW AND OPPOSITE **New movie technology has created a plethora of special effects to bring UFOs and their occupants onto screens across the world, giving celluloid reality to the vision of our cosmic cousins coming to take us up to heaven.**

The tradition of angels/extraterrestrials exists in prophecies of the Muslims, Hindus, and Buddhists as well. After his enlightenment Buddha Gautama sat under his Bodhi tree in radiant silence. On the seventh day "gods" came down from heaven to pay him a visit. The story goes that they persuaded him to renounce his silence and share his teaching with humanity.

Whether you think of them as devils, or as cuddly as Steven Spielberg's E.T., certainly something very strange is flying around in our skies. Someone or something is playing doctor with human abductees and coloring humanity's collective visions of life on other planets. Are there Merkabah waiting to land, or is this all just a mass illusion? Perhaps the next few decades of history will unlock the airlock of this star-fired mystery.

Many believe the collective signs of a cosmic rescue depict our time as one where we are collectively ready to commit global suicide. If that is true, and the signs are not just a self-perpetuating doomsday prophecy, then in the near future extraterrestrials are coming to do more than abduct cattle and probe a few chosen individuals like Whitley Strieber. Rather than simply ascending to the clouds as Saul of Tarsus believed, thousands – if not millions – of us could see ourselves beamed aboard spacecraft hiding in the clouds, where we will wait out the apocalypse until it is safe to land.

ABOVE **Steven Spielberg's E.T. stands in a long tradition of travelers from other worlds who bring messages or offer to rescue us from our earthly doom.**

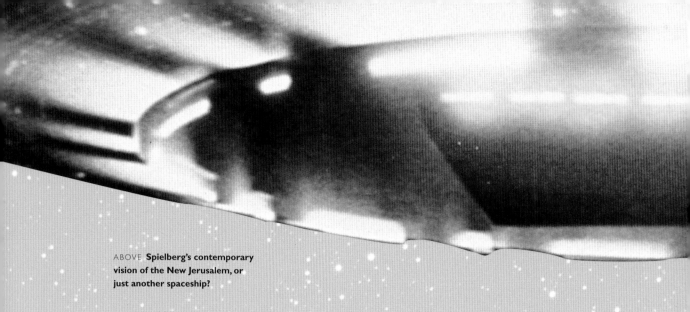

CASTLES IN THE CLOUDS

And I, John, saw the holy city, new Jerusalem, coming down from God out of heaven, prepared as a bride adorned for her husband.... And he carried me away in the spirit to a great and high mountain, and showed me that great city...descending out of heaven from God, having the glory of God: and her light was like unto a stone most precious, even like a jasper stone, clear as crystal; and had a wall great and high, and had twelve gates, and at the gates twelve angels, and names written thereon, which are the names of the twelve tribes of the children of Israel.... And the wall of the city had twelve foundations.... And the city lieth foursquare and the length was as large as the breadth.... the wall thereof, a hundred and forty and four cubits, according to the measure of a man, that is, of the angel.

And the buildings of the wall of it was of jasper: and the city was pure gold, like unto clear glass. And the foundations of the wall of the city were garnished with all manner of precious stones. The first foundation was jasper; the second, sapphire; the third, a chalcedony; the fourth, an emerald; the fifth, sardonyx; the sixth, sardius; the seventh, chrysolyte; the eighth, beryl; the ninth, a topaz; the tenth, a chrysoprasus; the eleventh, a jacinth; the twelfth, an amethyst. And the twelve gates were twelve pearls; every several gate was of one pearl: and the street of the city was pure gold, as it were transparent glass.

And I saw no temple therein: for the Lord God Almighty and the Lamb [a code for Jesus at his Second Coming] are the temple of it. And the city had no need of sun, neither of the moon, to shine in it: for the glory of God did lighten it, and the Lamb is the light thereof. And the nations of them which are saved shall walk in the light of it: and the kings of the Earth do bring their glory and honor into it. And the gates of it shall not be shut at all by day: for there shall be no night there.

ST. JOHN OF PATMOS (81–96 C.E.), RV 21:2, 10–12, 14–25

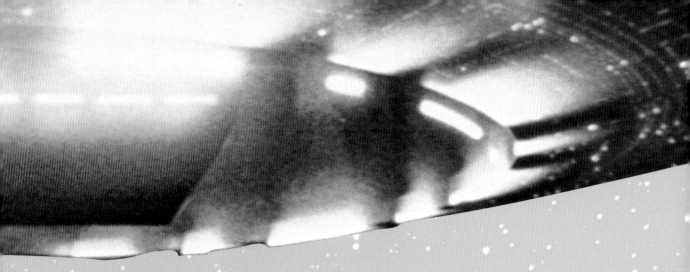

SAVED FROM MYSELF

What if someone plucked St. John out of his cave on the island of Patmos in the 1st century and planted him in a 20th-century movie house screening Steven Spielberg's *Close Encounters of the Third Kind*? How would he absorb the illusion that John Trumbull and his special-effects team created, depicting the vast, city-sized mother ship descending like New Jerusalem over Devil's Tower, Wyoming? If someone from the time of St. John could see a movie of a metallic-skinned and glowing mother ship of vast proportions with great clear glass observation decks, he might call such a thing a floating city of "pure gold as if it were clear glass." The maneuvering lights flashing in their multicolored splendor might look like walls made of the most fabulous gems and precious minerals to a 1st-century Christian. Might the technologically unsophisticated saint describe the luminous white beings stepping out of an eye-piercing light as "angels?" And when the alien-angels guide the main character into the light and inside the inner sanctum of the mother ship, would not St. John believe the angels were taking him to God?

Oh, Lord of the Rapture,
  Thou art my savior, deliver me from
  my own image.
Take me into the clouds,
  Take me away from the sight of my
  dysfunctions.
Let me escape from all the things I can't face.
  Deliver me from all the realities that
  don't match my dreams,
And save me from those who clip the wings
of my ignorance.
  Deliver me from what I do rather than
  from what I say,
And let your forgiveness wipe out my
responsibility.
  Oh Lord, keep my eyes bathed in your
  beclouded glory,
And save me from myself.

If something is terrible one should never leave it; one has to go through it. That's how one grows. Never leave any challenge. One has to fight the challenge and go into it. Never escape – an escapist never grows. And that's how there are so many juvenile people in the world, because everybody has escaped from challenges.

OSHO (1978), HAL

THE 1,000-YEAR REICH OF THE SAVIOR

And I saw the thrones, and they sat upon them, and judgment was given unto them: and I saw the souls of them that were beheaded for the witness of Jesus, and for the word of God, and which had not worshipped the beast, neither his image, neither had received his mark upon their foreheads, or in their hands; and they lived and reigned with Christ for a thousand years.

ST. JOHN OF PATMOS (81–96 C.E.), RV 20:4

THE 1,000-YEAR REICH ⊙F THE SAVI⊙R

After this I beheld...a great multitude, which no man could number, of all nations, and kindreds, and people, and tongues, stood before the throne, and before the Lamb clothed with white robes, and palms in their hands; and cried with a loud voice saying, "Victory to our God which sitteth upon the throne, and unto the Lamb."
  And all the angels stood round about the throne, and about the elders.... and fell before the throne on their faces and worshipped God.... And one of the elders...said to me, "These are they which came out of great tribulation, and have washed their robes, and made them white in the blood of the Lamb. Therefore are they before the throne of God, and serve him day and night in his temple: and he that sitteth on the throne shall dwell among them. They shall hunger no more, neither thirst any more; neither shall the sun light on them, nor any heat. For the Lamb which is in the midst of the throne shall feed them, and shall lead them unto living fountains of waters: and God shall wipe away all tears from their eyes."

ST. JOHN OF PATMOS (81–96 C.E.), RV 7:9–11, 13–17

And I saw the thrones, and they sat upon them, and judgment was given unto them: and I saw the souls of them that were beheaded for the witness of Jesus, and for the word of God, and which had not worshipped the beast, neither his image, neither had received his mark upon their foreheads, or in their hands; and they lived and reigned with Christ for a thousand years.

ST. JOHN OF PATMOS (81–96 C.E.), RV 20:4

For a thousand years religion will be taught, but then will come the end of the world. Fire will be followed by wind, destroying all we have built; then will come water to cover everything we know. Only a few will survive, in caves and in the tops of trees. The gods will come from Ganden Paradise and take those people back with them. They will be taught so that religion will not die, and when once again the winds blow the milk-ocean and once again the world is formed, these same enlightened ones, saved from the world before, will be the stars in the sky.

THUBTEN NORBU, 14TH DALAI LAMA'S BROTHER (*c.* 1980)

And when the thousand years have expired, Satan shall be loosed out of his prison, and shall go out to deceive the nations which are in the four quarters of the Earth, Gog and Magog, to gather them together to battle: the number of whom is as the sand of the sea.... And fire came down from God out of heaven and devoured them. And the devil that deceived them was cast into the lake of fire and brimstone...and they shall be tormented forever and ever. And I saw a great white throne, and him that sat on it, from whose face the Earth and the heaven fled away; and there was found no place for them. And I saw the dead, small and great, stand before God; and the book was opened, which is the book of life: and the dead were judged out of those things which were written in the books, according to their works. And the sea gave up the dead which were in it; and the death and hell delivered up the dead which were in them: and they were judged every man according to their works. And death and hell were cast into the lake of fire. This is the second death. And whosoever was found written in the book of life was cast into the lake of fire.

ST. JOHN OF PATMOS (81–96 C.E.), RV 20:7–15

The greatest and most ruthless decisions will have to be made. A barbaric measure for the unfortunate who is struck by it, but a blessing for his fellow man and posterity, the passing pain of a century can and will clearly redeem millenniums from sufferings.

ADOLF HITLER

A NEW HEAVEN, A NEW EARTH, A NEW WORLD ORDER

And in the days of these kings shall the God of heaven set up a kingdom, which shall never be destroyed: and the kingdom shall not be left to other people, but it shall break in pieces and consume all these kingdoms, and it shall stand for ever. [Dn 2:44]

And the Ancient of days did sit, whose garment was white as snow, and the hair of his head like the pure wool: his throne was like the fiery flame.... A fiery stream issued and came forth from before him: thousand thousands ministered unto him, and ten thousand times ten thousand stood before him: the judgment was set and the books were opened. [Dn 7:9-10]

As concerning the rest of the beasts [world leaders and/or empires and other religions], they had their dominion taken away: yet their lives were prolonged for a season and time. I saw...one like the Son of man [come] with clouds of heaven, and [come] to the Ancient of days, and they brought him near before him. And there was given him dominion, and glory, and a kingdom, that all people, nations, and languages, should serve him: his dominion is an everlasting dominion, which shall not pass away, and his kingdom that which shall not be destroyed. [Dn 7:12–14]

But the saints of the most High shall take the kingdom, and possess the kingdom for ever... .[Dn 7:18]

And the kingdom, and the kingly power, sovereignty, and greatness of all the kingdoms under heaven shall be given to the people of the saints of the Most High. Their kingly power is an everlasting power and all sovereignties shall serve them and obey them. [Dn 7:27]

DANIEL (*c.* 6TH–4TH CENTURY B.C.E.), DN CHAPTERS 2 & 7

"The Third Reich will rule for a thousand years!"

This notorious prophecy asserted by Adolf Hitler is not his original vision. A thorough indoctrination in biblical end-time prophecy may be the source for his own egomaniacal dream of being the world's savior, and the Nazi Empire – the Third Reich – being God's new world order lasting a thousand years.

Hitler attended Catholic school as a boy in Linz, Austria. The priests of the neighborhood cathedral introduced him to the Christian propheganda of Christ's Second Coming at an altar overshadowed by a façade emblazoned with swastikas. They preached that someday Christ would return as an all-powerful and benevolent king of the world, who would dictate his Father's divine law and love seated in a new world capital – a New Jerusalem – that was descended directly from heaven.

The papacy's views on democratic ideas around the turn of the century, when little Adolf attended elementary school, were definitely negative. Democracy was a threat to the sacred virtues of authoritarianism, and with this in mind, it is more than likely that the priests helped shape the intolerance of an impressionable boy toward democracy or religious freethinking.

Hitler conceived the Messiah as a dictator – benevolent, perhaps, but subject to blind obedience. Who would not bow down and give tribute for a thousand years to Jesus Christ waving his rod of iron like a field marshal's baton? What need is there for thinking for yourself or wanting freedom, when your leader – called "Führer" in German – is the Son of God?

ABOVE **Hitler's Third Reich sought to impose a new world order in which Hitler played the role of world savior.**

From an early age the boy cultivated a profound sense of his own special destiny, as do many who become our saviors. Where most Christian children take their Sunday school spoonful of biblical indoctrination and get on with the normal dramas of growing up, Hitler grew to adulthood thinking that he was the reincarnated Elijah – the same prophet who Christ said had returned as John the Baptist, his forerunner. It didn't matter that Hitler discarded Christianity for the beer-hall babble of Germanic pan-paganism; the biblical perceptions set in his mind at childhood became the foundation upon which he would build his dream-Reich of a thousand years.

Decades later, as master of Germany, he would commit himself body and soul to save the world from Godless democracy, Bolshevism, and the Jews. God, whether you call him Odin or Yahweh, had appointed Hitler as the one to fulfill the Prophet Daniel and St. John of Revelation's vision of a thousand-year Reich – or "realm" – of the savior. Once Hitler's war of Armageddon had purified the world, he would transform Berlin into *Germania,* his New Jerusalem.

Even before plunging the world into war in 1939, Hitler had already set his personal architect, Albert Speer, the task of building models for a great temple of his Nazi religion. Speer would construct a vast copper-domed edifice 825 feet in diameter and 726 feet high to cast its long shadow over New "Berlusalin's" skyline by 1950. The Nazi pantheon would be a shelter for rallies of worshipers – 180,000 at a time – paying homage to the savior of the master race for 1,000 years.

And he shall rule them with a rod of iron; as the vessels of a potter shall they be broken to shivers.

ST. JOHN OF PATMOS (81–96 C.E.), RV 2:27

It seems that every religion that depends on a final judgment of humanity as the cornerstone of its apocalyptic scripture instills in its followers a deep urge to surrender themselves to the Brave New World of the returned Messiah.

Is all well that ends well at the end of history?

Whether you call him Christ, Maitreya, or Rudra Cakrin; whether he's the Mongolian World King, the White Burkhan, or the 12th Imam ushering in a new world order of righteousness – it doesn't matter how many religions share the vision – "He" will walk and talk with us, rule and make judgments for us for a thousand years, and you and I had better live on His righteous side.

ABOVE **The phenomenon of the Third Reich was an entire nation hypnotized by the voice of one man who entertained messianic delusions.**

You will be sheep – He is your shepherd, and there will be no need for another.

The leader/Führer principle requires obedience. The Messiah as Master of the World will not spare his rod of iron and spoil his children of the golden age. But who would rebel? It's not ever going to be someone like Hitler. This is Christ, or it's Buddha returned, or it's any name you put on your most beloved deliverer, and that's an important difference, say those who look forward to his millenary dictatorship. When Hitler's people gathered in their millions to adore their Führer, crying "Hail victory!" ("Sieg Heil!") in hypnotic waves of sound were not the same as the cries of "Hail victory" and the "Hallelujahs" rumbling from the multitude before St. John's vision of the Christ, the Lamb of God.

When the blessed sheep of the Messiah begin to gather in New Jerusalem in the great rallies to come, say our current millennialists, their feverish eyes will not be those of the Hitler Youth raising the blood flags of the false Führer, but the wide, adoring gaze of those reborn by the blood of the Lamb. But consider: when people surrendered their minds to herd around the counterfeit messiah of Linz, Austria, they enjoyed the euphoria of being free of responsibility for their lives. Hitler carried their burden if they but believed in him and obeyed.

Look where it got them.

In 1945, World War II ended with 988 years left to go in Hitler's 1,000-year Reich. The Allied forces obliterated a messianic empire.

It won't be that way with Christ, because he's our true savior. The crowds who will gape at him at his rallies won't be mindless cultists, but believers overwhelmed with adoration for the Lamb of God. As good sheep breathing in the elixir of his forgiveness, we will be entranced by his loving light. Only from the outside could we be accused of being unreasoning fanatics.

All the dictators in the world are created by us because we want somebody else to tell us what to do. There is a very subtle reason for it: when you are told by somebody else what to do, you don't have any responsibility for whether it is right or wrong. You are free of responsibility; you don't have to think about it; you don't have to be worried about it. The whole responsibility goes to the person who is giving you the orders to do something.

This has been the case – [people] always looking to the politicians, looking to the priest; looking to neurotic-type people who proclaim themselves prophets, the son of God, messengers of God.... People [who] don't want to take any responsibility immediately fall into their trap.

OSHO (1987), INVT

THE DICTATORSHIP OF THE FORGIVEN

And he that...keepeth my works unto the end, to him will I give power over the nations.

ST. JOHN OF PATMOS (81–96 C.E.), RV 2:26

Allah has promised to those of you who believe and do good that He will most certainly make them lords on the Earth as He made rulers those before them, and that He will most certainly establish for them their religion which He has chosen for them, and that He will most certainly, after their fear, give them security in exchange. They shall serve Me, not associating ought with Me; and whoever is ungrateful after this, these it is who are the transgressors.... Think not that those who disbelieve shall escape in the earth, [for] their abode is the fire; and certainly evil is the resort!

MUHAMMAD (*c.* 620–630), QUR 24:55–57

And they sung a new song, saying thou art worthy to take the book, and to open the seals thereof: for thou wast slain, and hast redeemed us to God by thy blood out of every kindred, and tongue, and people, and nation; and hast made us unto our God kings and priests: and we shall reign on the Earth.

ST. JOHN OF PATMOS (81–96 C.E.), RV 5:9–10

When I was a teenager and the 1960s were drawing to a close, many an acid freak became a Jesus freak. I chanced upon a stack of doomsday cartoon books in a popular Christian head shop of the day. The books painted black-and-white messages of good and evil in the loud colors adored by adolescents, and as I was one at the time, I couldn't help being drawn into the comic-book version of Armageddon and the Judgment Day to come.

The illustrations still color the chameleon of my memory with images such as the faceless Lord God, sitting on his throne judging what looked to me like the assembled throngs of humanity's last nudist Nazi rally. The people here lined up before the robed and faceless God cheek-to-derrière in their birthday suits.

I was suspicious of the thin veil of self-righteousness covering the cartoonist's libido. Though he proclaimed his salvation on the book jacket, I couldn't help noticing that he had a habit of drawing all the naked women as if they were centerfold models plucked by the Rapture from Hugh Hefner's Playboy mansion. The illustrator gave me the idea that females, whatever their age, will face God and the lake of fire forever in the firm and perky flower of full frontal bodaciousness arrested forever at the age of 18.

Memories of adolescent titillation aside, the one image more pertinent to this chapter started with a cartoon sequence of people all over the world disappearing. In the twinkling of an eye and faster than you could say "Kryptonite," thousands of people just "poofed" out of sight, from a pilot flying a jet airliner full of passengers over the Pacific to Aunt Sally vanishing in mid-clip as she hung out Uncle Bob's underwear on a clothesline in Pittsburgh.

ABOVE **The 1960s saw a generation of hippies who combined liberal values with notions of a post-apocalyptic paradisal land.**

RIGHT **In the 1980s born-again Christians peddle a different message: judgement day leads to heaven _and_ hell.**

ABOVE **Christians calling on their Lord to make sure they are in good shape when the boarding announcement comes.**

Where did they go?!

I turned to the next page and beheld illustrations of happy, squeaky-clean Americans soaring up into the clouds. Here was Aunt Sally delivered from the clothesline, and there was the airline pilot ascending to glory while I imagined his planeload of abandoned passengers plunging somewhere into the Pacific. All kinds of happy escapee filled the sky: secretaries, kids, Fuller Brush salesmen, moms, dads, grannies, and a token black or two, all ascending toward a luminous Christ like bedazzled moths taking a bead on beatitude's bug zapper.

That's when I slammed the comic book shut.

It was only later, after making some inquiries, that I discovered how many of my Christian acquaintances and relations (at that time) devoutly believed in what that cartoon book illustrated – all cartoonish exaggeration aside. At the appointed time, God will choose to make thousands of people vanish from the earth in a twinkling of an eye. Perhaps Saint Scotty has beamed them up to the Starship *Enterchrist* until the auspicious hour that James T. Jesus calls upon them to descend with him from the clouds as his glorified priests, priestesses, pedagogues, lawmakers, paper pushers, politicians, and policemen. The returned and forgiven ones running Christ's world government will teach us few billion surviving sinners how to get on with life properly in the new world empire of the Son of God.

Ever since the day I read that comic book I have had a recurring – if somewhat whimsical – nightmare. Imagine a world ruled by the forgiven – people like those folks on Sunday school TV shows who promote the idea of the Rapture with the most passion. If they are right about the Rapture, then, we must all prepare to be ruled by Christ's presidium of sweaty television evangelists and their corseted, uptight, blue-haired, weepy, and whiny wives dripping mascara.

SING PRAISES
FOREVER, OR ELSE

And it shall come to pass, that every one that is left of all the nations which came against Jerusalem shall even go up from year to year to worship the King, the Lord of hosts, and to keep the feast of tabernacles. And it shall be that whoso will not come up of all the families of the Earth unto Jerusalem to worship the King...even upon them shall be no rain...there shall be the plague wherewith the Lord will smite the heathen that come not up to keep the feast of the tabernacles. This shall be the punishment of Egypt, and the punishment of all nations that come not up to keep the feast of the tabernacles.

SECOND ZECHARIAH (*c.* 160 B.C.E.), ZEC 14:16–19

The banner of Shambhala shall encircle the central lands of the Blessed One. Those who accept him shall rejoice, and those who deny him shall tremble. The decriers shall be given over to justice and shall be forgotten. The warriors shall march under the banner of Maitreya.

THE PROPHECY OF SHAMBHALA (BEF. 800)

For I know their works and their thoughts: it shall come, that I will gather all nations and tongues; and they shall come, and see my glory. And I will set a sign among them, and I will send those that escape of them unto nations...to the [distant] isles, that have not heard my fame, neither have seen my glory; and they shall declare my glory among the Gentiles. And they shall bring all your brethren for [a tribute] unto the Lord out of all nations upon horses and in chariots, and in litters, and upon mules, and upon swift beasts, to my holy mountain Jerusalem, saith the Lord.... And I will also make [some of the Gentiles] priests.... For as the new heavens and the new Earth, which I will make, shall remain before me.... And it shall come to pass, that from one new moon to another, and from one Sabbath to another, shall all flesh come to worship before me, saith the Lord. And they shall go forth, and look upon the carcasses of the men that have transgressed against me: for their worm shall not die, neither shall their fire be quenched; and they shall be an abhorring unto all flesh.

THIRD ISAIAH (4TH CENTURY B.C.E.), IS 66:18–24

What if the interior decorators of New Jerusalem are the same ones who decorate the average Trinity Broadcasting Network talk show? Picture it: voluminous curtains draped around Kmart-quality stained-glass windows with images of cheeky cherubs. Christ's bureaucrats descending from heaven to land on ostentatious Louis XIV-cum-Grand Old Opry chairs. And the music! Endless Praise the Lord concerts sung by chubby sopranos in Eisenhower-era ballroom gowns. Overjoyous tenors straining their lacy tuxedos as they belt out the wobbly high notes.

Picture a thousand years of *700 Club* reruns, Pat Robertson telethons, and Billy Graham TV specials. Claudia Schiffer and Cindy Crawford will trade in their thongs for pleated dresses with puffed sleeves. And dye your hair mauve, girls! In my worst nightmare, Jesus Christ returns as Jesus Kitsch.

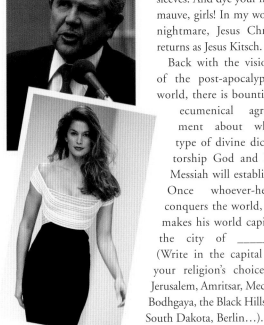

Back with the visions of the post-apocalyptic world, there is bountiful ecumenical agreement about what type of divine dictatorship God and his Messiah will establish. Once whoever-he-is conquers the world, he makes his world capital the city of _____. (Write in the capital of your religion's choice – Jerusalem, Amritsar, Mecca, Bodhgaya, the Black Hills of South Dakota, Berlin…).

The anti-Semitic Hitler described a vision of submission and pageantry remarkably similar to the visions of Jewish prophets like Zechariah and Isaiah. Clearly Hitler drew inspiration from his childhood Bible sessions when he dreamed of the nations paying tribute for a thousand years to the Nazi messiah and his successors in the world capital of Germania.

ABOVE **If Pat Robinson had his way Cindy Crawford would be dressed quite differently.**

Of course anyone can take a prophecy meant for someone else and make it theirs. Hitler turned out to be a lousy messiah, and World War II ground his dreams of tribute and Germania into rubble. Many of my readers may feel insulted that I even let him stand near a Buddha or a Jesus as a potential candidate for a messiah. Perhaps their criticism is right, and for their sake let me for once be fair and defend divine dictatorships, be they Christian, Hindu, or Buddhist versions. A mass murderer like Hitler could never be a fair-minded potentate governing the world. If there must be an absolute monarch ruling this planet after disposing of the devil, let it be the Son of God (if he's a Western messiah), or a pure incarnation of God in human form (if he's an Asian avatar). If I'm to surrender my fundamental democratic freedom of worship, freedom of choice, freedom of movement – yes, even my freedom of thought and feelings – then let them all be surrendered to a benevolent dictator direct from the Lord of Hosts.

Perhaps eternal salvation is worth losing my equality under the law, my personal responsibility – yes, even my mind. I can see how life in the age of the Messiah on earth would be much happier if people didn't have to think for themselves. Hey, being a sheep in a herd isn't bad at all, if the shepherd is the Lamb of God.

In the coming brave new world there is only one religion. If Kalki rules, then we'll all become Hindus. If it is Maitreya, you will adopt the red robes of the Buddhists. If the 12th Imam restores the world to Allah, don your turbans, men, and pull on your ankle-length chadors, ladies, for life in the world Taliban reich. If the ruler turns out to be Christ, then you have about a 300-to-1 chance that conversion to someone else's sect of Christianity will be the first Messiah directive, because there are at least 300 predicted versions of Christ's Empire of the Son of God on Earth.

Submit, and the Messiah will protect you – under his ever-watchful eye he will see that everyone is happy. The promise of the Golden Age, whether it's ruled by Shambhala, Immanuel, or Christ, is that you will live longer, happier, and holy lives. Just submit to the King and there will be no disease, no want; he will build the autobahns, and the trains will run on time. Submit and you will be repaid with eternal happiness. How can anyone turn away from the security of so many people living in bliss, all moving as one mind, one body, all dedicated to God's Great Leap Forward, marching hand in hand with the Messiah?

Forever let us bow down to him and sing: One Realm! One People! One Leader! Hail Victory!

Respect in the hope of reward
is the outcome of fear.
In love there is no fear.

J. KRISHNAMURTI (1963), LIAH

A THIEF IN
THE NIGHT

It is very difficult to recognize a contemporary master.

His fate is to be condemned, condemned by

all quarters, in all possible ways.

He is not respected – he is not a respectable person.

It takes time, thousands of years, for people to forgive

him; only then do they start respecting him.

When they are free of guilt of having condemned

him once, they start respecting him, worshiping him.

OSHO (1981), GLM

A THIEF IN THE NIGHT

The flames of hell have been made to blaze, and heaven hath been brought nigh; the celestial gardens are in flower, and fresh pools are brimming over, and paradise gleameth in beauty – but the unaware are still mired down in their empty dreams.

The veil hath fallen away, the curtain is lifted, the clouds have parted, the Lord of Lords is in plain sight – yet all hath passed the sinners by.

'ABDU'L-BAHÁ, PARAPHRASING MUHAMMAD (c. 1920), SLC

Be ye therefore ready also: for the Son of man cometh at an hour when ye think not.

Y'SHUA (c. 30–33 C.E.), LK 12:40

The day of the Lord so cometh as a thief in the night.

SAUL OF TARSUS (51 C.E.), 1 THES 5:2

When I look at photos of criminals standing for their mug shots, some of them flash the hurting glow of crucified looks. And when a few of them display just the right angular noses, high cheekbones, shoulder-length hair, and beards to play Jesus look-alikes on the cross, it makes me wonder – what if Christ has already returned, and we've locked him up? They arrested him last time, right? If he didn't fit in with the expectations of his own times, then why do so many of us automatically assume we will welcome Christ if he appears in our near future?

A long time ago my mother drove me past Christ standing on the roadside. No B.S. I saw him standing on the road on my way home from Ridgecrest Junior High School one afternoon in 1968. Our huge brown boat of an Oldsmobile station wagon floated past a barefoot man on the side of the road dressed in a long cream-colored robe. He had dusky shoulder-length hair and a short pointed beard. He really turned my head. I never saw a man look and feel so much like Jesus Christ. He held outstretched arms and he gazed blissfully at the skies as if he were ready to embrace the fog- and smog-fetid heavens over the Palos Verdes peninsula.

"Jesus," as I later found out, had stood there without moving from that rigid crosslike stance all day, with his square-jawed Jeffrey Hunter face turned to the sky. There were no cameras or filmmakers around, so police from the Palos Verdes Sheriff's Department reckoned this character meant blissful business. Of course the police reasoned that he couldn't be the real Jesus returned, even though one could argue that the claimant and the real article were both hippies of their day. In the case of this Jesus (and given that this was 1968), the police assumed the divine grace of LSD was afoot, and they eventually called in the straitjacket brigade to take Jesus of Palos Verdes, California, away.

It is a good thing the guys in white suits didn't live in Jerusalem 2,000 years ago. They'd have nabbed the real Jesus for sure. Imagine, if you will, some guy today saying his mom was a virgin and his papa was God. What do you think a patrol of paramedics would do with Buddha, sitting under a Bodhi tree for years, wasting away, doing nothing except watching his breath go in and out? The story goes that he subsisted on one hemp seed a day for years. When I lived in India I saw statues of him sitting in the lotus position with his bones and veins ready to burst out of his tight, emaciated skin. Imagine what modern health-care workers would do with a man suffering from such a bad case of spiritual anorexia. I think they'd probably carry him away for a good force-feeding.

One night the Greek philosopher Socrates, a near-contemporary of Buddha, walked into a field underneath the stars, looked heavenward, and froze exactly the way Jesus of Palos Verdes did 25 centuries later. Socrates later explained that the stars glistening in their thousands had sent him into such chills of ecstasy that he forgot himself and froze in that position, unblinking, for the entire night. Only in the morning did his disciples find him and shake him out of his reverie, otherwise Socrates might still be standing there. It's a good thing for Socrates that Plato and the rest of the boys were doctors of philosophy and not doctors of mental health.

ABOVE **Miracles are well and good in their place –
preferably a foreign country 2000 years ago – but
there's no room for them in our modern sensibilities.**

It is okay to have the finger bone of Buddha in your
temple, but Nirvana forbid the whole Buddha should
come through the door in the flesh. It is okay to heal the
sick and raise the dead as a messiah of a two-dimensional play of light on a movie screen, but suspicion
automatically arrives when we are face to face with a
flesh-and-blood man of enlightenment. Christ can live
safely in the present Vatican halls as long as he's an oil
painting by Raphael or hewn in Michelangelo's marble,
but there would be hell to pay with the Swiss Guard if
the real cross-lugging Christ passed under the Barberini
gates into the Vatican Piazza to stake his claim on
Christendom's greatest cathedral, St. Peter's Basilica.
Jesus of Nazareth would suffer the same fate as Jesus of
Palos Verdes.

For those of you who think you'll be able to recognize
the returned Jesus or Buddha because they can perform
miracles, think again. If a messiah is really coming, and if,
as so many of the prophecies imply, his miracles will
prove he is the true savior, how is even an authentic
raiser of the dead, or materializer of water out of wine or
bread out of stones, going to pass the scrutiny of
modern human beings who already enjoy the special

effects of movies like *Star Wars: The
Phantom Menace* or the lifelike resurrection of dinosaurs in *Jurassic Park*?
If someone really did roll an alien out
of cold storage after he/she/it
crashed in Roswell, New Mexico,
no one would believe it. We are
ever more jaded to miracles thanks
to Hollywood hoaxes using cutting-edge special effects.

Can faith in the dream-mes-
siah make us view the real
article as flimflam? We close
Part I, "The Second Coming
Syndrome," with an exami-
nation of the pathology of
messianic projections and
how they blind us to the
real person we mistake as
our savior. If we under-
stand this pathology,
perhaps we can recognize the messianic appearances that have
already come and are, according to
prophecy, yet to come just a few
years from now.

ABOVE **Could the modern
equivalent to the changing of
water into wine be the special
effects of films like** *Jurassic Park*
where dinosaurs return?

MESSIAHS MISSED

People in biblical times labeled Jesus a cult guru. So was Buddha. Rather than uphold the traditional hopes of priests and followers of their religions, Christ and Buddha are two historical examples of how great spiritual teachers disappoint the contemporary expectations of all but a handful who wait for their coming.

BUDDHA GAUTAMA SIDDHARTHA:
THE EXPECTATION

A passage in the *Srimad Bhavatatam Purana* recorded in 3000 B.C.E. foresaw "the birth of a supreme being" in "Gaya," a town in Bihar province, East India, as "Lord Buddha," the next avatar to come 25 centuries after Krishna. The prophecy implies that he would reject Vedic traditions of holy sacrifice because at the time of his rebirth unclean and unholy people would pervert the custom. Because of this vision and other Puranic prophecies, the Hindus expected the next avatar would restore Vedic Hinduism to its roots.

BUDDHA GAUTAMA SIDDHARTHA:
THE DISAPPOINTMENT

Siddhartha Gautama was born in Nepal, but he experienced his second birth as "the Buddha" (the awakened one) in Gaya, Bihar (India), around 560 B.C.E. After his enlightenment he dropped out of Hinduism and led a heretical new cult for 42 years. He rejected the traditional caste system and angered the Hindu priestly caste (the Brahmins) by declaring anyone a "Brahman" who can attain to buddhahood, whether he's born into the high caste of the Brahmins or the lowest cast of the Sudras (untouchables). Worse yet – Brahma forbid! – he invited women to become disciples.

Buddha was diametrically opposed to the Hindu belief that the seeker attains the superself through *Mosksha* (liberation). He also denied the traditional worship of millions of gods. Instead, Buddha declared that there are no gods, and promoted an ultimate state of "non-attainment" of the "no-self" he called Nirvana ("splitting the thunderbolt"). Soon he drew into his ranks of monks the cream of Hindu society's educated and affluent, who abandoned Krishna's religion and adopted a life of renunciation.

JESUS CHRIST:
THE EXPECTATION

Messiah-watchers in Palestine used calculations in the Book of Daniel to pinpoint the time of his arrival on earth, sometime around 2,000 years ago. The Jewish people of that era expected a militant messiah king from the line of David, born in Bethlehem. He would lead Israel in a holy war, casting out the Romans with his "rod of iron" – after which he would promote the traditions, uphold the Law of Moses, the holy Torah, and restore Israel to its past glory. The Jewish people would return to God's grace, prosper, and triumph over all the peoples of the world.

JESUS CHRIST:
THE DISAPPOINTMENT

Jesus fulfilled prophecy by being born in Bethlehem under the bloodline tracing back to King David, but the ministry he established was unkosher to traditionalists across Judaea. He didn't uphold the Law of Moses, but reinterpreted its tenets. He suggested the people tolerate the Romans. Jesus promoted love, not holy war. No messiah in shining armor was he; only a simple Galilean preaching that God is love.

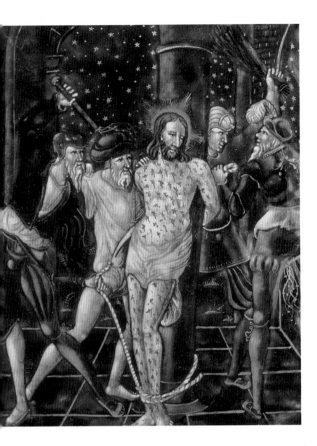

ABOVE **Judas is shown here in his role as supreme betrayer, yet without him the Christian message would have been lost.**

Jesus went to the Temple in Jerusalem, but not to swell the religious egos of the Pharisees. He started a riot in God's holiest house. He threw out the money changers, but did not promote rebellion against the Romans as the new Jewish spiritual king. Jesus would not become the political and spiritual "Messiah" of the Jews. His kingdom was abstract, subtle. It was within.

This wasn't what the rabbis in the synagogue had prepared the believers for. The message of Jesus – later called "Christos" – was all Greek to them. Finally the mainstream Jewish culture rejected the heretic and later the cult of Jesus because it didn't restore Israel or Mosaic law. Instead it eventually established a worldwide religion with mostly non-Jews.

Even a close disciple, Judas Iscariot, wanted Jesus to fulfill his role as freedom fighter and warrior messiah. In a way Judas was a sincere spiritual terrorist trying to do in his time what some in ultra-right-wing Christian militias or fundamentalist Islamic terrorist organizations want to do in our time. Judas wanted to force the issue and make the Messiah show himself to the world. Judas delivered his master to the Pharisees, perhaps assuming Jesus would finally reveal himself by using his supernatural powers. What did Jesus do? Nothing! He passively went off as a captive of the Pharisees and their soldiers. Later he let himself be tortured, whipped, and crucified. There was no miracle, Jesus did not command his chains to break, nor did the nails pop out of his wrists or ankles so he could float to earth before half of Jerusalem. Jesus died as any ordinary man in the same bare-naked and gory circumstances would have. Judas was devastated. He suffered the ultimate prophetic disappointment and hanged himself.

All are so prone to think of just a few days making such changes [the physical and spiritual changes coming to humanity], but the preparation takes time – and we are usually forewarned by the nature of things, but realize it after it has passed.

EDGAR CAYCE, IN A LETTER TO
A FRIEND (*c.* EARLY 1940s)

Very rarely does a buddha exist in the world, so even if you meet him you will not understand his language. Most probably you will misunderstand him. You know misery, and he is talking about bliss. You know wounds, and he is talking about eternal health. You know only death, and he is talking about eternity.

OSHO (1989), ZNM

Christ will arrive at the beginning of the new era.... But it will not be the man who was once incarnate and known as Yeshua, or Jesus. It will be another Wise One.... This Wise One will give the next set of signposts to humanity, just as Yeshua left us a set of signposts, and it took two thousand years for humanity to begin to see the wisdom of what he was really saying.

SPIRIT GUIDES OF RUTH
MONTGOMERY (1979), AMG

A PLAGUE OF PARROT PUNDITRY

Who teaches the followers of each religion to recognize their savior when he comes?

The religious leaders.

Has any mullah, ayatollah, shankaracharya, pope, Dalai Lama, or Rinpoche alive today met a messiah face to face?

No.

They come across him in a story passed down the generations for thousands of years, through a thousand interpreters. The factual memory of what the Messiah was and what he said is like water sent down a bucket brigade to put out the new millennium's threatening fire. One generation of theologians splashes the story into the bucket of the next, letting droplets of recollection spill and be lost. By the time the present generation receives the story, the water of truth has all but splashed away and only a dry wooden bucket of dogma remains to contain a trace of the wet truth, rapidly evaporating from its wooden strictures. The wooden container of truth is all we have left to throw on the fire.

Why is Jesus missed? When he is present, he himself says, "You don't look at the Living One." And then when he is dead, millions of people close their eyes and see him and enjoy him, the same people who crucified him when he was here in the body. The same people go on imagining and thinking about him – because this imagination is not a fire, it is a consolation.

OSHO (1974), MST

If the Teaching becomes ineffective and the community fails, then that Source of Truth is dead. Then the Teaching simply becomes part of the mass of solutions and consolations that have appeared in human time. It is just a relic and a fetish. Even during the Guru's lifetime, the Teaching may function that way for many.

ADI DA SAMRAJ (*c.* 1975), WYIT

Organized religions – whether it is Christianity or Hinduism or Mohammedanism – have not been seekers of truth. In two thousand years, what truth has organized Christianity added to the statements of Jesus? So what is the need of this organization? It is not increasing religiousness in the world; it is simply repeating what Jesus has said…. In twenty-five centuries, how many Buddhists have searched for the truth, or have found the truth? – just a long line of parrots repeating what Gautama Buddha has found.

OSHO (1987), HISP

Many people first expect life to improve before they themselves become good. This would mean that the idea of the good should first be applied in life and then in human beings. This is not possible. People expect the Kingdom of God to come from outside before it enters into them. They expect it to come from outside in some spiritual way and that they will immediately acquire the right to citizenship in this kingdom. But this can never happen. The Kingdom of God is within people and not outside them.

PETER DEUNOV (1935), ROYL

To understand God, you must first understand your own mind – which is very difficult. The mind is very complex, and to understand it is not easy. But it is easy enough to sit down and go into some kind of dream, have various visions, illusions, and then think that you are very near to God. The mind can deceive itself enormously. So, to really experience that which may be called God, you must be completely quiet.

J. KRISHNAMURTI (1963), LIAH

DANGEROUS BEINGS

Think not that I am come to send peace on Earth: I come not to send peace, but a sword. For I have come to turn "a man against his father, a daughter against her mother, a daughter-in-law against her mother-in-law – a man's enemies will be members of his own household."

Y'SHUA (c. 30–33 C.E.), MT 10:34–35, QUOTING MICAH (c. 721 B.C.E.), MI 7:6

They shall forget the meaning of the word, teacher. But then shall the teachers appear and in all corners of the world will be heard the teaching. To this word of truth shall the people be drawn. But those who are filled with darkness and ignorance shall set obstacles.

PROPHECY OF SHAMBHALA (BEF. 800), ALTAI

From the beginning of the world until the present time each [Divine] "Manifestation" sent from God has been opposed by an embodiment of the "Powers of Darkness."
This dark power has always endeavored to extinguish the light. Tyranny has ever sought to overcome justice. Ignorance has persistently tried to trample knowledge underfoot. This has, from the earliest ages, been the method of the material world.

'ABDU'L-BAHÁ (1911), PARIS 33:1–2

Leaders of religion, in every age, have hindered their people from attaining the shores of eternal salvation, inasmuch as they held the reins of authority in their mighty grasp. Some for the lust of leadership, others through want of knowledge and understanding, have been the cause of the deprivation of the people. By their sanction and authority, every Prophet of God hath drunk from the chalice of sacrifice.

BAHÁ'U'LLÁH (1858), IQN

It is very difficult to recognize a contemporary master. His fate is to be condemned, condemned by all quarters, in all possible ways. He is not respected – he is not a respectable person. It takes time, thousands of years, for people to forgive him; only then do they start respecting him. When they are free of guilt of having condemned him once, they start respecting him, worshiping him.

OSHO (1981), GLM

In the realm of religion there are three categories of dangerous beings.

CATEGORY 1:
The Rebel Masters

On the whole, the founders of our present-day religions did not come to sustain the status quo of their contemporaries. The inventors of new religions threaten the established faiths and their hold on power by questioning their tenets. Lord Krishna disrupts Indian society and incites a war of purification. Buddha breaks away from the Hinduism that Krishna purified. Muhammad overturns the stone idols in Mecca and puts the kibosh on pantheistic Arab cults. Nanak the Muslim founds the Sikh religion, and starts a spiritual rebellion. He seeks a balance against the excesses of Hinduism and Islam. Moses parts the Red Sea and unites the Jewish people under the Torah. Jesus parts the Jewish people with a schismatic new religion and unites the Gentile world under the banner of his cross.

The path the founders of religions take cuts against the grain of their-contemporary morality. Krishna, God's incarnation, celebrates holiness and hedonism equally. He is not a renouncer; he is not celibate, either. God's incarnation happily seduces 12,000 wives. Buddha allows wives to become monks just like men. Muhammad's first disciple is his wife, who is at least 15 years older than he is. Nanak, on his *hadj* (pilgrimage) to Mecca, sleeps with his feet pointing toward the Kaaba. The devout complain that he blasphemes God by pointing his dirty feet at Allah's holiest Islamic shrine. Nanak replies, "You can move my feet where you like, but first answer me this, where can you point my feet where Allah is not?" A crowd led by mainstream priests in Jerusalem corners a presumed adulteress near where Jesus was resting. The laws of Moses require them to stone her to death. "He who has not sinned cast the first stone," says Jesus, and the words of the hobo holy man upset the pious Pavlovian pitch of their stones.

Someone armed with nothing more than refreshing new insights can undermine a thousand years of religious equilibrium. Therefore vision, by its very definition, is a sworn and potent adversary of religious tradition and order.

What do you do if you are Caiaphas, the "pope" of your religion, the leader of the Sanhedrin, the "cardinalate" of that day, when a poor, Aramaic-speaking young man from Galilee declares himself the son of God? Rather than give respect to the head of the Sanhedrin and your traditions as he is predicted to do, this Galilean shuns you, criticizes you, and questions that which cannot be questioned – the Law of Moses. Does this vagabond carpenter sleep in the houses of the high, the kosher, the righteous? No. He spends his days with the dirty peasants drying the tears of whores and tasting wine with fishermen and tax collectors.

ABOVE **Jesus challenged the accepted order by whipping the money changers out of the Temple.**

What do you do if you are one of five shankaracharyas – the "popes" of Hinduism – and a hippie calling himself a Buddha disrupts the status quo of caste, questions the very existence of the gods, and opens the path of liberation to everyone? What do you do in ancient Persia to a man called Zarathustra, who burns away the smoke of nebulous and indistinct mythologies of gods with the odd revelation of one spark of divine fire dwelling in all things? What does Pharaoh do with a Moses – kiss and make up? Or does he unleash his chariots to trample him down? Does Caiaphas sit in Herod's Temple and let some longhair kick his money changers around, or does he sic the Romans on the troublemaker? Can Persian pantheists sit by and let their religion be purified by Zarathustra's flame, or do they incite their people to put out his fire with the thrust of a dagger into his heart?

CATEGORY 2:
The Mainstream Mobs

Once upon a time there lived a most twisted and gnarly tree in the cosmic forest. Its black branches were more warped and tangled than the matted hairs of a Rastafarian tress. No bird nested on them; no squirrel dared explore the dark labyrinth of branches. Once in a thousand years or so there grew on the branch tips of this most confused and ugly tree one or two flowers of the rarest beauty. Whenever the great mass of the tree became aware of the flowers' existence, it became horrified. It cut off the flow of sap and shook them off.

The mass of semiconscious humanity is like this tree. If the rare flowers of its highest potential do blossom from time to time, the contrast is too shocking. The tangled and warped-minded mob cannot stand the loving glow of alien petals. When dangerous beings like rebel masters flower too brightly, they are often cut down and trampled by the dangerous beings that constitute the mainstream mob.

Only once was a great master pruned by accident. Lord Krishna was killed by a spaced-out member of the masses, a peasant hunter. Where the Greek Achilles had a weakness in the heel for death's arrow, Krishna was killed by an arrow shot through the sole of his foot.

OPPOSITE **Krishna, riding his mythic bird, met his match in battle with the peasant Indra.**

BELOW **After the trial, Christ's death was demanded by a bloodthirsty mob.**

Other avatars and founders of religions were not so lucky. Zarathustra was stabbed to death. Buddha was threatened by Hindu mobs and assassins at least eight times during the four decades he taught. His death from extreme dysentery may have been caused by some Hindu sympathizer passing holy cow dung into his food. A mob of Egyptian charioteers tried to run down Moses. A mob shouted for Christ's crucifixion and got their wish. Muhammad was poisoned by his detractors and lingered in agony for seven years.

It makes me wonder why Jesus would want to come back and face another nailing. Why should the 12th Imam come out of hiding? The god Vishnu, who once incarnated as Krishna, would have a foot up on unconscious people if he never incarnated a foot, a body, and a target for the crosshairs of a future hunter.

The founding flowers of new religious insights are not the only ones crushed by a mob's rocks, crosses, and arrows. Pythagoras fashioned a new paradigm of Greek mysticism and saw himself and his commune burned to the ground by a mob. Socrates so hurt the mob's religious feelings with his simple and penetrating questions that they demanded that this 70-year-old man should see his inevitable departure hastened with hemlock. Bodhidharma, the Indian Buddhist master who brought Buddhism to China, survived being poisoned by a jealous disciple in a fit of pique. The mob beheaded Sarmad, a Jewish mystic and ecstatic ecumenist wandering through India. Mansoor, a Sufi, was slowly dismembered for innocently declaring that Allah and he were one. (In other words, Allah is the whole universe and everyone and everything in it; Allah is all-ah-round and inside his creation.)

The forerunners of a new religion have been persecuted even in more recent times. For instance, the Shah of Persia's entire regiment of bodyguards herded together to shoot the Bab (meaning "the Gate"), the forerunner who paved the way for the loving Bahá'í world teacher, Bahá'u'lláh. He in turn was imprisoned for most of his adult life; his son and successor, 'Abdu'l-Bahá, was then locked up for 40 years.

The truth wish of the dangerous masters collides with the death wish of the dangerous mob.

ABOVE **During his time on earth, Buddha was constantly under threat from Hindu mobs and assassins.**

CATEGORY 3:
The Myth-Makers

Who baits the mob to persecute and kill the dangerous men of vision? The most dangerous beings of all. They are the ones who appear after the mob has done away with the Messiah. These are the priesthoods who organize religions over the tombs of the departed masters. They are the revisers of eyewitness accounts. They are the priests who gather in Nicaea centuries after the death and purported resurrection of Christ and decide to censure one set of gospels inspired by God in favor of another, as if men who defend their Bible as the word of God one day can edit God the next. They are the people around the tomb of the recently departed Muhammad who "knew" which one of the 32 versions of the Qur'an was correct and decided to burn the other 31. How they came to this conclusion is not known, yet it is certain they made it without consulting the author/channeler of Allah's message, the late Muhammad. The day after Buddha Gautama died from an assassin's dung dollop in his begging bowl of a last supper, his grieving disciples split his new religion into 32 sects. It seems that even his enlightened disciples hadn't considered writing down their master's words until he was dead.

Buddha's cousin-brother, Ananda, was the only monk by Buddha's side for his entire life as an enlightened master. He heard everything Buddha said, but there was a catch. Ananda had not attained enlightenment, and even though he would later catch the nonexistent flowers of Nirvana with the grasp of his nonexistent inner hand – the one hand that makes the sound of one hand clapping – the enlightened Ananda had only his unenlightened memory to call up an interpretation of what Buddha had said over those 42 years they wandered together.

LEFT **Buddhism was divided into 32 different sects the moment Buddha Gautama was dead. Only then were his words written down.**

Let a few centuries roll by and you see the priesthoods of 32 sects of Buddhism, armed with Ananda's ego-tainted memories, slowly reinterpret their founder's statements and make them more digestible to the coming millions of future unenlightened followers. Let 325 years or so pass after Christ physically vanished from this earth, then let Roman Emperor Constantine convene the Council of Nicaea to gather the third category of dangerous beings to put the last touches on Romanizing and centralizing what had been a more free-styled and antiestablishment Christianity. After the organic faith becomes an organization, Rome fashions for itself a new mainstream religion by taming a living organism of faith into an organization of doctrine. Wait for the final blink-out of the light of Allah's open and ecstatic prophet-receptor before you gamble on a 1-in-32 chance that you saved the right Qur'an and burned the 31 fraudulent ones.

So now we come to the third category of dangerous beings. This category consists of those who make their religious founders palpable and tasteful to the mainstream. St. Paul makes Jesus more Hellenized and more appealing to the Gentiles. He adopts popular aspects of the most in-vogue pagan mainstream religion of the day, the Persian Cult of Mithras. Suddenly there's a distinctly un-Jewish and un-Y'shua-bar-Youssefian doctrine getting the average Roman citizen's attention.

was Alexander, the Macedonian tyrant – a person so inwardly insecure that he could not conquer his feelings of emptiness unless he conquered the world and proved to himself that he could subject millions of other human beings to his will. Just as countless prayers have been sent to the wrong address for two millennia – to the home of "Jesus" rather than "Y'shua" – so have countless millions of Buddhists prayed to representations of their awakened founder that are based on the face of a vainglorious aggressor. It would be like all the Christian artists of the next 20 centuries basing their icons and other images of the peaceful Christ on the handsome face of a more contemporary world conqueror such as Napoleon Bonaparte.

ABOVE **Napoleon would be a glamorous, if unlikely, model for pictures of Christ.**

Almost as soon as the dangerous visionary who founded a religion has departed, there come self-proclaimed authorities who believe it is their duty to tame the organic and spontaneous qualities of the new religion. Usually the job of turning an orgasmic vision into an organized religion requires a *coup d'église*. The authoritarians argue that a religion cannot sustain its founder's vision without establishing a hierarchy that preserves the "true" messages of the Messiah. There must be order!

Things like the Mithraic Holy Eucharist ritual of the Last Supper pop up in the creed, along with alien mysteries like a Persian-Zarathustra-style apocalypse. It isn't Saoshyant who comes to earth in triumph to win the final battle between good and evil, it is "Christos," the new name St. Paul gives to Y'shua in an attempt to make him more appealing to pagan anti-Semites and Judeo-clueless Gentiles alike. St. Paul makes "Christos" a miracle worker, born of a virgin, because Mithras – his chief messianic competition – is also born of a virgin.

If a Hebrew messiah can become the God-man of the Gentiles, the priests that later come to institutionalize Buddhism can help promote their savior and founder all over Asia with a sculptor's mistaken makeover. Where Y'shua became "Christ," Buddha became Alexander the Great!

The face modeling for the all-compassionate Buddha seen on millions of statues across Asia is based on the busts of another man, a supreme egoist. He

RIGHT **The despotic Alexander the Great, the face that launched a thousand mistaken Buddha likenesses.**

Bearing personal witness to the transformative effects of a master's love must be taken out of the individual's hands and standardized for his or her protection by specially trained and initiated "priests." In a sense, the very sorts of people a master like Christ rebelled against become the Caiaphas and Sanhedrin of the religion projected in his memory. To keep the people's attention, the dead religious founder must become more God-man than simply a man. (And one thing is certain in this generally patriarchal civilization of the past 5,000 years: your founder had better not be a woman!) Thus, the original Hebrew word for a simple, innocent young woman is mysteriously translated as "virgin." Mary, the mother of Jesus, surrenders herself to the transcendental gynecological ministrations of the Holy Ghost.

ABOVE **Hindu culture may still resist Buddhist philosophy and compromise the power of the Buddha.**

Buddha can't be born in a normal way, either. We must standardize his memory. Make him remarkable. Buddha comes out from between the legs of his squatting and suffering mother, landing on his feet and taking seven steps before he declares, "I am the most enlightened man who's ever walked the earth!!"

Muhammad can't just die like everyone else. Before he departs the earth he has a final dream wherein he foresees himself astride a supernatural horse that is rocketed to Paradise from the launch pad of Jerusalem's Temple Mount.

The march of time itself warps the memory of the departed savior. A new hierarchy promotes a new dogma and hastens the facts into the outhouse of myth. Our man becomes God-man, avatar, Messiah-king. He becomes someone to be worshiped, not understood.

The keepers of a messiah's memory want all of us to be static – lulled by the base wave of their dogma. Their teaching is like a white noise that hums for centuries, stilling the mobs with repetitive and pleasantly hypnotic mantras and comforting them with the drone of an unchanging oscillation of doctrine broadcast from the pulpits. The hum of their hymnal myths seems quite effective in keeping the majority of any religion's followers cuddly and complacent for thousands of years between the sudden, short, and uncomfortable radio spikes that are the lives of living messiahs.

The white noise of dogma, applied to generations from their earliest and most vulnerable formative years, can produce the mobs needed to resist and destroy any new messiah's advent. That is why the mainstream Jewish culture could demand Christ's crucifixion; that is why Hindu culture could eventually banish Buddhism from India after a few hundred years. Afterward the Hindu Brahmins buzzed believers into complacency with a rationalization that Buddha had indeed fulfilled the Srimad Bhagavatam prophecy. He was a bona fide Hindu avatar, but he hadn't come to revise Hinduism. Buddha was the god Vishnu pretending to be evil so he could test the faith of the Hindus.

Putting it in a more kinesthetic way, the hierarchy dispatches the messiah, then theological myth-makers go to work on calming and soothing the inflammation of rebellion among their followers. They soften the muscles of doubt by using the vibrator of comforting myth. But there's a problem with vibrators. If you apply one to the same spot for too long, it leaves the area numb and senseless.

It is something very natural to the unconscious state of humanity. The living Master is a danger, but the dead Master is no more a danger. The living Master can wake you up; you cannot dodge him, he simply goes like an arrow into the heart. But a dead Master is a dead Master. He is just a memory, he is no longer there.

And now the disciples start worshipping him. Why? It is out of a feeling of guilt that they never heard him while he was alive? They feel guilty, they repent. Now they have to do something to get rid of the guilt. Worshipping is out of guilt....

People crucified Jesus, and the same people started worshiping him. It is repentance. They started feeling a great pain, a great heaviness, a great anxiety. They had done something wrong; they had to compensate, they had to worship this man. They condemned him as a criminal and they worshiped him as a God.

...When you worship a Master you start creating a Master to your own idea – hence the myth springs up. The myth comes from your unconscious. The Master is physically dead, now you want him to be spiritually dead, too. The myth will do it: he will become spiritually dead, too. Your myth is a lie! And the more the Master becomes surrounded by myth and fictions, the more and more unreal he becomes.

That's why it is very difficult to believe that Jesus is a historical person.... It is because of the mythology that has been created around him: he walks on water, he turns water into wine....

The people who created these myths are really getting rid of the reality of the Master.... Death has destroyed his body, myth will destroy his spirituality. He will become just a mythological figure, utterly impotent, useless.

...No living Master ever fulfills anybody's expectations; he lives his own life. Whether you accept him or you reject him makes no difference. You can kill him, you can worship him, it makes no difference. He goes on living his own way, he goes on doing his own thing. He cannot be forced to fulfill your requirements of him.

OSHO (1979), WHT

NEW EYES, NEW EARS

But ye, brethren, are not in darkness, that that day should overtake you as a thief.... Therefore let us not sleep, as do others, but let us watch and be sober.

SAUL OF TARSUS (51 C.E.), 1 THES 5:4, 6

Watch ye therefore: for ye know not when the master of the house cometh, at [evening], or at midnight, or at the cock crowing, or in the morning: Lest coming suddenly he find you sleeping. And what I [say] unto you I say unto all, Watch.

Y'SHUA (c. 30 C.E.), MK 13:35–37

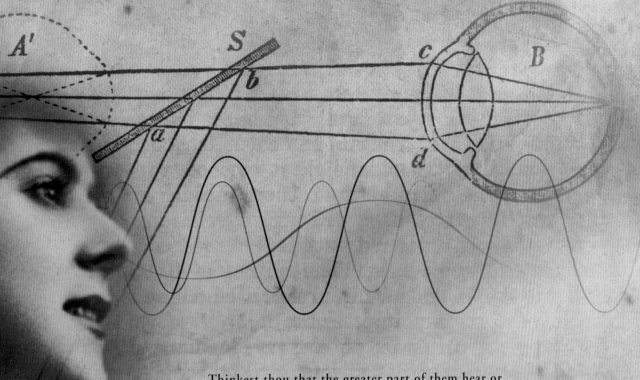

Thinkest thou that the greater part of them hear or understand? They are even like unto the cattle! Yea, they stray even further from the path! (Qur 25:44) Hearts have they, with which they do not understand, and eyes have they with which they see nothing! (Qur 7:179)

MUHAMMAD (*c.* 620–630)

Watch therefore: for ye know not what hour your Lord doth come. But know this, that if the good man of the house had known in what watch the thief would come, he would have watched, and would not have suffered his house to be broken up. Therefore be ye also ready: for in such an hour as ye think not the Son of man cometh.

Y'SHUA (*c.* 30–33 C.E.), MT 24:42–44

Having eyes, see ye not? and having ears, hear ye not? and do ye not remember?

Y'SHUA (*c.* 30–33 C.E.), MK 8:18

Those who have eyes in Christendom see Jesus in their dreams and in their near-death experiences. Those who are Catholics add a visualization of the Virgin Mary, and it is her voice they hear speaking the mother tongue of their birth. The Tibetan listens to the apparition of Tara. The Hindu in a near-death experience falls down the dark tunnel toward the being of light but sees no Christ. Instead, Lord Krishna is waiting there. The Buddhist never encounters Krishna at the terminus of the near-death experience, because there stands the luminous Lord Buddha.

It doesn't take a prophet to predict that humanity with all of its various views of the savior is about to undergo a near-death experience. We sustain a desire for infinite excess of numbers and consumption that is taking us collectively down the dark tunnel of a near-death destiny, a mere ten, twenty, or thirty years into the new millennium.

What will humanity see at the end of a tunnel of ecological breakdown, global famine, and social collapse? Will a savior be waiting there, lighting the end of history's tunnel? And if so, who will it be?

The new millennium has each religion expecting to meet only their messiah and no one else. Each Native American nation expects its own specific version of a half-thousand tribal variations of Quetzalcoatl to stand at the end of time's tunnel. He will save them from the whites who raped their land. The whites expect any number of Christian versions of the returning Christ to save them from their own rape and pillage of the earth. The Hindus wait for Kalki to save them from the sins of

Western influences. The Tibetans wait for the Shambhala King Rudra Cakrin to shamble down the Himalayan peaks like a battling Yeti, throwing out the Chinese by force of arms. The communists wait for a new Lenin to raise the red banner once again. The Jews wait for Immanuel to save them from the influence of Jesus Christ and the Arabs. The Arabs wait for the 12th Imam to save them from the Christians and the Zionists. Nazis want a second Hitler standing at the exit of their tunnel, blistering his vocal cords with a shriek of Sieg Heil. Theists want to see God's son, while atheists wish that no one will stand at the end of their tunnel.

The momentum of religious prophegating almost predestines humanity to weaken its resolve to save itself. How can a sense of personal responsibility swim up a river of collective conditioning

that marks us as victims of original sin before we are even born? A sinner before birth cannot save himself. He needs a savior.

With this programming in mind, when I read that messiahs and avatars in the past warned me to look with open and fresh eyes and listen with new ears, I become aware of how I nod obediently. I see a mind lulled to complacency by the static dogma of my culture. I notice how, for much of my life, I took in that phrase "Have new eyes and ears" only as deeply as my mind, preset at an early age, could receive its implications. The priests have taught me to wink conspiratorially at the two-dimensional icon image of my savior and think, yes! I understand. It is a given that my religion already has the new eyes and ears to recognize the true savior the other people cannot see.

Descartes can think, therefore he is. But I've been programmed to think that if I simply believe, I will therefore be saved by my messiah.

The 1990s close with your author finishing a marathon of over 500 radio interviews on three continents. Most of these interviews averaged two to ten call-ins per show. There is nearly always a point in the debate where someone – usually a devout member of his or her religion – will phone in and defend (often angrily) their religious indoctrination with the following declarations:

ABOVE **Rodin's *Thinker*** personifies the modern spirit of intellectual autonomy and self-realization.

✢ God's going to test us in the catastrophes to come, and we must obey the tenets of our religion without question, otherwise we will fail the test and be judged.

✢ We MUST stay faithful to the message and identity of our deliverer as the religious authorities have revealed him to us.

✢ Therefore, do not question, and do not listen to anyone who casts doubt upon our doctrine.

I pondered for years over this almost universal brushoff of critical inquiry, and I've come to see that a sincere attempt to uphold the faith can go fundamentally against the founder of that faith. If all you need is to follow the tenets of your religion and respect the religious laws without question, then you live like no founders of religions ever lived. No founder of any great religion ever followed such advice. Spiritual masters like Krishna, Buddha, Muhammad, and so on, all lived in times that suffered religious turmoil just like our own. Faced with this they didn't hold on to the faith of the time. They disobeyed their priesthoods and questioned everything. These men had new eyes and new ears.

Follow the accepted interpretation of messianic prophecy, and I suspect you will miss what's really coming. It is time to clean our eyes and unplug our ears. If an assumption must be made, we might first assume that what we expect is most likely not what will happen. A religion that trains its followers for thousands of years to see the world as something sinful and necessary for God to judge and destroy will train its people to seek the dead and discarnate teacher over the living. The dead master cannot overturn a money changer's table. A hidden Imam or an ascended master is not able to tap your local Brahmin priest on the shoulder and tell him he's full of Brahma's bullshit. The true sages were never respectable when they were alive, or welcomed in their day. It is only reasonable to assume that there are sages and future founders of religions walking among us today whom we'd like to crucify just as readily as good people of Christ's or Buddha's day attacked new world teachers in order to preserve their traditional religions.

Perhaps right now, this very moment, there are strangers among us with the consciousness and love of a Christ walking on the same earth as you and I. Some of them may have already overturned our table of doctrinal beliefs, and we didn't like it. It made us angry. They attacked our religion! History, however, shows us that even the spiritual rebel who is least in harmony with our established beliefs today can be hailed as the founder of a great religion tomorrow. Perhaps most of us don't open our eyes and ears to rebellious seers because we assume our eyes and ears are already open. It seems that our great spiritual teachers often pass in and out of our times like thieves in the night. They are always ahead of our time and our understanding.

We are entering religiously feverish and expectant times, and someone or something is coming to a head, a God-head. If the Messiah comes, perhaps we need new eyes and new ears washed clean of everything our religious authorities have taught us to expect from him, or her. Rather than have faith in what our religious leaders have taught us to hear and see, a new messiah of the 21st century may require us to face those interpretations for what they are, impediments to the authentic mystical experience to come.

Even the Antichrist may be a misunderstood new Christ. Was not the first Christ an anti-Moses for the Jewish religion, and an anti-pagan to the Romans? It is only natural that the established religions condemn the next messiah, for to embrace the new Christ would threaten their hold on our hearts and minds.

BELOW **Krishna, like many other spiritual leaders, is reported to have lived in times of turmoil and religious change.**

The Prophets of God should be regarded as physicians whose task is to foster the well-being of the world and its peoples, that, through the spirit of oneness, they may heal the sickness of humanity.... Little wonder, then, if the treatment prescribed by the physician in this day should not be found to be identical with that which he prescribed before. How could it be otherwise when the ills affecting the sufferer necessitate at every stage of this sickness a special remedy?

BAHÁ'U'LLÁH (D. 1892), GLE

People are waiting for some savior to come and deliver them from all this misery. The savior is not going to come, but half of their waiting is right: they are waiting to be transformed. If they go on waiting for the savior they are waiting for Godot, who has never come, who will never come. They have to drop this idea that tomorrow somebody is going to come and deliver them from their suffering, misery. No, it is not going to happen. You have to become a savior of yourself.

OSHO (1985), FTOT

PART TWO

THE APOCALYPSE OF THE AWAKENED ONES

PART TWO
THE APOCALYPSE OF
THE AWAKENED ONES

Arise, shine; for thy light is come, and the glory of the Lord is risen. For, behold, the darkness shall cover the Earth, and gross darkness the people: but the Lord shall arise upon thee, and his glory shall be seen upon thee.

THIRD ISAIAH (4TH CENTURY B.C.), IS 60:1–2

After each 25 centuries the world comes into a state of Chaos. Man becomes uprooted, starts feeling meaningless. All values of life disappear. A great darkness surrounds, sense of direction is lost. One simply feels accidental. There seems to be no purpose, no significance. Life seems to be just a byproduct of change. It seems existence does not care for you. It seems there is no life after death. It seems whatever you do is futile, routine, mechanical, all seems pointless.

These times of chaos, disorder, can either be a great curse...or they can prove a quantum leap in human growth.

OSHO (1979), PHLS

A savior is a dream for some, a holy nightmare for others. He is someone who never seems to exist in the here and now. He's always coming. He already came. He lived and performed his miracles for someone else before I was born, and there's a good chance he will delay his return long enough so that he misses putting his miracles under my scrutiny during my lifetime.

He seems unidentifiable except for the footprints he leaves in the sanctuary of myth. He is a thing of tales and declarations told by people who never knew him. Centuries of woolgathering have stuffed the heads of theologians so full that you can spin a mighty fine "Lamb of God" yarn out of what were once the story and insights of a real human being.

Every time we gain a messiah, we seem to lose touch with the man.

The redeemer needs redemption. We have lost him in the clouds of our expectations and religious indoctrination. We have perverted his apocalypse with our misunderstanding of that word, reducing him and his revelation to a thing of divine retribution, bloody moons, sackcloth skies, and doom for the world.

Apocalypse is Greek for enlightenment.

This is what comes to mind when I hear the word "enlightened." It is light, delight, awake, free, liberated, naked, fresh, eternal, a twinkle. It doesn't whip itself in a dark monk's cell. It doesn't repress, it impresses. It doesn't point fingers at oversights, it is the finger pointing at the moon of insights. Enlightenment is the miracle of being natural and normal in an unnatural and extraordinarily egoistic world.

Apocalypse is also Greek for revelation.

Perhaps revelation is all Greek to the established religions.

If that wasn't so, then why does every new and potent spiritual voice terrify the religion of its day with its apocalypse? If the establishment was always in tune with the times, then there would never have been a Christ rubbing a sandaled foot against the cobblestones of Hebraic law, or a Buddha dropping out of Hinduism, or a Muhammad upsetting statues of animist deities in Mecca square.

History certainly repeats itself. Why then should we expect any different behavior from the established religions of today?

Great teachers often come just at the time when human history is about to spin a new turn of events on the wheel of a new era. The more fearful the future, the more ripe the climate for mystics to unsettle the dreams of ruling religions.

Predictive astrology says we are at the dawn of such an age, the Age of Aquarius, the age of science and rebellion. Unlike its predecessor, the Piscean Age (the age that has been dominated by the Christian "fish" religion), the next 20 centuries of the Aquarian Age will see the abandonment of superstition and faith-based religions in favor of a more scientific examination of human being.

In the Aquarian Age we may even see the most hallowed of prophetic subjects – the Messiah – undergo a death and resurrection.

Part Two looks at hundreds of censored and overlooked messianic prophecies that do not fit comfortably into current mainstream apocalyptic expectations of the Second Coming syndrome. They generally promise that humanity in the 21st century will reinvent itself and bring an end to its violent and fear-ridden childhood. If these more radical visions are correct, there will be no doomsday for the world, just an end to one of religion's longest-running expectations.

In the final days the Messiah dream dies, so humanity can be free.

> The new culture is on the way! Human thoughts and feelings have to be regulated and then those called the "geniuses of humanity" will come and undertake the upliftment of humanity. That is great work! The uplifting of humanity is not the work of one person alone.
>
> PETER DEUNOV (D. 1939), EVRY

ПOAH'S ARK OF COПSCIOVSПESS

*He whose mind is unsteady, who knows not
the path of Truth, whose faith and peace are ever
wavering, he shall never reach fullness of wisdom.*

BUDDHA GAUTAMA (*c.* 500 B.C.E.), DHM 3:38

ПОAH'S ARK OF
CONSCIOUSNESS

And, lo, there was a great earthquake: and the sun became black
as sackcloth of hair, and the moon became as blood; and the stars
of heaven fell unto the earth, even as a fig tree casteth her
untimely figs, when she is shaken of a mighty wind. And the
heaven departed as a scroll when it is rolled together, and
every mountain and island were moved out of their places.
And the kings of the Earth, and the great men, and the rich
men, and the chief captains, and the mighty men, and every
bondman, and every free man, hid themselves in the dens and
in the rocks of the mountains; and said to the mountains and
rocks, Fall on us, and hide us from the face of him that sitteth on
the throne, and from the wrath of the Lamb. For the great day of
his wrath is come; and who shall be able to stand.

ST. JOHN OF PATMOS (81–96 C.E.), RV 6:12–17

This world is indeed in darkness, and how few can see the light!
Just as few birds can escape from the net, few souls can fly into
the freedom of heaven.

BUDDHA GAUTAMA (*c.* 500 B.C.E.), DHM 13:174

Man is now living in his most critical moment and it is a crisis of immense dimensions. Either he will die or a new man will be reborn.... It is going to be a death and resurrection. Unless human consciousness changes totally man cannot survive. As he is right now he is already outdated.

...During this period there will be every kind of destruction on Earth including natural catastrophes and man manufactured auto-suicidal efforts. In other words there will be floods which have never been known since the time of Noah, along with earthquakes, volcanic eruptions and everything else that is possible through nature. The Earth cannot tolerate this type of mankind any longer. There will be wars which are bound to end in nuclear explosions, hence no ordinary Noah's ark is going to save humanity.

...The Holocaust is not going to be confined to certain places, it is going to be global so no escape will be possible. You can only escape within and that's what I teach. I do not teach worship of God or any other ritual but only a scientific way of coming to your innermost core.

OSHO (1983)

LEFT **The evolution of nuclear warfare may fulfill the prediction of a global Holocaust from which there is no escape.**

The mother of all travails is unavoidable. There will be famines, plagues, and global disasters, whether seers have used the gift of true providence to forewarn us of signs of the end times, or have conditioned us to make the end times happen. A tribulation is coming, whether it is the end of the world or the birth pangs of a new age. The next 50 years will see unprecedented stress brought to bear on human civilization and earth's ecology. There will be wars, global warming, and unrest. By the 2020s there will be billions of young people expecting a better future, but they will be disenfranchised by their own excessive numbers. They will see the job market and the world's resources collapse. The basics for happiness in life will be denied them. They will not enjoy a good education, or a roof over their head. They will be denied food, water, and hope. The young will be prime targets for the harangues and hate-mongering of not one but dozens of messianic Hitlers preaching an apocalyptic solution.

If only they could catch a ride on a Rapture cloud – if there were one. The more practical person might dig a survivalist's ditch and wait out the tribulation to come, but escape may not be possible when the whole world is going to feel the pain of this multifaceted travail. If food runs out during a protracted global famine, the survivalists will be the first doomsday moles rooted out of their holes by the desperate who are rooting out the last of the hoarded supplies. No one will escape. You may choose to leave the rising coastlines of California for a religiously pure and safe area like the desert town of Sedona, Arizona; but rather than drown from rising oceans, you may desiccate when the potable water in that New Age Mecca runs out.

ABOVE **There are getting to be just too many of us for the brave new world we have made.**

The coming decades of the early 21st century could see all of us writhing under an Internet of history's first global emergency. No region, no nation, and no person on earth will be exempt from the effects of another person's misuse or overuse of the planet. The next 30 years will endure floods not seen in recorded history – if not directly from weather, then from rising coastlines. Prophets foresee earthquakes, volcanic eruptions, and even many scientists predict natural disasters of a scope and magnitude never before encountered. It will be as if the earth were rebelling against a humanity that chooses to remain retarded while it waits for the saviors to fix them. Nostradamus and other seers have predicted a plague of 70 wars across the world, triggered by the breakdown of water and food resources caused by rampant overpopulation. Many of these wars will end in nuclear explosions and the unleashing of biological and chemical-weapon plagues.

Attempts to escape may not only be futile but result in a missed opportunity. A major theme promoted by more renegade redeemers – those mystics who do not toe the mainstream antilife and pro-afterlife line of the Second Coming syndrome – is that you cannot escape from yourself. No matter how high the Rapture carries you into the clouds, no matter how many Himalayan mountains you pull over your head to escape the disasters, the problem comes along for the ride.

You are the problem.

And you could be the answer.

The answer to averting the tribulations to come may arise out of each individual understanding and transcending the problem he or she has become.

Individual salvation requires something else entirely, a totally new vector. While some continue to wait for

rescue in the form of a new ark of a New Jerusalem to mother-ship them out of harm's way, there are visions that act like irritating flies dancing on the nose of such deliverance dreams, disturbing their reverie. These visions buzz with images of a travail from which there's no escape. They say that the coming disasters will force all people to stand face to face with a heartbreaking and dream-breaking reality: No saints or saviors are coming to save us from ourselves.

We will have to become our own saviors.

One of the renegade mystics, Osho, believes the next Noah's ark needed to save humanity is a "Noah's Ark of Consciousness." It is not a UFO mother ship of nebulous construction built for one to wait out the seven years of tribulation behind a comet's tail. It isn't a cave city for survivalists. It is a hideaway so secret that you'd never guess how close it nudges against where you live even at this moment. It hides right behind the source of your existence.

This safe haven is a place that spiritual survivalists retreat to.

It is the ark of consciousness within each of us.

The pathway to this "ark" can be found by remaining silent and centered exactly in the middle of the cyclone of the coming times.

BELOW **As ecological and population pressures build up, the historically familiar human recourse to war and aggression in an effort to preserve what we have will inevitably follow.**

THE COMING MIND BROIL

Many native prophetic traditions the world over share a vision of the world's physical and psychic energy fields rising a third or more in intensity in the coming century. They contend that the earth's energy band began its increase between 1983 and 1991, and will attain to its higher vibration around 2012. It is said that this new frequency of energy will be a blessing to those who can embrace the unknown, and who are open to innovation, adventure, and meditation. However, the native seers and shamans warn that those who hold on to fear and contraction will find life after 2012 hard to endure. Some will enjoy mind-liberation, while those who cannot change will suffer a mind-broil. Those individuals who cannot abandon fossilized ideas and traditions will be so subconsciously terrified by the new energies of new times that it is said they will drop dead from their own fear.

Tribal people will tell you that thoughts are things, and that modern humankind uses the subtle forces of thought most irresponsibly. When there were relatively few of us, this didn't have a serious impact, but now the unprecedented appearance of unaware and mechanically conditioned humans contributes more aberrant and unconscious thoughts than ever before. When the critical mass of so many unconscious thoughts may cause a foretold psychic trauma, only the ark of a silent mind may keep its cool in the brainstorms to come.

He whose mind is unsteady, who knows not the path of Truth, whose faith and peace are ever wavering, he shall never reach fullness of wisdom.

BUDDHA GAUTAMA (*c.* 500 B.C.E.), DHM 3:38

The coming…years are going to be of constantly accelerating momentum. They will drive many people crazy because no one will be able to live comfortably, because a great longing will arise in every soul. It will be almost like a fire – it will burn people.

OSHO (1977), WHIS

In the evil days of the ages full of turbulence
There will be many fears and dangers;
There will be men possessed by devils.

NICHIREN (*c.* 1271)

A moment comes when you start realizing that nothing is going to happen. Then there is the state of anguish. In anguish, only one thing seems to be there: somehow to get out of this circle of life – hence suicide, the increasing rate of suicide. And an unconscious desire of humanity that the third world war happens…. "So I am not responsible that I committed suicide…the world war killed everybody, and killed me too."

OSHO (1987), HISP

In the age of Kali, people's minds will always be in turmoil. They will become emaciated by famine and taxation, and will always be disturbed by fear and drought. They will lack adequate clothing, food and drink, they will be unable to rest properly, have sex or bathe themselves, and will have no ornaments to decorate their bodies. Actually, the people of Kali-yuga will gradually come to appear like ghostly haunted creatures.

THE SRIMAD BHAGAVATA (BEF. 300 C.E.)

There are periods in the life of humanity which generally coincide with the beginning of the fall of cultures and civilizations, when the masses irretrievably lose their reason and begin to destroy everything that has been created by centuries and millenniums of culture.

G. I. GURDJIEFF (c. 1916), MIRA

Then the kings will divide the world among themselves; there will be great hunger, great pestilences, and much distress on the Earth. The sons of men will be enslaved in every nation and will perish by the sword. There will be great disorder on Earth.

Y'SHUA (BEF. 5TH CENTURY C.E.), AOFT

Leave them to entertain themselves with their desires! (Qur 6:91).... They are seized by the madness of their vain fancies. (Qur 15:72)

MUHAMMAD (c. 620–630)

No believer has real gratitude toward these messiahs, avatars – no, because what have they given to you? Just beliefs...unfounded, ungrounded. How can you feel grateful to them.... On the contrary, if you search within yourself, you will feel anger. You will be surprised when I say that all Christians, deep down, are angry with Jesus. He promised to redeem them, and nothing is redeemed. He promised, and he was saying, "Soon you will be in the kingdom of God, soon you will be with me in the kingdom of God." And two thousand years have passed, [and] that "soon" has not yet been completed....

There is anger in every Christian against Jesus. And because of this anger he shows too much fanaticism for Jesus, so that nobody knows that he is angry. In fact he does not want to know that he is angry, that he has been deceived, that he has been given a bogus belief, that for two thousand years millions of people have lived with this belief and died with this belief – attaining no growth, reaching nowhere, finding nothing. One is afraid of this anger, this rage. To suppress it, he goes to the church, he prays to Jesus, or to Krishna, or to Mohammed.

But every believer, sooner or later, is going to be frustrated because belief is not going to give him the truth. It is not going to give him the living waters of life.

OSHO (1984), MTOE

SH✟T HAPPENS
TO SLEEPWALKERS

Belief is blind. It has no rational proofs for it. It is based in your psychological need.... You want to believe, because without belief you feel empty...so utterly empty that you can't even dare to live. Look withinwards; that emptiness looks like death.

It is your psychological need that somebody should give you a hope, a belief, some kind of opium, so you can go to sleep. At least for the time being, you can put aside all your fears. You have the messiah with you, the son of God – now, what fear is there?

He gives you meaning, he gives you hope, and he has authority. But these are all projected by you...and exploited by him. It is a mutual phenomenon.

...Do you see the vicious circle? He becomes more authoritative, more determined, more fanatic. And the more he becomes authoritative, determined, fanatic, the more people are bound to fall in the trap because they need authority. They need a father figure, somebody to lead them. On their own they don't know where to go, what to do, what to be.

OSHO (1984), MTOE

The bigger the lie, the more people believe in it.

ADOLF HITLER

One night a man opens his eyes, rolls out of bed, and starts walking to the kitchen. He passes his wife coming out of the bathroom on her way back to bed, says good morning – then bellies up to the kitchen counter and relieves himself in the trash can under the kitchen sink.

That's when he wakes up.

I was once a witness to an experiment in autosuggested somnambulism at an after-high-school party. A young woman agreed to go under hypnosis. The hypnotizer suggested that she had now gone home and it was time to take a shower. Before my disbelieving eyes, the woman began to disrobe in front of us. She did so with complete innocence. It wasn't an act. She was alone behind the door in the bathroom of her mind. The 15 equally embarrassed and amazed onlookers did not exist to her. We stopped the experiment, and the hypnotizer asked her to button up her blouse before she exposed herself further. Once awakened from the trance, she had no memory of what she had done and thought we were all joking.

People function remarkably well while they are sleepwalking. They can assume the illusion of full cognizance, especially when under the spell of someone else's hypnotic suggestions.

With that in mind, relax, please relax...r-e-l-a-x...let your eyes follow the pendulum of my words back and forth...back and forth... Allow your mind to open, slowly...s-l-o-w-l-y...as I suggest to you the following bedtime story:

Once upon a time, in another life, I was born into a world where everyone I knew, from the first moment of life onward, conspired to put me back to sleep. I lived in a land where parents, pedagogues, and priests taught me that slumber was wakefulness. I was a good pupil, because I had no understanding of the difference between being awake and dreaming of being awake. The more seemingly awake I became, the more the spell of dreaming deepened.

In that life they taught me to make every waking aim and effort a means to catch hold of noble illusions such as success, happiness in love, fulfillment in children, contentment in possessions – and last but not least, they taught me to dream of being moral, virtuous, and worthy of God's salvation.

LEFT **Nothing wrong with family values just as long as you embrace them with your eyes open.**

RIGHT **How to get ahead in business? Keep your head down, your eyes shut, and follow the dream that you have been given.**

BELOW **Our one and only true love is a noble pursuit, and an illusory one.**

They taught me to see things upside down from what they were. For instance, the priest waved his smoking censer back and forth, back and forth in blessing...b-l-e-s-s-i-n-g...telling me repeatedly that Christ was my savior, Christ was my savior, believe...b-e-l-i-e-v-e...believe only in Him. Shut out all the suggestions of other religions and you will be saved.

As I was growing up, each of my parents taught me the difference between right and wrong, waving a mesmerizing finger from side to side. The teacher instructed, waving her chalk stick back and forth before my eyes before putting it into my hand to chalk out her somnambulistic mantras for being a dutiful matriculate.

I began to fill my empty ledger of a soul with hypnotizing dictums, such as to honor and obey without question ideas and traditions you never had a hand (or a say) in creating – especially if they uphold traditions your hypnagogic demagogues never questioned yet held in dumbfounded respect. I was especially spellbound by the Word of God and the promised return of his Messiah. In Sunday school I fumbled for my Bible and they helped me relax...relax...and count back from Psalms 150 to 1. They counted me back through all the verses of all the holy books until my "I" was mesmer-I-zed to automatically do good deeds – not for the simple joy of just doing them, mind you, but to gain something in return, to earn a place in the last and best dream: heaven.

If I was to get by in a society of somnambulism it was necessary to have my priests and teachers gas me up to dream the world in black and white. They therefore implanted many delayed reactions to anything that would compromise the dream. The priests and therapists helped me make contracts on love. I played Ken in pheno-Barbie-doll dreams about love and marriage.

Above all, they programmed me to expect. Expect... e-x-p-e-c-t... deeper... and... deeper... beyond the intelligence that doubts...beyond the heart that senses...to sink deeper beyond the kith and kinesthesia of the body's natural instincts...to fall into the cruise control of expectation. Expect others to love you...to fulfill you. And if they don't, then always...a-l-w-a-y-s...blame the other.

Naturally good dreams have a way of snuggling next to nightmares. This fact wasn't overlooked by my Svengali social programmers. If my worldly dreams remained unfulfilled, that too was kept under control by deeply implanted suggestions, like "getting religious."

Renounce Barbie as plastic! Renounce the catalepsy of this world. Dream a higher dream. Be narcotized by the glory of God. Go beyond this physical dream body. "Phantomize" about the paradise promised to you in the other world. Reject the dream of the hedonist and sinner for the dream of the renouncer and the saint. Having once been completely engrossed by greed for money, I now rolled over in my slumbers to obsess over cultivating my love of God.

There was nothing I couldn't do in the land of Nod, as long as I didn't wake up. Above all, I was not to doubt the dream. I was even free to visualize anarchy and rebellion as long as I stayed within the dreamscape. Revolutions are welcomed in the world-dream as long as they sustain an illusion of progress, as long as they only decorate the tight lips of established power with a new lipstick. Revolutions are rubbed into the stiff upper lip of power periodically to change the pigment of history's fancy. Yesterday it was communist red, today it is capitalist red, white, and blue.

To protect me from the apocalypse of awakening from my sleep, my religious and social educators painted bitter salve on the hangnails of my doubts to sour any impulse to bite and chew on them.

I somnolently lived out my life in the land of Nod, one more citizen of the nation of "as if," worshiping the God of "around-and-about the truth." And before my death woke me up, I dreamed of waking up in heaven.

Come back...come b-a-c-k.... On the count of one...two...three millenniums of sleepwalking through history.

One...two...three....

Snap out of it!

Come back to full consciousness.

Wha...what's this?! Am I pissing in the kitchen trash can? Am I mechanically exposing myself in front of leering voyeurs beyond the walls of my make-believe shower stall? Somebody's put me under the trance of three hundred religions. Their hypnotic suggestion has me thinking we're all alone and fine in our bathrooms, stripping off our sins and earning points for heaven when we might instead be peeling off our awareness and intelligence, exposing ourselves to trouble.

One…two…three…at the count of 2000 C.E.

Return me to humanity before it is too late. Or else I may never wake up from an overdose of doomsday suggestion pills.

Many rebel mystics (some of whom are quoted in the following pages) tell us that for most of human history people have lived a somnambulistic life. For such people history is just something that happens. They are so much leafy debris cast helplessly into the fateful fling-about of history's whirlwinds. The winds blow them *hither* into the storm clouds of their wars and dark ages, and *yawn* into still, quiet heaps of momentary idleness in times of peace. Their eyes are as opened as those of the blind who reason that Providence has led them one day to stumble into a bed of flowers rather than a tiger trap.

The consequence of unconsciousness may not be a punishment by God-somebody, but a self-created breakdown of individuals and systems. End time may be a hypnotic suggestion fulfilled by potentially conscious beings if they live life in a sleepy and robotic way. They pop the sleeping pill – perchance to dream that their planet can endlessly tolerate their abuse. And if it can't sustain civilization in the 21st century, then they inhale a whole bottle of tranquilizing prophetic promises that a messiah will save them.

Now two thousand years have passed and Christians are waiting for the savior to come. I tell you he is never going to come, for the simple reason that what he has promised he cannot deliver. Krishna has promised that he will be coming, but it is strange that nobody wonders why these people did not redeem humanity while they were here. What is the point of postponing it for the future, for the next time when they will come?

People were as much in misery then as they are now, people were as much ignorant as they are now – so what was the reason to postpone? Jesus could have redeemed the whole world, Krishna could have enlightened everybody. But it was a very subtle game: they took responsibility – and helped you to remain a prisoner till they come back. Just go on praying…one day he is going to come.

This has taken away not only your responsibility but your freedom. It has taken away your very individuality and your uniqueness.

Let it sink deep in your hearts. Only you are capable of awakening. Because only you are capable of falling asleep. Nobody else is responsible for your sleep.

OSHO (1987), TAH

SAMSARA'S TORNADO

Mystics from southern Asia describe the unconscious turning of past, present, and future history – both personal and collective – as the revolving wheel of Samsara. We spin around cycles of war-peace, love-hate, and good-evil, caught in Her hurricane-wheel of desire. We dreamers orbit Her cyclone of misery caught in Her spokes. What follows are quotes from those who would like to hold the smelling salts of their insights under our noses so we can get off Her misery-go-round.

All beings are from the very beginning buddhas. It is like water and ice; apart from water, no ice. Outside living beings, no buddhas. Not knowing it is near, they seek it afar. What a pity! It is like one in the water who cries out for thirst; it is like the child of a rich house who has strayed away among the poor. The cause of our circling through the six worlds, is that we are on the dark paths of ignorance. Dark path upon dark path treading, when shall we escape from birth-and-death?

HAKUIN, THE ZEN MASTER

Man's consciousness has not grown with the same pace as his scientific progress, and that has been the cause of all the old civilizations destroying themselves. There was no outer cause, no outer enemy: the enemy was within man. He created monsters as far as machines are concerned. But he himself remained very retarded, unconscious, almost asleep. And it is very dangerous to give so much power to unconscious people.

OSHO (1987), RAZR

One lives in the past, all knowledge is of the past. One lives there, one's life is there, in what has been – concerned with "what I was" and from that, "what I shall be." One's life is based essentially on yesterday and "yesterday" makes us invulnerable, deprives us of the capacity of innocency, vulnerability.

J. KRISHNAMURTI (1972), URTHW

Your own consciousness has no wounds...knows nothing of misery.... Your own consciousness is innocent, utterly blissful.... The mind contains all your misery, all your wounds. And it goes on creating wounds in such a way that, unless you are aware, you will not even find how it creates them.

OSHO (1989), ZNM

Man such as we know him...cannot have a permanent and single I. His I changes as quickly as his thoughts, feelings, and moods, and he makes a profound mistake in considering himself always one and the same person; in reality he is always a different person, not the one he was a moment ago.

G. I. GURDJIEFF (*c.* 1916), MIRA

Have you ever observed the "observer" as different from the observed?... Thought brings about this division. You look at your neighbor, at your wife, at your husband or your boyfriend or girlfriend, whoever it be, but can you look without the imagery of thought, without the previous memory?
...If there is a division between the "observer" and the "observed" that division is the source of all human conflict. When you say you love somebody, is that love? For in that love is there not both the "observer" and the thing you love, the observed? That "love" is the product of thought, divided off as a concept and there is not love.

J. KRISHNAMURTI (1972), URTHW

This world of love is a different world – there is no calculation in it. When you love with the idea of ambition or profit, with the desire to achieve or with any other motive, your love is poisoned in the same ratio. This is why your love does not bring happiness, only suffering happens.

OSHO (1976), SHWR

The fool who does evil to a man who is good...the evil returns to him like the dust thrown against the wind.
...A wrong action may not [always] bring its reaction at once, even as fresh milk turns not sour at once: like a smoldering fire concealed under ashes it consumes the wrongdoer, the fool. And if ever to his own harm the fool increases in cleverness, this only destroys his own mind and his fate is worse than before.

BUDDHA GAUTAMA (*c.* 500 B.C.E.), DHM 9, 125; 5: 71–72

If you recognize the reality of truths of life, you will find that if you want to make somebody suffer then it is necessary that you suffer first. Before giving poison you have to drink it first. Before killing somebody, a killer commits suicide first. He has already died. So your love must be false, otherwise this world would be a heaven.

OSHO (1976), SHWR

The ego is clinging, dependent, self-indulgent, resistive, reactive, adolescent, reactively moved toward independence, wanting to affirm without intelligence, wanting to believe without inspection, wanting to be religious without self-knowledge and self-overcoming.

ADI DA SAMRAJ (1987), HBUS

These imprisonments are spiritual and psychological; that's why you don't see them. Otherwise what do you mean, when you say, "I am a Christian," or "I am a Hindu," or "I am a Buddhist"? It means that "I believe Gautam Buddha is going to be my redeemer"; that "I am waiting simply for Jesus Christ to come and redeem me."
You have dropped every effort to transform yourself – and that is the only way there is for any kind of transformation. All these redeemers have created only prisons for people. And the priests go on representing those dead redeemers.

OSHO (1987), ZARD

If a blind man leads a blind man, they will both fall into a pit.

Y'SHUA (c. 30–33 C.E.), GOFT #34

You do not realize that one has to learn
to speak the truth. It seems to you that
it is enough to wish or to decide to do so.
And I tell you that people comparatively
rarely tell a deliberate lie. In most cases
they think they speak the truth. And yet
they lie all the time, both when they wish
to lie and when they wish to speak the
truth. They lie all the time, both to
themselves and to others.

...Nobody ever understands either himself
or anyone else. Think – could there be such
discord, such deep misunderstanding, and
such hatred toward the views and opinions
of others, if people were able to understand
one another? But they cannot understand
because they cannot help lying.

G. I. GURDJIEFF (*c.* 1916), MIRA

Ignorance is the cause of
all religious conflicts....
Ignorance has its roots in
the ego, it does not see
[the Divine] in all things.

GURU NANAK (1521)

Conflict exists as long as there is effort, as long as there is contradiction. So, is there not a contradiction between the "observer" and the "observed" – in that division?...When I say "I am a Hindu," "I am a Brahmin," this and that, I have created a world around myself with which I have identified myself which breeds division. Surely, when one says one is a Catholic, one has already separated oneself from the non-Catholics. All division, outwardly as well as inwardly, breeds antagonism.

J. KRISHNAMURTI (1972), URTHW

[The religions] have created guilt in you, and through guilt they have enslaved you, because when you are guilty you want to be freed, saved from the guilt. The messiah, the savior is needed. His agents go on creating guilt in you and then he comes to save you.

OSHO (1985), DTOD

Mankind is absurdly concentrated upon the symptoms of its own distress, and, thus, human beings collectively and individually pursue knowledge of, and the power over, the conditions which confront them in body and mind. They feel confronted and confined by the world as a force at both the objective and subjective levels of consciousness.... Therefore, the pursuits of mankind are a kind of warfare or struggle with phenomenal conditions, on the basis of a sense of confinement that is conceived as a lack of knowledge and perceived as a lack of power.

ADI DA SAMRAJ (1980), EGOI

Your mind is deranged on account of the burning that is in you, and sweet to you is the crown of your enemies' blows! And the darkness rose for you like the light, for you surrendered your freedom for servitude! You damned your hearts and surrendered your thoughts to folly, and you filled your thoughts with the smoke of the fire that is in you! And your light has hidden in the cloud of darkness...and you were seized by the hope that does not exist. And whom is it you have believed? Do you not know that you all dwell among those who want you to curse yourselves as if your hope were nonexistent? You baptized your souls in the water of darkness! You walked by your own whims!

Y'SHUA (BEF. 250 C.E.), BKTC

You are unreal – as you are you are unreal. Let me remind you. Man can live in two ways: real, unreal; natural, artificial. Unreal everybody has become. It takes great effort to remain unreal; hence, unreality is agonizing. It is very arduous to remain unreal. It is a constant work, because you have to go against nature. It is going up current, it is pushing the river; with your tiny hands pushing the gigantic river. You feel tired, you feel washed out, you feel dissipated. And sooner or later you will feel defeated – the river will possess you and you will be thrown with the current of the river.

OSHO (1978), TITE 1

You hide death. You hide hatred with love. You have become skilled in covering everything with nice words. Now expose these words and see the reality of things, because by seeing the reality transformation begins in life. If you don't cover your hatred with love, then you will not be able to hate because hate brings only suffering: it certainly brings suffering to the other, but it also brings suffering to you. Before you make someone else suffer you have to give suffering to yourself. Before you start destroying someone's life you have to destroy yourself. When you put thorns on someone's way they get stuck in your hands.

OSHO (1976), SHWR

Only a man in the highest state of being is a complete man. All the others are merely fractions of man.

G. I. GURDJIEFF (1922), VWS

People...put great value on the level of a man's knowledge but they do not value the level of a man's being and are not ashamed of the low level of their own being. They do not even understand what it means. And they do not understand that a man's knowledge depends on the level of his being.

G. I. GURDJIEFF (c.1916), MIRA

SAFE IS THE CENTER
OF THE CYCLONE

Outside, the freezing desert night.
This other night inside grows warm, kindling.
Let the landscape be covered with thorny crust.
We have a soft garden in here.
The continents blasted,
cities and little towns, everything
become a scorched blackened ball.
The news we hear is full of grief for that future,
but the real news inside here
is there's no news at all.

MEVLANA JALALUDDIN RUMI (1207–1273) IN THE POEM "THE TENT"

formative years enduring many nights under the elements and days of hardship, uncertainty, and hunger as he wandered westward with his family across the devastated lands and burned-out cities of the Persian Empire. Veled and his family finally settled in the relative safety of Konya, Turkey, where Rumi would eventually grow to manhood and succeed his father as the head of the local medrese (dervish-learning community).

Konya was the cosmopolitan gateway to the famous Silk Road. In those days, the city lived in a state of constant religious agitation. When political intrigue and

LEFT **Genghis Khan, leader of the infamous Mongol hordes who attacked the Persian Empire.**

When Mevlana Rumi was 12, his father, Bahauddin Veled, a noted Islamic scholar and teacher, led his family out of Balkh (Afghanistan) as refugees from the thundering hooves of the Mongol hordes of Genghis Khan. Starting in 1219, the savage Mongolian horsemen descended on the Persian Empire from the Central Asian steppes. Wherever the Mongols rampaged, whole cities were burned to the ground and their entire populations of men, women, and children were slaughtered.

The boy who would become one of Sufism's greatest enlightened mystics and poets spent a number of his

religious pontificating failed, different religious communities often settled disputes with clubs and knives over whose creed or prophet was better. Strangely enough, all the warring factions accepted Rumi, in part because of his loving inclusiveness and acceptance for all.

It is said that he had an aura of silence and calmness that was unflappable and infectious. He composed the poem opposite sometime in the late 1250s, when terrified traders riding down the Silk Road to Konya from the East exacerbated the civic strife with tales of a new wave of apocalyptic devastation coming from the descendants of Genghis Khan. The Mongol horse armies of his grandsons would unleash their own version of Operation Desert Storm, obliterating Islam's glorious Abbasid capital of Baghdad.

When the news reached Rumi and his disciples that Mongols were riding up and down the plains and deserts of the Near East with impunity, there was indeed reason to fear and grieve for the future. Yet his recorded observations on the matter testify to how little impact the negative effect of childhood traumas had on his inner peace.

Rumi the man, like Rumi the former child refugee, viewed the outside world from the silent haven of his inner "ark" of consciousness.

Where Christ suffers famously on his cross and complains to his father-God in heaven about it, al-Hillaj Mansoor – a little-known 10th-century Islamic mystic – faces a crucifixion many times more barbaric and cruel without complaint. He presses prayerful hands to God one last time before the headsmen chop them off. He thanks the butchered feet piled before his leg-

ABOVE **The Baha'í house of worship in Wilmette, Illinois, consecrated by 'Abdu'l-Bahá, is the only one of its kind in the U.S.**

stumps for taking him on his journeys of self-discovery. He gives his crying disciples, the jeering mob, and his murderers equal regard. He looks upon them with happy and loving eyes until the moment those eyes are gouged out of their sockets. After this al-Hillaj turns his head to heaven. The head no longer has a nose, or ears – the executioner has already sliced them off. But al-Hillaj still has a rapturous smile. He gazes heavenward without eyes, spreading his arm-stumps as if they still possess open, beseeching hands in praise of Allah.

Al-Hillaj sings the following verse: "Love of the One is isolation of the One. Those that believe not therein seek to hasten it: but those who believe in it go in fear of it, knowing that it is the truth."

After this they pull out his tongue.

The executioners would have wished to do more to al-Hillaj, but the evening prayer time was at hand. So the mob of true believers pressed the torturers to cut off the heretic's head so they could go to the mosque and pray. As the sword came down, al-Hillaj flashed a loving, blood-soaked smile.

It was a smile that somehow rose through the sirocco dust devil of physical pain and surrounding violence from an unfathomable depth in the center of the cyclone.

There are many other stories of a peace that passeth understanding being the axle in a whirlwind life of suffering and persecution. In far more recent times, the Bahá'í prophet 'Abdu'l-Bahá lived in less physically harsh, but no less psychically crippling circumstances as an inmate in a Turkish prison cell.

BELOW **Silk traders make the treacherous journey across central Asia to Konya bringing stories of devastation wrought by the Mongols.**

At a lecture in Paris in 1911, 'Abdu'l-Bahá shared with an attentive crowd his secret for surviving incarceration.

"I myself was in prison forty years," he recalled. "One year alone would have been impossible to bear – nobody survived that imprisonment more than a year! But, thank God, during all those forty years I was supremely happy every day. On waking, it was like hearing good tidings, and every night infinite joy was mine. Spirituality was my comfort, and turning to God was my greatest joy. If this had not been so, do you think it possible that I could have lived through those forty years in prison?

"Thus, spirituality is the greatest of God's gifts, and 'Life Everlasting' means 'Turning to God.' May you, one and all, increase daily in spirituality, may you be strengthened in all goodness, may you be helped more and more by the Divine consolation, be made free by the Holy Spirit of God, and may the power of the heavenly kingdom live and work among you."

Slightly more than a half-century later another controversial founder of a new religion was recorded on a prison video monitoring system. You could see him sitting in a feces-smeared jail cell in Charlotte, North Carolina, seemingly undisturbed, sipping his water as if he were riding comfortably in one of his Rolls-Royces.

This was the same man who, as a young boy in Gandarwara, India, enjoyed jumping off a 60-foot-high railway bridge into the swirling, monsoon-swollen waters of a flooded river. Where other athletic adults had drowned, this slight lad happily navigated the strong currents and even allowed the river's notorious whirlpools to suck him down toward what could have been a silty, earth-brown death.

The boy didn't fight the current – he relaxed.

Such was the case if death came or not, he reasoned. Drowning in the river was preferable to drowning in a lifetime of fear.

The closer death came to him – knocking its arrival on his compressed lungs, pressing watery hands over his tightening throat – the more the boy simply gave in, surrendering himself to the current and into relaxation. Eventually he found his body circling around the center of the whirlpool's liquid tornado. There at its base, he discovered that the current is so weak that all one needed to do was step out of it and rise to the surface, alive and well.

The boy would grow up to become a professor of philosophy and later one of the late 20th century's most controversial Indian mystics. He would also gain inspiration from the poem of Rumi, and contribute the following interpretation:

"Rumi is saying: The news we hear is full of grief for the future. But the real news inside, is there's no news at all. Everything is silent and everything is as beautiful, peaceful, blissful as it has always been. There is no change at all; hence, there is no news.

"Inside it is an eternal ecstasy, forever and forever.

"I will repeat again that these lines may become true in your lifetime. Before that happens, you must reach within yourself where no news has ever happened, where everything is eternally the same, where the spring never comes and goes but always remains; where the flowers have been from the very beginning – if there was any beginning – and are going to remain to the very end – if there is going to be any end. In fact, there is no beginning and no end, and the garden is lush, green, and full of flowers.

"Before the outside world is destroyed by your politicians, enter into your inner world. That's the only safety left, the only shelter against nuclear weapons, against global suicide, against all these idiots who have so much power to destroy.

"You can at least save yourself." (OSHO [1987], HISP)

ABOVE **The mystic Osho taught meditation as the "Ark" one needs to navigate the coming global disasters.**

RIGHT **Osho gained inspiration from the poet Rumi and taught his followers to reach within themselves.**

Men who are foolish and ignorant are careless and never watchful; but the man who lives in watchfulness considers it his greatest treasure.

BUDDHA GAUTAMA (*c.* 500 B.C.E.), DHM 2:26

And the Savior answered, saying, "Blessed is the wise man who sought after the truth, and when he found it, he rested upon it forever and was unafraid of those who wanted to disturb him."

Y'SHUA (BEF. 25 C.E.), BKTC

As a man who has no wound on his hand cannot be hurt by the poison he may carry in his hand, since poison hurts not where there is no wound, the man who has no evil cannot be hurt by evil.

BUDDHA GAUTAMA (*c.* 500 B.C.E.), DHM 9:124

The wise man who by watchfulness conquers thoughtlessness is as one who free from sorrows ascends the palace of wisdom and there, from its high terrace, sees those in sorrow below; even as a wise strong man on the holy mountain might behold the many unwise far down below on the plain.

BUDDHA GAUTAMA (*c.* 500 B.C.E.), DHM 2:28

Steadfast a lamp burns sheltered from the wind;
Such is the likeness of the Yogi's [the awakened one's] mind
Shut from sense-storms and burning bright to Heaven.
When mind broods placid, soothed with holy wont;
When Self contemplates self, and in itself
Hath comfort; when it knows the nameless joy
Beyond all scope of sense, revealed to soul –
Only to soul! and, knowing, wavers not,
True to the farther Truth; when, holding this,
It deems no other treasure comparable,
But, harbored there, cannot be stirred or shook
By any gravest grief, call that state "peace"....

KRISHNA (*c.* 3000 B.C.E.), GITA 6:19–23

THE UNBEARABLE LIGHTNESS OF BEING ORDINARY

May each one of you become a shining lamp,
of which the flame is the Love of God.
May your hearts burn with the radiance of unity.
May your eyes be illumined with the
effulgence of the Sun of Truth!

'ABDU'L-BAHÁ (1911), PARIS 5:21

THE UNBEARABLE LIGHTNESS OF BEING ORDINARY

The Indians don't have messiahs. We have wise men and powerful medicine people, but no messiahs. We don't have anything like salvation, like heaven and hell. Just to pay the rent is hell.

GRANDFATHER SEMU HUARTE, CHUMASH NATION (1983)

A man walked the earth, but there was no solid gold nimbus from an altar image weighing down upon his head. A man spoke a sermon on the mount, but there was no Cinemascope to widen the horizon. A man on a donkey rode into Jerusalem surrounded by a crowd with palm fronds. Alfred Newman, the legendary movie score composer, didn't magnify the emotional impact of the entry with a melodious chorale, and there was no Hollywood sound mixer to edit out the people singing off-key.

In the reenactment of this moment in Christ's life in the movie *The Robe,* there's a close-up shot of Victor Mature, who played a Greek slave on the roadside watching the man on the donkey pass by. The chorus suddenly stops its prancing song and the voices assume solemn hallowed tones that shiver and brighten along with the widening gleam of Mature's eyes as the passing donkey rider regards him off-camera. But in the actual historical event there was no Mature looking like a timid deer frozen in the floodlights of a God-man's eyes. No orchestra and chorus were there to augment the donkey passenger's presence or ghetto-blast his aura with an angelic atmosphere that could raise God-sized goose bumps.

Everyone looks better in a movie adaptation. Buddha is sexy thanks to Keanu Reeves's portrayal in *Little Buddha.* Jesus looks like the John Wayne of messiahs because of Jeffrey Hunter's square-jawed Aryan looks in *King of Kings.* Over time you have to Charlton Heston your Hosanna. Even in Islam, a religion that frowns on any physical portrayal of the

LEFT AND BELOW **Jeffrey Hunter, Keanu Reeves and Victor Mature all bring a certain Hollywood glamor to the sometimes mundane world of religious belief.**

Prophet Muhammad, the actors and extras in the movie *The Message* regard him off-camera with respectful drop-jawed gapes.

The movies didn't start the trend. They are the most recent artistic collusion in the habit of deifying and distancing future followers from their saviors. The icons of Christ stare us down with flat and superhuman portraits. How can the sweaty and dusty man on the flea-bitten donkey match Michelangelo's clean, white, and unblemished marble facsimile of Jesus Christ in the Pietà? He lies draped forever in crucified ecstasy in the lap of his ageless mother of the immaculate marble face-lift. Countless statues of Buddha in perfect repose make it hard to imagine he ever stood with the wind, peeing in perfect repose like the rest of his monks. You never see Lord Krishna in his dirty underwear, and the cows and cowgirls he frolics with are always dung-free and sparkling clean.

A messiah's makeover makes sense. If Superman is the man of steel, saving the world, then my savior can't be just another four-eyed Clark Kent. Can I worship someone who's on my level? Can someone just as frail, reeking of garlic, and as faulty as myself rule over the world for a thousand years? A mere political leader looks down at us from the dais; a simple priest or preacher stands high and mighty at the pulpit above his flock. How much more rarefied and otherworldly must be the returned world redeemer? My religious leaders teach me to obey a higher authority. Therefore it is only natural that I feel more inclined to submit myself to someone who is extraordinary. Whether the founder of my religion is a model of modesty or megalo-messianism, he must be either higher – or humbly lower – than I could ever be. He can't just be an ordinary man.

Mahavir, the 24th divinely incarnated master of Jainism and Buddha's contemporary, is said to have attained his God-manliness while squatting in a field in the yogic position called Milking the Cow. Let no one even suggest that Mahavir at that moment was also attaining another more basic and down-to-earth-making form of liberation.

Ordinariness undermines all that is holier than thou. If extraordinary insight into the divine mystery can sprout from flea-bitten donkey riders and people

Religions have done a great harm to humanity by claiming extraordinariness for their founders – because if Jesus is the son of God, then of course, he can be silent. But we are ordinary human beings; how can we attain to that height? That is his special privilege. All that we can do is worship him. We can be Christians, we cannot be Christs.

…Krishna is God's incarnation, so perhaps he can make it possible to be a no-mind. But how can we make it? – we are just ordinary mortals, we are not incarnations of God.

These foolish ideas, that their founder is special, have been promulgated by all religions, propagated by all theologies. Once you make the founder of a religion special then he becomes absolutely useless and disconnected from humanity.

I am a very ordinary person, just like you: no son of God, no incarnation of God – all that is bullshit.

OSHO (1980), MRCL

pooping in a field – if enlightenment can make a superman out of every schlep of a Clark Kent – then where is the need for anyone presuming religious authority and extraordinariness over others? What religious hierarchy could keep dictating how we think and feel about godly redeemers if the truth got out that godliness was as everyday and normal as carrying water, fetching firewood, eating, breathing, and defecating?

THE MAN BEHIND
THE GOD-MAN MYTH

Each divine revelation [a messiah] is divided into two parts. The first part is essential and belongs to the eternal world. It is the exposition of Divine truths and essential principles. It is the expression of the Love of God. This is one in all the religions, unchangeable and immutable. The second part is not eternal; it deals with practical life, transactions and business, and changes according to the evolution of man and the requirements of the time of each prophet.

'ABDU'L-BAHÁ (*c.* 1921), NWER

RIGHT **There has to be a connection between the messianic vision and the practicalities of life.**

When Krishnamurti dies, which is inevitable, you will set about forming rules in your minds, because the individual, Krishnamurti, had represented to you the Truth. So you will build a temple, you will then begin to have ceremonies, to invent phrases, dogmas, systems of beliefs, creeds and to create philosophies. If you build great foundations upon me, the individual, you will be caught in that house, in that temple and so you will have to have another Teacher come and extricate you from that temple. But the human mind is such that you will build another temple around Him, and so it will go on and on.

J. KRISHNAMURTI (1985, D. 1986), FTNW

I have met a few rare individuals who hid the whole sky in their eyes. They filled the atmosphere with the silent aura of their "ordinariness" melting my heart, baffling my brain. They had an extraordinary sense of relaxation. They were nonserious people, but profoundly sincere. I never felt judged in their presence, even though some of these people cut my ego to the quick with a passing remark, a giggle, or when they quietly ignored me when I was being needy. These people were adults – some were near my age, some were pushing 90 – but where I was at times childish, they were ever childlike. To them, being ordinary was just like being innocent, open, fresh – and their intelligence seemed to capture the fragrance of youth and vitality, even if they were physically very old and infirm.

What they defined as ordinary were things I considered miraculous. For instance, they said it was natural and normal for a human being to live in the fulfillment of "effects" without needing a "cause." In other words, they didn't seek lovers, they were love; they didn't seek fulfillment, they came to understand that they were fulfillment itself. When others became abusive of them, they did not respond in kind with anger or crumple in victimhood. It was as if the poison rising in the abuser had no bridge to the abused, therefore there was no one abused. They didn't suffer the cyclone of life because they didn't identify with it.

But when I say this, don't think I mean they were renunciates, holier than thou, and high above the struggle of life. The mystics I have known loved life, and they lived it to the fullest. They danced, they made love, they enjoyed life's moods and its beauties, but they didn't seem to carry expectations.

To people of tremendous seriousness and importance, these mystics were unbearable. People wanted them to get caught up in their drama, and they just wouldn't behave. These mystics had ignore-sense, rather than ignorance. They seemed ever able to sniff out the truffles of truth from the forest floor of illusion. It was as if they saw something we didn't see, but *could* see if we just had the right sense to see it. It was as if these "ordinary" people – once colorblind like ourselves – had rediscovered how to see and celebrate life in full Technicolor.

They saw death in full color, too. In one case I watched one of these self-proclaimed "ordinary" men, Osho, blissfully face his approaching death over a six-month period. On the night of January 19, 1990, I helped take his body down to the burning ghats on an Indian river for cremation. The man faced death as he faced everything: in a state of "such is the case." He was not for it, he was not against it.

Things seem to meld together in the consciousness of such "ordinary" people. Where we see "love," they see "love/hate." Where we see "death," they see "death/life." Where I see irreconcilable opposites, the ordinary man sees complements.

Dr. Amrito, Osho's personal physician and my friend, related to me his experience of Osho's final moments. On the last morning, Amrito said the body showed signs that Osho's heart was about to fail. He told me his patient nodded and spent the rest of the day making his final arrangements as if he were merely preparing for a weekend trip. At one point Amrito began to weep. The dying man looked at him, almost sternly – a rare expression for someone who was always so joyous. Osho frowned at the tears and said, "No, this is not the way." When my friend stopped crying, the "ordinary" man gave him the sweetest of loving smiles before he peacefully died.

ABOVE **Osho's followers enjoyed life to the full rather than quarreling with its demands.**

Osho had a love of expensive Rolls-Royces. When cornered by someone who disapproved of a religious man driving luxury cars, he shrugged a reply: "I *am* a simple man – I simply love the best."

This "simple" man also dressed in fantastic robes made by his female disciples. The robes were woven out of the finest fabrics, and often his knitted caps were ringed in rows of simply beautiful precious stones and pearls. When I visited his commune in Oregon and his ashram in Pune, India, I'd see him driving the cars and wearing a new expensive gown almost every day.

I have to admit that I was a bit skeptical about Osho's "ordinariness."

For skeptics such as myself, I am reminded of the following ancient Hindu fable Osho often told to help us understand his unique brand of ordinariness:

News reached an Indian maharajah that a famous *sadhu* (religious renunciate) had come to sit under a tree in his kingdom. The maharajah had heard so much about this mystic's spiritual transcendence of all illusion and worldly things that he drove his chariot over to visit him. He found the sadhu sitting under a tree, naked as a "Jain" bird, meditating in silent ecstasy.

Out of politeness, the maharajah invited the sadhu to come to his palace and enjoy its luxuries as his guest. Just as it was the social custom of the time for a maharajah to offer, it was the custom for the renunciate to lovingly refuse, to show his transcendence of the world.

ABOVE **A sadhu, a holy man who renounces wordly pleasures, painted with traditional markings.**

The sadhu's eyes popped open, and he stood up and said, "Okay, let's go."

The naked man climbed onto the chariot and, grinning, motioned the stunned maharajah to have his driver whip the horses to a gallop for the palace.

Over the next few weeks the sadhu taught the maharajah about renunciation, meditation, and spiritual liberation while he happily sampled his best food, dressed in his beautiful robes, and enjoyed the company of the maharajah's most beautiful palace courtesans.

The maharajah sulked until he could stand it no longer. One day he found the mystic living the life of Lord Krishna, lounging on a divan enjoying the garden and its peacocks, while maidens lay at his feet serenading him with songs and sitars.

"You are a fraud! How can you call yourself a renunciate? A religious man should abandon worldliness," sputtered the maharajah.

The finely robed sadhu was unfazed. "I have been expecting this," he said. "Frankly, I am surprised at how long it took you to let fly your displeasure. So extraordinary are your ideas of what being religious is."

The sadhu hopped from the divan and began walking out of the garden. "Come on, bring your chariot, it is time for me to go."

The sadhu directed the maharajah to drive him to the edge of his kingdom. Once they reached the border, he descended from the chariot and gave back all the jewels and beautiful clothes until he was once again the epitome of a naked renunciate. He said good-bye and began to walk away.

Seeing him naked as the day they first met, the maharajah could sense the sadhu's spiritual aura, and he felt ashamed. He fell at his feet asking for forgiveness.

"Please return to my palace. Now I understand that you are indeed a holy man."

The sadhu stopped and turned around. "No, I will not return," he said firmly, but with kind eyes. "If I go back I will put on your robes, enjoy your food, and celebrate life with your ladies-in-waiting, and you will again feel that this man is a fraud. Then you will once again demand that I leave.

"My poor beloved friend, you cannot see the natural man before you. You only see your ideas of how a holy man should be. There is no need to renounce things. One only needs to renounce the attachment to things. I am free to enjoy everything – or nothing – because the source of my enjoyment is free of any cause or any effect. Therefore I can leave your palace and be naked again in the wilderness. It doesn't matter, nor does it affect my liberation."

LEFT **Osho did not resist arrest or struggle with his imprisonment in America; he accepted his situation with grace.**

The day came when tragic events put the gist of this fable to the test.

In late October 1985, I remember one day seeing Osho in his fine caps and robes driving his Rolls-Royce slowly past a line of thousands of his adoring and celebrating disciples. The next day I saw him on television, after U.S. federal agents arrested him, alone, sitting behind bars in faded and rough-woven prison dungarees. There was no car, no silken robe, no pearl-lined cap to cover his balding head, but I perceived that nothing had changed inside him. He was cool and relaxed. Now he was like the naked sadhu, but he exuded the same relaxed "such is the case" gaze he showed when richly attired.

I'm not saying he was enjoying being arrested. Rather, I'm saying he was not letting his arrest disturb his joy. His incarceration had cruel and unusual aspects. For one thing, the federal marshals had arrested him without a warrant or a publicly announced indictment in a case that the U.S. prosecutors later admitted they couldn't actually prove. When they jailed this aging, "ordinary" man, the federal marshals forced him to drag himself around in leg, wrist, and waist irons "for his protection."

About six months after Osho was deported from the United States – and it was clear that his commune had become Oregon's newest ghost town – the chief prosecutor of the case, Charles Turner, admitted in public and in print that the arrest was politically motivated, just to get the guru out.

Despite his ordeal, I recall Osho reflecting on his arrest, pointing out that even in the outwardly worst circumstances, a person can live in the suchness of their ordinary divinity and even make music "dancing to the clinking sound of your chains."

i-DIOCY THE EMPTY SKY?

LEFT AND BELOW

A Trabant or a Rolls Royce, it is all one to the "ordinary" man.

I struggle with the word ordinary.

Applying this label to mystics like a Krishnamurti or an Osho seems so inadequate. The word "ordinary" is a boring, black-and-white word. It is Rice-a-roni compared to gourmet Italian risotto. "Ordinary" is a clunky Trabant or a working-class Subaru when I want to drive an appellation that roars like a Corvette Sting-Ray or purrs like a Rolls-Royce Silver Spur sedan.

Well…what to do?

I'm not qualified to talk about being ordinary, because I am an extraordinary personality.

Or, putting it more bluntly, I am an idiot.

This Greek word comes from the root *idios,* which stands for "identity." An extraordinary life requires that I *I*-dentify with emotions, thoughts, and things. I am "John." I am an "American." I love this. I hate that. I hope, I fear, I do the *I*-diot.

Idios also means being "special" or "distinct" from other personalities. *I*-diocy is what you get when society seeds the empty skylike being of a child's soul with the dark rain clouds of a borrowed identity. Nevertheless, if one is aware, one sees that for any identification to exist, it requires its opposite. If society and religion can program you to *I*-dentify, there is a chance that you can deprogram yourself from religious and societal conditioning and experience dis-*I*-dentification. Society conditions us into ego personified through a hurricane of beclouded thoughts and feelings. But however dark and roiling this hurricane may be, it must rotate around a profoundly becalmed inner eye at its center. That eye in the idiot's storm can be a window to the larger sky we have forgotten. It is a reminder of the unbearable lightness of being infinite.

A spiritual master is like that endless sky.

You and I are also that sky, but there's a difference. Every moment, waking or sleeping, a master remembers what we keep forgetting.

In an ever-empty sky the storm clouds of hate and fear may froth and curl and exhaust their rage, while at other times love clouds of delightful sunrise and sunset colors dance, but behind all the nice and nasty cloud-play – sky.

A spiritual master is a sky that remembers itself.

You and I are a sky that forgets, and identifies with the clouds.

Now, what if a spiritual teacher, remembering the "skyness" of being, felt a compassion to convey that "remembrance" to other parts of the sky, parts still caught up in identification with clouds?

How will that empty sky communicate its awakening to the beclouded sky?

What language will it use?

Certainly it cannot expect the beclouded sky to understand cloudless communication. The empty sky will have to speak the other's language. It will have to wax foggy. The empty sky will have to wear a mask – maybe even a cumulonimbus-sized mask of a messiah.

Communication cannot by definition be one-sided. For even if the beclouded sky can become a disciple, it must wonder if there is more to those rare blue holes that disturb the overcast topography of its personality. Toward such overclouded skies the cloudless master calls, wearing a nebulous mask. The master approaches, enticing the beclouded sky to become its disciple. Then the master shows this disciple infinitesimal glimpses of the blue vault of liberation beyond its cumulus mask. The disciple doesn't understand but is intrigued, and wants to see more holes in the gray gloom of its life.

The empty sky, as a master, must be careful not to reveal too much of its burning blueness all at once. The disciple still thinks the master is there to make the halos in the translucent cloud-forms brighter and more spiritual, when the master is really a thief from the cloudless night, working to dispel all the disciple's misty illusions.

The disciple believes itself to be the clouds.

The master knows the disciple is the sky itself.

The master must tread cautiously, or the disciple will see too soon where this emptiness leads – to a complete evaporation of its cloudy raison d'être. If the disciple isn't ready to see the *all,* it will retreat deeper into the cloud-illusion.

The empty, clear sky is patient. Over time the sky-master mixes more holes of its true blueness into the cloudy bait and the cumulonimbus-savior promises.

The disciple over time becomes acquainted with existence beyond the low, middle, and high-level clouds of its identification, until there comes a moment when the fabulous void is yawning wide enough through the clouds for the disciple to finally understand that there is no master. There is no disciple, either. They were formlessness sustaining the form-play of idiotic clouds.

There is only one sky.

If our great teachers down through history are guilty of playing along with some of our messiah myths and salvation expectations, they did it because we were unable to see their ordinariness with our extraordinary and idiotically cloudy perceptions. Still, those few who understand what is hidden from most of us will continue to persuade us to follow them as our guides to enlightenment. They are not our saviors as such – they are fellow travelers. They are friends who have traveled a little farther down the road than you or me. That's all.

To heed the call to follow a friend like the Galilean or the Buddha takes but one small hole of blue memory disturbing an idiot's overcast soul.

After that, it takes guts, and unconditional trust.

BELOW **The master has to find a language which the disciples will understand, so the ordinary has to become extraordinary.**

THE PATH OF TRUST

God Himself appears as the guru.... A World teacher is one who diverts man from the path leading to death and puts him on the path of Immortality. He who does this is the inner Guru. Once the guru has accepted a disciple, He will never leave him until the Goal has been attained. The question of leaving does not arise at all. Where can the Guru go? Does He dwell in the realm of coming and going? Therefore, if one calls Him 'Guru', it has nothing to do with the body that is transitory. The Guru resides within. So long as the inner Guru has not been revealed nothing can be achieved.

ANANDAMAYI MA (1896–1982), MATRI

The living Master, even if he allows you to worship him, allows you to worship him only so that you can come closer to him, that's all. He allows you to worship him so that you can come close and he can really destroy your ego. He wants you to become intimate with him. If this is the only way you know...and this is the only way you know, because you have always been worshiping Buddha, Krishna, Jesus, Mohammed.

ABOVE **The prophet Muhammad ascends to heaven in this exquisite 16th-century Persian print.**

You have been worshiping, so when you come to a living Master, the first thing that you can do is worship him. He allows you to worship him so that you can come closer, so that you can be caught into his net.

OSHO (1979), WHT

The word *Guru* is a new victim in the serial killing of beautiful words by pop culture. Apply it in titles like "guru of golf," or the "gurus of Washington wonk" and you have secularized this Hindu term for a religious teacher to fit any Svengali of politics, sports, or the arts. The technically correct dictionary translation of the Sanskrit word "guru" is the "venerable one" or the "spiritual master," but that definition is a dead statue to anyone who has known and loved the real living and breathing article. The seeker touched by the presence of the guru knows a far more poetic definition.

A guru is like a great cloud, heavy with rains. So burdened is the rain cloud that it cannot contain itself. The heavy cloud must give the rain to the earth. The guru cloud doesn't put conditions on where it deposits its rains; the guru cloud will share its bountiful showers equally with the sterile rocks and the fertile, thirsty soil.

A guru is a giving phenomenon.

A guru drowns its parched recipient with a monsoon of love, a cloudburst of refreshing awareness.

ABOVE AND RIGHT **A guru, like the Maharishi Mahesh Yogi, is not a leader but offers his being to anyone who wants to accept it.**

A guru doesn't do anything. Just as the cloud doesn't decide when or upon whom it releases its showers, a guru releases the heavy, bountiful silence and peace of his presence on everyone. And as with the rain, most people will just "open their umbrellas" and ignore this intrusion, while a precious few find the "soaking" inspiring.

In this latter group are the people who seek out gurus. They gather around the guru's tranquil eye in the center of a cyclone that is an *ashram* – the guru's spiritual community, or college campus of seekers and disciples. Dozens or tens of thousands of disciples can surround the guru of an ashram, and it can appear to outsiders and followers alike that he is their leader. It can appear that he is doing something to influence them. But a guru is not a doer. You could say he is filled to the brim with *being*.

Is-ness is his business.

The rain cloud doesn't make an effort to grow flowers. Let the flowers and the rocks respond as they like. They are the doers. The rock does the drying off and forgets the rain; the seeded earth does the blossoming.

A guru is a catalytic agent. He or she precipitates a process in disciples without being involved in or changed by the consequences. He may walk and sit and eat and do the things other people do. He may help precipitate a transformation in his disciples as a result of committing some action that might surprise and shock the disciple to attention. A guru can be like a thunderclap – a rain cloud thunders whether or not anyone is there to be jolted to attention. The doing – or lack of response – to the guru's thunder is up to the disciple.

Each seeker of a spiritual teacher must bear witness to this mystery in his or her own unique way. I can say from my own experience that you know you are in the presence of an authentic guru when just his presence, his silence, is enough to bring new context to your existence. Just the fragrance of the master's "Is-ness" can resurrect a forgotten knowing. Just his aura of no-worry, no-body-ness can nourish new buds of a lost innocence sprouting in a life lived in the drought-cracked land of society's conditioning.

The guru is full of an emptiness you once had: a cleanness of mind and spirit you had forgotten. The guru is a catalytic agent for remembrance of a time when your brain wasn't a dustbin for other people's ideas and emotional baggage.

The master's call is like the first kiss of humidity against the cracked and desiccated land. It is the electricity in the dry season's stifling heat preceding the guru thunderstorm. You are expectant like the land. You trust that wet kiss on your cracked and desert-like face more than all the so-called better judgment dumped into you by your society's mentors and tormentors. Something magnetic awakens inside and it draws you to his presence. Your heart leads the way, dragging the ego along like a cluster of cans clattering behind a honeymoon carriage. You go to the guru dragging your rusty bits of better judgment, ideas of love, and mental training along for the ride.

You go to your master. You take a risk.

Maybe society is right, and your guru is indeed a madman, like a Hitler, or Jim Jones, or an Ashahara. Still you gamble that this one will not exploit you for his or her own messianic ego trip. You put your trust in your guru as being God's madman, or as Godliness itself, wearing a persona or masquerading as a fly lure for the Infinite Fisherman to catch your heart.

Once it becomes clear that you have, for better or worse, already thrown your "deity dice" on this person's craps table, you become your master's disciple – you become someone willing to learn. This is 50 percent of the journey down the path of trust. In the second half the guru helps you take two more steps on the path.

RIGHT **Amida Buddha, whose devotees will be reborn in the transcendent Pure Land.**

STEP ONE:
The Master Becomes Your Deprogrammer and Your Inspiration to Experiment

Real trust has no conditions attached. A real guru is an inspiration, not an enslaver. He nurtures a trust in experimentation, rather than nourishing your blind belief. An authentic master won't give you a belief to follow. A messiah like Adolf Hitler demands blind belief. A real master strives to make you aware of many unconscious pathologies that keep you unblissfully unaware of your true nature. You know you are in the presence of a real guru when you find all your expectations exposed while living with him. If you don't let them go they will be, figuratively speaking, rubbed in your face.

Usually incidents with other disciples reveal your ego trips in the day-to-day affairs of life in the master's spiritual community. At the same time, a real ashram also gives you a safe haven for going through what are often painful revelations, because you can see that you are not alone. Everyone's ego trips are being exposed there. Also, you feel encouraged to look deeper into yourself because you see how many around you are becoming happier and more integrated human beings.

ABOVE **A genuine guru encourages painful, self-healing revelations.**

The ashram is a hard place for ego trips to sustain themselves, but it is a garden that nourishes one's rise to clarity and happiness. Being a member of a real master's community of disciples doesn't make you dependent or turn you into a spiritual slave. If at first he requires you to surrender to him and to the regimens of his ashram, it is no more unreasonable than a surgeon asking you to remain on the operating table until he finishes the operation.

It takes great intelligence to surrender yourself to a guru. He can say or do something outrageous, even unjustified, but if something he says or does as a device causes you to leave his presence in the middle of the operation, you are the loser. You have chosen trifles over transcendence. The master doesn't care about being politically or religiously correct, he cares about *you*. He wants to upset all your judgment ducks, set in a neat row by your society. He has the compassion to poke a stick into the spokes of your finely tuned morality. He's there to show that both good judgments and bad are worthless if they are borrowed.

A true master wants to destroy the chains connecting you to all arranged marriages with hand-me-down knowledge. He wants to pull the plug on your past and short out your fossilized traditions. He's out to turn off your ego's TV so the empty screen will reflect the couch potato pundit that idiotic life has made you. A master holds up a mirror to your face, risking his life for you, because most people don't want to see their true reflection. They can break the mirror, persecute, and even kill, its holder. A true disciple, however, may cringe at the image of himself or herself, yet be grateful that the master cared enough to show the reflection of an adopted persona – a mask – no matter how ugly it may be. If the mask isn't exposed by someone, how can you take it off and see your original face?

In the first step toward becoming unbearably light with ordinary being, the master is your surgeon. Sometimes the operation to relieve you from conditioned habits and borrowed identities is as painful as peeling off your own skin. The "honeymoon" with the guru may be over, yet one who is willing to learn must trust this mysterious doctor. You must follow the instructions of the master-midwife and bear down on the waves of contractions as you give birth to your own lost understanding of who you really are.

After the cathartic work is finished, the master's next job is to pose experiments that the disciples must test for themselves. In my own case, my master admonished me gently but firmly to always remember that if during self-observation I dislike what I see coming up out of my unconscious, then face it. If I want to avoid something in life – never avoid. When fear stands up to paralyze me – go into that fear.

"That's the only way to finish it," my master said, "otherwise it will haunt you like a shadow."

Anger, greediness for this and that, fears, pride, phoniness, etc. – name your worst nightmares from the ID (your IDiot nightmare), then see them come at you

BELOW **Enlightenment leads to true clarity and lightness – an acceptance of your ordinariness.**

ABOVE **Modern society encourages greed, overconsumption, possession.**

like a demon. Don't shrink back. Do exactly the opposite of what your society's conditioning says you should or should not do. In my case, I faced – and still face – my demon programs. The ego, when faced straight-on rather than avoided or repressed, simply vanishes. I watch these programs as my master instructed, without judgment for or against, mindful of my breath, relaxing. What is watched isn't "my" thoughts and feelings, they are "the" thoughts and feelings, passing in and out. They are mental traffic on the mind's freeway, and I'm sitting by the side of the road. Sometimes the freeway is empty; sometimes there's a traffic jam of thoughts and emotions. The trick is not to get caught in the traffic, but just to watch the "cars" go by. Let the cars of thought honk and weave and fender-bend after their own destinations. Putting it another way, my being – my "watcher" – is like the sky. There is a "seeing" of clouds floating by – puffy, white, and smiling, or dark and thunderous – across empty sky.

ABOVE **The idea of self will alter once you have faced your fears and anxieties.**

A real master doesn't want you to believe his or her statements. Belief to a true master is a cuddly euphemism that masks a state of blind ignorance. A master teaches you to either know something as your own experience, or to accept all that is unknown. Above all, he lays before a disciple the hypothesis that you can celebrate everything – happiness, sadness, life, death, all of it. He teaches acceptance of yourself, of others, even acceptance of nonacceptance.

A master will tell you often that he is just an ordinary human being, like you. He's no messiah or God-man or avatar come to take up your sins or your responsibilities.

He'll say you don't need saving. You need "waking."

That's the only small difference between you and the master. You are extraordinarily sleepwalking through life, and he is ordinarily awake.

Once a sleepwalker, now an awakened one, the master will declare, "If I can wake up, so can you."

Love is compassion and the ability for empathy. But not as empathy which includes only a few people. And not an ability of empathy only applied within your own field of people. Love is not always there to caress your hairs [Swedish saying], but many times it means you have to brush the hairs against the grain. In this way love does not want anything. The one who wants to be loved and act accordingly is not loving but rather is calculating, consciously or unconsciously. People can disgrace themselves as much as possible to be liked and accepted, but the one who feels true love to his fellow human being and the world will be perceived by many as very uncomfortable and even as an enemy because he or she will say things and act in a way that breaks the borders of covenants, laws, and life patterns. Such a human being is never out to hurt, or has never any ulterior goals in her actions. She is not looking for any personal gain, or any goods and therefore her actions are straight and clean because she gave of her knowledge and her wisdom only to share what she has discovered and she does this without any demands.

AMBRES (1986)

STEP TWO: Union, Gratefulness, No-Knowing

It has been 19 years and counting that I've been testing my master's experiments, and I haven't really figured out anything. In the beginning I had many questions. When my master responded, he didn't answer them as such; it was as if he made my questions vanish. Over time the clouds of questions slowly disappeared and left behind just a sky made of *answer*.

Not all of his hypotheses agreed with me, but that was not a problem. My master always encouraged me to follow my own way, to celebrate being as equally unique a human being as he was. If something didn't work, it only meant that we still needed to find techniques in meditation or therapies that harmonized with my individuality. The essential hypothesis he suggested to me was that ultimately existence itself is the teacher.

Life is the master.

When I also discovered this through my own experimentation, I began to see the master's sutures of insight slowly become my own.

Thus I begin to understand the second step a disciple takes with a master. You begin to experience union with him or her. In the beginning you fall into a rhythm with the master as your most cherished beloved, but it is not a romantic affair of soulmates. The one-on-one coupling I've shared with women in this life, as rich and fulfilling as it has been, is nothing compared with the disciple-master relationship. It is one-ego-on-no-ego. It is one *I*-diot in love with a Nobody. It is a one-on-zero affair. You are somebody. You are trying to be something, whereas the master is a no-thing being. And there's the mysterious paradox. He is full of this emptiness, he is a monsoon cloud bursting with rain, and like rain his emptiness nourishes a thirsty soul. Even the pitter-patter of his showers on the roof of your resistance is comforting to you.

The master is an empty void that has a bright awareness about it. You feel that he has arrived. Yet he is a vacant, nonpresent presence. A body walks up to you and talks to you. A man dances with you, but even though the body is total and animated in its moves, it appears just as empty as a corpse. You dance with him and become aware that this corpse is far more alive than you. It is as if the sky decided one day to hide inside the shell of a human body so it could relate to you and love you. The only hint of the sky's masquerade is the bright and penetrating emptiness of his eyes.

You find yourself falling in love with zero. It is like the legend of the great lovers, Tristan and Isolde. They adored each other with such intensity that they both disappeared into that love. They became so aware of love that they became love. Love liberated them from being egos, from being limited in time or confined in sexually identified minds and bodies. They became love's eternity, love's endless sky. In the same way, by staying close to a master you begin to disappear into his state of union and nonseparation. Tasting his no-thing-ness, your starved soul begins to become wet with his nectar. Once this has happened, once the master gets his emptiness under your skin, his physical existence becomes irrelevant. The sky was not the body. It was just visiting you. You are not the body either. In those moments when the master merged with you, he showed you that you are also the sky hiding behind form.

To merge with a master is called *Satsang*. There is no appropriate translation in any Western language for this Sanskrit word. I can say this, from my own experience: Satsang happens when you come close to a master, so close that his emptiness helps you to dissolve into "it." Suddenly, unexpectedly, you disappear into his whole in the clouds. The mind and all its thoughts fall away; the emotions and all their turbulence of hurts and expectations vanishes. You become light and lightning-bright with the same focusless attention of the master. Satsang is a coupling. He has disappeared and so have you. For a moment there is no master, no disciple. No-thing.

At this juncture prose must be left behind. The language of books is a language of the clouds, of the idiots; its expression is extraordinary. Language separates, distinguishes. Words and sentences are like Tristan-and-Isolde egos before they dissolved into no-ego. Language dissects the flower of a master-disciple union into its parts. Language divides and dismantles the mystic flower of Satsang until it lies in pieces on the floor, killed. The only way to understand what I'm saying is to find a master, sit with him or her and disappear into his love and awareness.

ABOVE **Tristan and Isolde adored each other into pure, timeless, ego-less love.**

A look with no intention.
A robe of green, fluttering,
　　　like a poplar tree sage in a desert.
A moonlight leaf,
　　　causing the cockerel to purr in the
　　　almond tree.

The hum held in your hands,
The eyes wide open gazing backwards
　　　at something beyond the seen:

　　　The one you recognize in me.

A rocking moves my frame from nowhere,
　　　and meeting draws closed our eyes.
And you never saw me.
And I never saw you.
　　　　So that we could re-member.

Through moments of Satsang with my master I have tasted the essence of the Apocalypse of the Awakened Ones. As far as I understand it, this is one of their secrets: no messiah as such is coming to save us. The savior sleeps within each of us.

Worship not the awakened mystics. Understand them as the reflections of your own divine potential. Their physical sojourn on this earth is an invitation to ignite the fire of your sleeping consciousness. To indicate this truth, they led you from the periphery of the outer apocalypse to the untapped majesty hiding within self.

And Jesus said: "He who will drink from my mouth will become like me.
I myself shall become he, and the things that are hidden will be revealed to him."

Y'SHUA (*c.* 30–33 C.E.), GOFT #108

The Guru actually emerges from within. When genuine search takes effect,
his genuine manifestation is bound to occur; it cannot possibly be otherwise.
The One, assuming Himself the shape of the Guru, of his own accord
brings about his manifestation or becomes manifested.

ANANDAMAYI MA (1896–1982), MATRI

Each night one embraces a Buddha while sleeping,
Each morning one gets up with him again.
When rising or sitting
Both watch and follow one another.
Whether speaking or not
Both are in the same place.
They never even for a moment part,
But are like the body and its shadow.
If you wish to know the Buddha's whereabouts
In the sound of your own voice
There is he.

ZEN SAYING

In that moment there is no Master, no disciple.
Just two flames have come so close to each other,
they have become one flame.

The disciple starts smelling of the same fragrance
as the Master. His eyes start showing the same raw
light as the Master. His vibe becomes the same as
the Master.

And then the tremendous gratitude: the gratitude
that this man did not give me a belief, otherwise I was
lost. This man did not make me dependent on him,
otherwise I was lost. This man did not exploit me
psychologically in any way, for his own ego, otherwise
I would not have been able even to find what is
happening.

Because I was sick, I was needful, he could have
easily exploited my needs for his own ego. He could
have created the vicious circle of fulfilling the ego:
you fulfill the Master's ego, the Master fulfills the
disciple's ego.

OSHO (1984), MTOE

The master or the teacher can never put himself above his disciples. Unfortunately disciples have a tendency to put the teacher on a pedestal and some masters or teachers are falling for this admiration and are bound by his disciples and them to him. And then arises a situation which is not fruitful. Where the teacher and disciples are all the time verifying each other they create a sect. Many times I have said that if someone says, "this is the only teaching," then run as fast as your legs can carry you because he's a charlatan. But if someone says, "I am a door to the truth," then stay and listen because then you can find golden truths. A master never preaches from above to his listeners, he is the lowest of them all. He or she tries to lift them from within with his knowledge and his wisdom. The master is not sitting on the top of the trees, he is wandering in the grass. He knows that everyone has the same knowing he has, but unlike others he has woken up to this knowing; therefore, he must transmit what he has found. He follows the precept of giving, the precept of love. For millennia people have followed the masters and teachers who have incarnated on this planet. But the crowd of listeners has also increased during this time. Seeds have been sown for coming crops and there is no darkness which is so thick that in the long run it can put the light out. A new time is coming, a new human being, a new man is being born.

AMBRES (1986)

MANY CANDLES – ONE FLAME

In the new Aquarian Age, the individual's spiritual journey will be nurtured by the cumulative impact of millions of other individuals seeking enlightenment on an unprecedented scale. This global wave of spiritual seeking will occur, say the more rebellious prophets and mystics, only after individuals break free from the shackles of greed for heaven, fear of hell, and all the other life-negative dogmas of the dying religions of the closing Piscean Age.

The new dispensation will also free the enlightened master from the shackles of messianism. As we abandon our myths about saviors, those upon whom we have projected that myth will find themselves liberated from their masks such as the God-man, Avatar, Messiah, 12th Imam, or Redeemer. When at last we see their original faces, these individuals will simply become our teachers, our friends.

If one candle can light millions, the flame of one awakened human being can light millions of unlit souls.

> When the disciple brings his unlit flame close to the master, the master's lit flame jumps to the unlit flame and lights it. The master loses nothing and the disciple gets everything.
>
> OSHO (*c.* 1977)

> May each one of you become a shining lamp, of which the flame is the Love of God. May your hearts burn with the radiance of unity. May your eyes be illumined with the effulgence of the Sun of Truth!
>
> 'ABDU'L-BAHÁ (1911), PARIS 5:21

Once you have tasted your own immortality, you start spreading an invisible fire...no intellectual argument, but people will be immensely touched by your very presence, by your aroma, by your fragrance, by your love. We need in the world more love to balance war.

OSHO (1987), NEWD

Our task is to bring about the Kingdom of God on Earth. We want to be conductors of the divine law. May that law rule all minds and hearts; may all men and women become sons and daughters of the divine kingdom and may they begin to live on the Earth accordingly!

PETER DEUNOV (1927–1928), DIVT

ABOVE **The flame of one enlightened person can spread infinitely.**

...Those who desire to understand, who are looking to find that which is eternal, without beginning and end, will walk together with greater intensity, will be a danger to everything which is unessential, to unrealities, to shadows. And they will concentrate, they will become the flame, because they understand.

J. KRISHNAMURTI (1929), FROM THE MANIFESTO: TRUTH IS A PATHLESS LAND

LEFT **Traditionally the gate to Heaven is narrow, while the gate to Hell is wide; but the rebellious prophet says we must break free of these binary oppositions to attain enlightenment.**

THE BUDDHAFIELD

Under the immeasurable discomforts that mankind are faced with today, security of an individual as well as of a nation is far from probable. There is only one choice left in order that mankind should escape this plight. That is, the whole mankind must come reunited into one whole being-unity and cope with the task for redress. This task is far beyond the capacity of any one nation, any one organization, any one ideology, or any one religion.

TAMO-SAN (1960), MOOR

THE BUDDHAFIELD

Just as death faces an individual, similarly death shows its dark face before the collective consciousness of an entire civilization. And that civilization's collective mind becomes ready to go deep into the realms of religion and the unknown..... This can repeat itself again; there is a complete possibility for it.

OSHO (1971), DMBY

Never before was the search so acute, so intense, because never before was man in such an anguish as he is today. The search always comes out of anguish. Whenever there is great anguish, the anguish becomes a challenge, one has to search for something which is so meaningful that the anguish can be dissolved through it. When the darkness is very very deep, only then does one search for light.
And the darkness is really deep. This is one of the darkest ages: never before has man been in such a disturbed, confused chaos. Because all the old values have disappeared,. Man is no more rooted in the past, there are no more any goals in the future, all utopias have failed. Man is utterly desperate now to know what to do and where to go.

  In the past it has happened many times that a certain value became valueless, another value took its place, it was substituted. One religion died, another took its place. One idealism was found futile, another better vision, more golden, was immediately available. What has happened this time is that all the ideals have failed and there is no more any substitute. It is not that one value has failed and another has come into being: that is not much of a change. This time, value as such has failed and there is utter darkness, nowhere to go. This is the greatest challenge to human awakening. Hence I say, for the first time in history, the time is right for a great Buddhafield.

OSHO (1978), LTG

The time of the God-field has come. [We] need to make this world entirely new. And it is like washing and clearing all things in this world. And if they do that peace will come to this world. The eternal world of God will be realized in the end.

DEGUCHI NAO (1892), FIRST DECLARATION

ABOVE **The conception of an earthly paradise does not seem beyond our grasp; the Aquarian Age is one of hope and promise that refuses global destruction.**

The Aquarian Age will see humanity take a quantum leap beyond what we currently know and believe. It will not be an era of father-figure gods sending their only begotten children to be persecuted and to preach salvation. It may see the end of messiahs as we have known them. They could be replaced by what many Aquarian Age prophets have foreseen as a "Christ" or "Buddha" force field. The savior of the 21st century could be a collective spiritual environment generated by thousands of awakening individuals who in turn were launched on their inner journey of self-discovery by one enlightened fellow traveler as their catalytic agent. Consequently, as more individual seekers gather together, they nourish this force field of collective awakening and intensify its presence and blissful vitality. This in turn attracts many more individual spiritual seekers into its ambiance.

Thus, the momentum created by so many individuals working and meditating to free themselves from the distortions of the past could create a field of energy that turns human destiny in a new direction, away from destruction and toward a life-affirming new era. Many prophets of this future potential foresee the arrival of a paradise on Earth 250 to 700 years from now – that is, if the Buddhafield is allowed to spread its presence across the world.

ESCAPING THE MISERY FIELD

LEFT **The "misery field" is where we all scratch around trying to make our piece where there is no peace.**

Most of us live life in a "misery field." There are moments of love, brief encounters with happiness, and all-too-short plateaus of fulfillment. For the rest of our lives we endure a spiritual climate that is generally negative. The daily grind draws most of our creative energy into the whirlwind of competition for money, food, and prestige. The struggle to survive against competitors dominates most of our day, from the nuclear family level all the way up to the family of nations. The things people have become more valuable than the people themselves. In the richer misery fields you are your car, your lace bra – your secrets are Victoria's Secret. You are your job.

In a culture of misery, life must be a hell to make heaven more appealing. No wonder popes as recently as the beginning of the 20th century were declaring social progress in world democracy a vehicle of Satan. The children brought into this misery biosphere soon see their bright and questioning beings dulled. The children of each generation learn how to be miserable through their lifetime education in the three Rs: Rote education, Robotic belief, and Regret.

You know you are lost in a misery field when laughter is a disturbance, when duty dulls the divine innocence, when burdens become virtues. People videotape their lives rather than live them. Memories are always sweet because the present situation in a misery field always sucks. You know that misery rules when people can't be alone and will compromise themselves to live in dysfunctional families and marriages. They will surrender to the will of national bodies, and sell their souls to religious pathologies.

Stillness and silence irritate the ambiance of a misery field. Even in places where talk is obviously not necessary, people must cluck and fuss. For instance, on Super Bowl Sunday in January 1999, I hiked to the summit of Mt. Si in Washington state. The sun colored the snow powder, marbling the cracks in a 300-foot outcropping known as "the haystack" as if it had veins of golden filament. Above the haystack ice clouds lined up like celestial celebrants twirling in a cirrus dervish dance in an unfathomable blue sky. The pine trees, wearing their snowy-white mime faces, sighed in the wind. I planted my boots knee-deep in a snowdrift and hugged the scene with my being, my senses pressed against the still wonder like naked newlyweds.

Soon there were others reaching the vista, huffing and puffing and chattering about this and that. Until the others arrived, the vista point and I enjoyed a brief interlude away from the world's misery field. The new people brought their mental static with them even though the miracle of sun and snow-play upon rock and tree continued.

"Look, Mildred, golly it's sure cold up here…Brush that snow off or you'll get cold…Oh! That's pretty…Yep, but not as pretty as the last time…*blah, blah*…. My hands are getting cold…Why didn't you put on those extra glove liners like I told you?…Ah, you never listen to me, serves you right…Hey, Bob? Quick get a picture of it before the clouds come back…*blah, blah*…. I'm hungry…*blah, blah*…Okay, let's get down in time to see the Super Bowl…*blah, blah, blah*…."

They jabbered while Mt. Si and I communed in silence. Even with all the chatter going on, the others sneaked suspicious glares at me for not blabbing along with them. My silence was politically incorrect.

At that moment I was more than a dropout, I was a step-out, an ecstatic. *Ecstasy* is the ancient Greek word for a state of extreme and intense sensitivity when one has suddenly exited from the world of the mundane.

It is not easy to keep a childlike sense of ecstasy alive in this world. When you are out in public, allow a relaxation into blissfulness without a "cause" and see how self-conscious you become. See how out of step you are. Note the fearful looks of some and the mean-spirited putdowns of others. See how something like a lead weight drags down your blissfulness once you allow it to emerge and be. The self-consciousness ends when your eyes resume the same dullness of the crowd and your body language assumes the plodding disposition of everyone else. It is at such moments when you return to the fold that you sense the worldwide thought field that keeps people down.

ABOVE **Getting up into the high mountains is a time-honored way of putting the misery field behind you.**

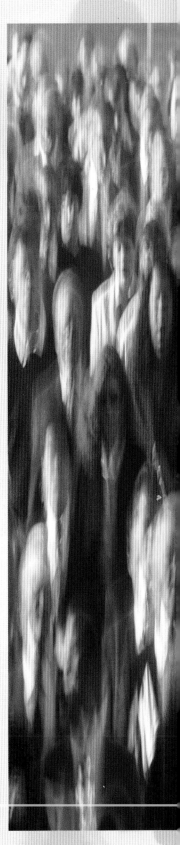

We are trained to generate it. It isn't anyone's fault, it is everyone's affliction, learned from cradle to corporation to crypt. The majority of us move through life in the misery field's automatic gear. Yet a handful of us over the centuries slip out of gear. Some of those who don't fit become religious seekers. Later on we mistake a handful of these misfits as our messiahs and avatars.

The mystically inclined have always required a spiritual retreat away from the magnetic influence of the misery-field worldliness. It is not by accident that there are monasteries far from the madding crowds. Spiritual seekers look for an oasis in the misery and violence of every era. They come out of the desert to drink at the well of a sacred place. They leave the noisy cities, they abandon the well-traveled roads. They wander off into nature, into the mountains, into the Himalayas. They appear antisocial when they are really antimisery.

Where people locked in the misery field may collectively project a myth of off-world salvation and an escape into the clouds, there are those among us who seek a "Rapture" away from the world's loveless and negative thought field.

THE COMING OF THE TRANSPERSONAL MESSIAH

Under the immeasurable discomforts that mankind are faced with today, security of an individual as well as of a nation is far from probable. There is only one choice left in order that mankind should escape this plight. That is, the whole mankind must come reunited into one whole being-unity and cope with the task for redress. This task is far beyond the capacity of any one nation, any one organization, any one ideology, or any one religion.

TAMO-SAN (1960), MOOR

A great, unheard-of experiment has to be done, on such a large scale that at least the most substantial part of humanity is touched by it – at least the soul of humanity, the center of humanity, can be awakened by it. On the periphery, the mediocre minds will go on sleeping – let them sleep – but at the center where intelligence exists a light can be kindled.

The time is ripe, the time has come for it. My whole work here consists in creating a Buddhafield, an energy-field where these eternal truths can be uttered again. It is a rare opportunity. Only once in a while, after centuries, does such an opportunity exist...don't miss it!

OSHO (1979), DMPDA

Whereas many people once or twice a year seek the peace and solitude of a vacation on an empty tropical beach, the few mystics of every generation take a somewhat different approach. They strive to create an alternative lifestyle, one where the spiritual vacation from the world never ends but deepens. It deepens so profoundly that even though the vacationer might return to the hurly-burly of the marketplace, he or she will not be *of* the marketplace. Instead the vacationer can become a center of cool and silent bliss in the cyclone of the misery field.

The mystics not only teach us that thoughts are a form of radiation, but that a higher state of "no-thought" can permeate a spiritual community and be like mists of a waterfall refreshing the surrounding forest with its healing presence. If fear and hate can haunt a place, so can love and compassion. The cumulative effect of silent, watchful minds and balanced, peaceful hearts can figuratively refresh the collective human spirit, enliven individual trees in the forest called humanity, and glisten the rocks of religious tradition with a new energy field.

ABOVE **The tropical paradise may be the nearest most people can get to peace. The real challenge is to find peace in the marketplace, not away from it.**

In the last year before the new millennium, three pyramids of obsidian black reflect the South Asian sky and loom over groves of scarlet-flowered flame trees and blue jacarandas in the Koregaon Park neighborhood of Pune, India. Below the canopy of trees, shaded from the Indian sun, you can see thousands of men and women from every race, dressed in maroon robes, coursing along the pedestrian thoroughfares of a multiacre campus.

The people weave through a network of buildings of modern, even avant-garde, construction. Many structures were once sprawling bungalows and mansions built during the days of the British Raj, but all the buildings are painted and marbled in black, with their windows tinted an iceberg blue. The contrast of the black buildings against the rivers of maroon-robed thousands and the surrounding subtropical gardens and forest canopy is strikingly beautiful rather than intimidating.

This is the Osho International Commune, today's largest buddhafield community experiment, which since the 1970s has been one of the world's greatest magnets for seekers and meditators. Tens of thousands of visitors arrive each year through the commune's Gateless Gate.

BELOW **The Osho International Commune in Pune, India, is a place of pilgrimage for Buddhafield seekers the world over.**

When night darkens the sky, the maroon robes of the people living here and visiting the commune are replaced by robes of white. They proceed down the thoroughfares of marble, illuminated by glass columns over emerald-green lights, on their way to Buddha Hall. It is a great dome, three stories high, made of arched girders and tent canvas that covers one acre in the center of the 32-acre campus. Throughout the year men and women file inside to sit cross-legged in rows on a vast polished marble floor for a nightly session of the White Robe Brotherhood. They sit, backs straight, unmoving, as flutes and sitars caress the air. They wait expectantly for someone who will never arrive – who was never born (nor ever died, so the communards say), who was just a visitor from the formless playing for a brief 58 years in a form of their beloved master, Osho. They wait before a podium topped by a richly upholstered white chair.

Each night by 7:00 P.M., a sea of thousands of white-robed men and women covers the marble floor. The celebration music intensifies and the White Robe Brotherhood begins dancing and singing. For 30 minutes a cyclone of celebration carries them away; nevertheless, their episodes of reverie and silent pauses for meditation hinge upon the axis of that empty chair.

Twenty-three years before the new millennium, a bald Indian mystic with a long white beard and flowing robe regularly sat upon another chair in the same spot every morning at 10 o'clock. A smaller crowd of his disciples, dressed in various vibrant colors of the sunrise, sat on a cement floor arranged around a grove of white cloth-covered poles suspending a far more rustic tent awning a mere 12 feet above their heads.

It is the morning of December 29, 1977. This is Osho's ninth discourse on Buddha Gautama's *Diamond Sutra*. On this morning, Osho (known at this time as Bhagwan Shree Rajneesh) will share for the first time his vision of the transpersonal messiah – the Buddhafield.

The word "Buddhafield" is of tremendous importance. You have to understand it, because that is what I am doing here – creating a Buddhafield. It is just to create a Buddhafield that we are moving away from the world, far away, so that a totally different kind of energy can be made available to you.

"Buddhafield" means a situation where your sleeping Buddha can be awakened. "Buddhafield" means an energy-field where you can start growing, maturing, where your sleep can be broken, where you can be shocked to awareness; an electric field where you will not be able to fall asleep, where you will have to be awake, because shocks will be coming all the time.

A "Buddhafield" is an energy field in which a Buddha matures beings, a pure land, an unworldly world, a paradise on earth, which offers ideal conditions for rapid spiritual growth. A "Buddhafield" is a matrix.

The world "matrix" comes from Latin. It means "the womb." From that world we get the words "matter," "mother," etcetera. The womb offers three things to a newly forming life: a source of possibility, a source of energy to explore that possibility, and a safe place within which that exploration can take place. That's what we are going to do. The new commune is going to be a great experiment in Buddhahood.

The audience listens, some staring in rapt attention at the man with the mirror eyes reflecting their faces, others sitting with eyes shut, enraptured by silence. All listen to the words; some even listen to the inner pauses between their master's slow and peacefully hypnotic cadences as he forms accented English words – sometimes with a soothing aspiration of "shhh" – from his trademark lisp.

The cuckoo in the gardens surrounding the hall calls out its rising glissandos of pure joy. A lonely train in the nearby station calls out a response, and Osho continues.

Energies have to be made available to you: possibilities have to be made clear to you. You have to be made aware of your potential, and you have to be given a safe place from where you can work; a place where you are not distracted by the world, a place where you can go on without any disturbance from the crowd, a place where ordinary things, taboos, inhibitions, are put aside; where only one thing is significant – how to become a Buddha [an awakened one]; where everything else simply disappears from your mind – money and power and prestige; where all else becomes insignificant, when all else becomes exactly as it is – a shadow world – and you are no more lost in the apparent.

Twenty-three years before the new millennium a much smaller campus, called the Shree Rajneesh Ashram, surrounded Buddha Hall. The umbrella canopy of soothing tree shade had huge holes for the sun to beat down on the green buildings and bake the gravel thoroughfares. In 1977 the sun was hotter, the hair and beards were longer, the robes a louder orange and red and more folk-hippie in style. In 1977 this was the commune of the "free-sex guru." A place of padded rooms where people wearing nothing more than sweat could take part in encounter groups, rebirthing sessions, and Tantric sex. This was the commune of the Rajneeshees of the Neo-Sannyas movement.

Osho had created the sect of orange-robed men (and women) that rubbed traditional and patriarchal Indian ideas of the renunciate discipline of sannyas the wrong way. These new sannyasins didn't renounce life, they renounced nonacceptance of life. They forswore traditional religious dogmas that divided heaven from the world, making one sacred, the other profane. They sought to experiment with Osho's hypothesis that an integrated human being is part earthy Zorba the Greek and part otherworldly Buddha Gautama. Osho called this synthesis a "Zorba the Buddha."

LEFT **What would we make of the Sermon on the Mount if we had it on video?**

The Orange People, as the press called them, experimented with the hypothesis that society programs inhibitions into us to retard our spiritual and material growth. To the Rajneeshees of that day, understanding your sexual energy was the key. Dive into it willingly and you might understand the root of life and unlock yourself from the inhibitions that stifle your life force.

Twenty-three years before the new millennium, when Osho introduced the concept of a new commune creating the force field of a collective buddhahood, the climate of their ashram was essentially neo-Tantric – a revision of the ancient South Asian sect of conscious hedonists. In Tantra nothing is denied. You live life with acceptance. You become a yes-sayer. Repress nothing – but Osho added one important proviso: be aware. Watch what you are doing, understand it. Use your witnessing consciousness to peel back all the layers of motivations that make you do everything you do each day, whether you are "doing" orgasm, misery, love, or hate – anything.

Osho asked his experimenting disciples not to believe him but to test his observations and insights. He invited them to experiment with his Ashram/Buddhafield's unique brand of active meditation techniques of self-observation tailored for the modern human being, who he claimed was too encumbered with thought and emotional repression to simply sit silently, doing nothing, like the disciples of Buddha 25 centuries earlier.

Those huddled close together on the cold cement floor on that December morning, listening to Osho expound the Buddhafield, were the vanguard of hundreds of thousands who would come to listen. Osho would give thousands of discourses over 20 years, covering everything under the sun: commentaries on all the religions and their enlightened men and women masters, as well as observations on the sciences, history, Western philosophers, politics, and sociology – and always laced with thousands of jokes. The audiotaped and videotaped transcriptions of his daily discourses would eventually fill 700 books.

If Osho was anything, he was progressive. He understood the mass media and their ability to record the utterances of future Christs and Buddhas. He understood that if Christ and Buddha had access to audiovisual technology it would have been much harder to make these extraordinarily ordinary and natural human beings into messiah myths. On videotape, the coming centuries would have seen them – warts and all – as ordinary people.

An audiotape or a home video showing what Jesus actually said during his Sermon on the Mount would have recorded *how* he said things. The subtleties of inflection, the pauses between words, would convey the nuances that no simple written record can capture. If his disciples had filmed Buddha's hundreds of discourses under the Bodhi tree, then for millennia to come future lovers of Buddha could have checked the accounts of his attendant and cousin-brother, Ananda, for any distortions.

Osho understood that new catalysts for the Buddhafield experiments of the Aquarian Age should use the objective evidence of audio- and videotape recording as one way to help root out self-proclaimed latter-day apostles who claim to have received "the truth." What luck would St. Paul have had when he broke ranks with Christ's brother James to proclaim Jesus to the Gentiles if videotapes existed showing Christ (or better, Y'shua) proclaiming his mission to be solely a Jewish revolution? If technology had existed to record the founders of religions, the Vatican empires, Hindu hierarchies, and any other religious middlemen would have had to base their authority on something far more substantial and objective than the thin air of faith and the fading light of ancient memories.

Twenty-three years before the new millennium, a tape machine at Osho's feet recorded one of his long and pregnant pauses before he continued speaking about what the Buddhafield would do to dispel illusion.

> *Maya* [illusion, sin] *is to be caught up in the apparent. That is the greatest illusion in the world. The apparent holds such sway on our minds. A "Buddhafield" is a place where you are taken away from the apparent.*
>
> *In the silence of a commune, in the uninhibited, untabooed atmosphere of a commune, the master and the disciple can enact the drama totally. The ultimate is when the master can touch the feet of the disciple, when the master and disciples are lost into one reality.*

In the year following this discourse, Reverend Jim Jones would lead his followers in a mass suicide. The world press tried to make comparisons between Jonestown and the Shree Rajneesh Ashram. Osho would explain that such a tragedy could never happen in his commune, because his people were there to celebrate life and renounce all that is life-negative. A false Buddhafield creates a Jonestown, or Hitler's Nazi utopia. The misery field can put on the mask of a Buddhafield while it magnifies the anger and fear. Paradoxically, a true master creating an authentic Buddhafield uses the collective love and meditation energy of its participants to forge equally unique individuals, not robots. It creates people to whom the master bows down in reverence – a new humanity.

Now understand: if somebody says, "I will create the Buddhafield," and the emphasis is on "I," then the statement is false, because a person who has the "I" still alive cannot create a Buddhafield. Only a person who has no "I" within him can create a Buddhafield. In fact then to say he creates is not right; language is inadequate.

The Sanskrit word for creation is far better. The Sanskrit word is "nirpadayati." It means many things. It can mean "to create," it can mean "to accomplish,"it can mean "to ripen," it can mean "to mature;" it can simply mean to trigger it into existence. That's exactly the meaning.

A Buddha does not create, he triggers. Even to say he triggers is not good; in his presence things happen, in his presence things are triggered, processes start. Just his presence is a fire, a spark, and things start moving and one thing leads to another, and a great chain is created.

The disciples attending that discourse were already well aware of the miracle of so much creative activity buzzing around their lazy Buddha's bones. The ashram was a beehive of active meditation groups, therapy groups, Sufi and devotional dancing sessions, and a theater department. In addition there was all the hustle and bustle of the daily chores involved in feeding, clothing, and cleaning for the thousands of guests and residents of the community – manning kitchens, running the medical center, clothing shops, and various other ashram industries.

Yet the man whose vision was responsible for all this activity did next to nothing all day. After rising in the morning he would shuffle over to his chair and spend most of his waking hours sitting in blissful silence by the window next to a garden shaded by a great almond tree. It was as if his purported enlightenment had brought his "doing" to a complete stop. His only major effort of the day was to leave his room (which he called his "cave") and shuffle off to the back seat of his chauffeur-driven Rolls-Royce, which carried him the few hundred yards to Buddha Hall and the waiting chair up on the podium.

He would come into the hall, lovingly greet his disciples with folded hands, sit, and discourse every morning for 90 minutes to two hours. Afterward he would rise, eyes glistening with a quiet tenderness, and fold his hands again to give his disciples a loving good-bye. The limousine carrying their guru would circuit the open walls of the tented hall, while the people within it followed its departure in hushed silence. The only commentary you could hear was the gravel against the tires, and the call of the cockerel as the car drove him back to his "cave."

In the evening, Osho would venture a few paces outside his room to a smaller pillared marble patio called Chang Tzu Auditorium, named after the ancient Taoist master, and give sannyas initiation to disciples. In 1980–1981, and just prior to his personal initiations coming to an end, Osho gave what he called energy *darshans* at Chang Tzu. He did nothing much more than sit in his chair and lay his long-fingered and finely sculpted hands on the brows of sannyasins.

The sessions would start with the candidates for the energy darshan being arranged around Osho sitting in his chair. At the right moment he would nod to the band, and guitars, sitars, flutes, and drums began stirring the air with ever more intense Sufi-zikur-style music. Around Osho and his candidates were a dozen red-robed female disciples dancing and moaning with abandon. This was a circle of the happiest, most energetic coven of witches one sleepy-eyed Indian warlock could ever hope to find himself among. The more relaxed he became, the more powerful was their dance, and the stronger the waves of music and energy coursing through Chang Tzu Auditorium and echoing through the entire ashram compound. Just as the surge of music and dancing reached its climax, someone would throw the master switch, putting out all the lights in the commune.

The unique experience of the energy darshans and the high-energy blackouts was still a year or two away for the disciples listening to Osho's first Buddhafield discourse. In the peace of that December morning they heard him accurately foretell things to come, how thousands upon thousands more seekers would gather around him, and how their combined spiritual urgency, love, and uninhibited celebration would somehow deepen and empower Buddhahood's force field.

That's how we have been going on. I simply sit in my room doing nothing, and seekers from all over the world have started pouring in. I don't even write a letter…just the presence. One comes, another comes, and the chain is created. Now the time has come when a Buddhafield is needed, a matrix is needed, because you don't know – thousands more are on the way. They have already moved, they are already thinking of coming.

The 1970s saw the Shree Rajneesh Ashram become the premier growth and therapy center in the world, but Osho found the semiurban and wooded neighborhood of Koregaon Park too confining and nestled too close to the four million people living in the misery field of the overcrowded Indian city of Pune. There was constant friction from the neighbors, some of it warranted. The Koregaon neighborhood of that day was too small to absorb the tens of thousands of Western disciples flooding its streets. They would overwhelm the limited apartment spaces and further crowd the riverside, establishing shantytowns of bamboo huts. The latter half of the 1970s saw his disciples comb India for properties far from population centers. Plans were made to build a new commune near the Rann of Kutch, a great marshland on the West Pakistani border. Then the sannyasins considered another site near the Himalayan foothill resort of Simla – but in both cases politicians and influential Hindu fundamentalists sabotaged the projects.

In 1981, Osho at 50 was ailing and prematurely aging. He traveled to the U.S., allegedly to seek medical attention for a lower back condition. He began a three-year self-imposed public silence at a newly purchased 64,000-acre ranch in the high desert of eastern Oregon.

Between 1981 and 1985 a city of 2,500 permanent residents with the capacity to house another 25,000 temporary summer visitors would rise out of the Oregon desert in the largest Buddhafield of the 20th century. An investment of $85 million, contributed from the communes and businesses of over 300,000 sannyasins worldwide, helped finance the construction of a city, a university, farming industries, and food and

waste recycling systems. A highly successful ecological rehabilitation project was also launched, to heal the overgrazed ranchlands and degraded watershed. A new 88,000-square-foot greenhouse was later converted into a meeting hall with a seating capacity of over 20,000.

The new Buddha Hall, known as Rajneesh Mandir, became the main gathering place for thousands of disciples flying in from all parts of the world every July for mass satsangs with Osho during their international summer festivals. Where 1,500 to 2,000 disciples sat on the cement floor listening to Osho introduce his Buddhafield vision in 1977, five years later a multitude of 25,000 people in red sat or danced on all-American vinyl before Osho on a podium, eyes closed, reclining in a chair under the vast roof of the Rajneesh Mandir.

I was one of the tens of thousands in that hall. One could feel the presence of an energy, a thrilling intensity in the atmosphere, whether the 20,000 meditators sat like statues or twirled and swayed, singing and dancing before Osho's podium. Was Osho's Buddhafield experiment another excuse for brainwashing?

BELOW **Osho's disciples sit on the floor of Rajneesh Mandir during a press conference, just some of the many thousands of visiting disciples at the Oregon Buddhafield.**

Yes!

A clean brain is much more fun to play with than one grimed with fossilized habits, fears, and hatreds. At the Oregon commune, surrounded by a red forest of thousands of individuals in meditation, it was easier to shake off all the dirt of the misery field. One lightens up in a Buddhafield. One smiles more, laughs more. Imagine living in a community where thousands of strangers accept you as you are, whether you are happy or crying, open or feeling closed and afraid. This is a place where it is easy to relax and be natural. You fall into synchronicity with its people, who in turn are emotionally and ecologically in harmony with their surroundings. You could leave your car or your front door unlocked, or forget your backpack on a downtown bench only to find it still there the following morning. Here was a city where you could forget crime, where you had universal health care – spiritual as well as physical. You forgot the rat race. You found it easy to discard the heavy, life-energy-draining burden of day-to-day survival stifling your happiness, your creativity.

Osho foresaw such a place on that December morning in Pune in 1977 and the cumulative effect of many candles being lit by one flame.

And the more people are there, the bigger the Buddhafield will be there, and the more powerful it will be. The possibility is that we can create one of the greatest and most powerful Buddhafields ever created in the world, because never before was there such search, because never before was man in such a crisis.

By the close of 1985, the experiment of the Oregon Buddhafield was over. Outside pressure from the surrounding misery field (known as the United States), along with the political intrigues of a small but powerful hierarchy infecting the commune itself, resulted in Osho's arrest, and the disbanding of the commune.

Back in 1980, Osho had publicly warned his unheeding disciples that if they chose to move him to America, his vision of the future, of religiousness without religion, would see him arrested and murdered. The prophecy may have found its mark five years later. Federal agents arrested him on rather flimsy and never-proven charges of immigration fraud and held him for 12 days in the U.S. prison system, three of those days incommunicado. His disciples claim that during those three days government operatives poisoned Osho's food with a heavy metal agent, Thallium, which hastened his death from diabetes and heart disease by January 1990.

In early 1986, Osho, with less than four years left to live, returned to his room in the Pune Ashram and resumed his daily discourses, every evening at 7:00 P.M. Where many sannyasins were bitter about the Oregon chapter, Osho saw his Buddhafield experiment there as a complete success, just a step along the way. It was the middle chapter of what some disciples close to him have told me was a three-step experiment.

BUDDHAFIELD 1

The Shree Rajneesh Ashram of the 1970s was the earthy foundation of the experiment. It was a place where disciples refined their primal energies and sexuality and began clearing a lifetime of tensions, hatreds, and primal fears through catharsis. The energy was often raw. Foundations can be ugly, but I suppose a catalyst must base higher work upon a solid – if also hard and even gross – foundation.

BUDDHAFIELD 2

In the commune city in Oregon, work became the meditation. Step two also dealt with issues of power and its abuses. People learned they had the power to work miracles when they collaborated in harmony. The commune was a microcosm of the world, and for the most part its ordinary citizens experienced what the world could be like in the coming golden age if love and meditation were everyone's core commitment. The world of the human communal family could work. It was creative, and ecologically and emotionally integrated. Wealth in all its dimensions – financial, spiritual, and emotional – can be abundant in a community that nourishes the Buddhahood aspirations of its individuals, no matter what corner of the world or what social or religious background they came from. Going beyond your limits was the revelation – even going beyond the limit of believing their second Buddhafield experiment could endure.

Old habits learned from life in the misery field eventually resurfaced to destroy its future. The citizens of the Oregon Buddhafield learned a harder lesson about the abuse of power when certain leaders of the ranch took advantage of Osho's public silence to twist his message of trust, send false messages in his name, and set themselves up as a little fascist regime.

When at last Osho broke his silence, he didn't confront the perpetrators like Moses coming down from Mt. Sinai lugging tablets. Over time the general tenor of his words at nightly discourses to the community at large did that for him. The talks exposed how out of touch the growing totalitarianism of the leadership appeared when compared with Osho's vision of a free and individually responsible new humanity living in a global Buddhafield.

As stated before, you can only sustain negativity in a Buddhafield for so long. Finally the ringleader and her followers pulled up stakes and left town. Osho and the new administration invited the outside state and federal police into the commune to investigate the crimes committed against its citizens by the previous leadership. This gave right-wing Christian elements in the Reagan administration the chance to turn on the victims and shut down Osho's second Buddhafield.

Many people abandoned Osho and his experiments after the Oregon ranch era. To them Osho had falsely promised paradise. He was a false messiah, a charlatan. At the very least, he was not upholding their expectations – something even these disgruntled disciples have admitted is the only real promise their master regularly said he'd keep.

Those disciples who rejected these spiritual sour grapes and stayed for the next step in the Buddhafield experiment generally explained to me that Osho was constantly cleaning house in an effort to get rid of negative and selfish people – or those who took Osho, his communes, and themselves too seriously, rather than sincerely.

A Buddhafield constantly needs to clear space for new experimenters willing to go deeper into the mystery of the Buddhafield journey. In other words, a Buddhafield is like a pond. People flow in and out, keeping it fresh. If people can't let the stale waters of their expectations constantly flow out of the pond, then they themselves stagnate, and the master provides them with reasons to flow out of the pond and seek their destiny elsewhere.

BUDDHAFIELD 3

Osho returned to his Ashram in Pune in early 1987. After his deportation from the United States in November 1985, he embarked on a world tour to meet his scattered disciples in their own lands. U.S. agents hounded his Lear jet wherever it went and succeeded in sabotaging his plans. Eventually he was either denied access to or thrown out of 21 countries.

Osho returned to India and for a time continued his discourses in an apartment in a northern suburb of Mumbai (Bombay). Eventually the controversies died down enough for him to set up his show at the Pune Ashram. By this time both the Indian and American governments had relented in their efforts to deny visas to his disciples.

The third stage of the Buddhafield takes us to the present day. One might surmise that the physical death of Osho, in 1990, would test the survivability of his Buddhafield. With their leader gone, the disciples must live his vision, rather than listen to him talk about it.

Before he died, Osho appointed an inner circle of 21 disciples to manage the affairs of his communes. In the years following Osho's death crises have come and gone concerning the direction of his vision. So far, it seems the momentum generated by meditation and the Buddhafield still works to soften disagreements between lay disciples and that inner circle.

The first month of the new millennium will see the tenth anniversary of Osho's death. Presently the third Buddhafield experiment, known as the Osho International Commune, continues to flourish. The Pune Ashram has exploded in growth. The 32-acre site now dominates Koregaon Park, and the commune offers visitors three dimensions of participation in the Buddhafield experiment: meditations are offered throughout the day; there are nine faculties of the Osho Multiversity, including martial arts, creative arts, healing techniques, and esoteric sciences; or you can choose a Zen working meditation, where I suppose you can experience whistling and witnessing while you work in daily activities.

Whatever your pleasure, the religious atmosphere at "Club-Meditation" (as the commune is playfully called by its managers) is always light and carefree. Perhaps the most radical aspect of Osho's Buddhafield experiments is the contention that religion is fun, and that humor is a sacred prayer. Seriousness is a disease of the misery field – enlighten up!

Osho clarified this and other aspects arising from phase three of his Buddhafield after returning to Pune in 1987: "When so many people are relaxing into the silences of their hearts, moving away from their minds, their past, their future, and are just remaining in the present, it creates a certain energy sphere, a certain vibe, a tidal wave that you cannot see. But if you are here, you will certainly be affected by the energy generated by so many people's silences…. This is the purpose of the whole gathering of seekers of the mysteries of existence. Without making any effort to help, their very being becomes a magnetic pull. I call this field the buddhafield, the field of awakening." (*The Rebel,* 1987)

The numbers of new seekers at the Pune Ashram today far exceed the crowds of the 1970s. The Global Connections office at the Ashram reports that the number of nations represented by visitors has jumped from 35 in 1990 to 110 countries by 1999. If such trends continue, Osho's movement could, over the coming decades, fulfill its founder's dream of spreading the presence of a Buddhafield across the world.

People turn to religious experimentation during times of crisis. The coming 30 years of the 21st century will see unprecedented strains on traditional society. If Osho's Buddhafields can continue to grow, there's every possibility that millions of people seeking alternative answers will crowd the growing network of Buddhafield communities in the near future.

Twenty-three years before the new millennium, a vision of such a future may have danced before Osho's eyes when in December 1977 he closed his first discourse on the Buddhafield with this declaration:

We are at the threshold of something new that is going to happen to humanity. Either humanity will die and disappear, or we will take a jump, a leap, and a new being will be formed. We are exactly at the same point as millions of years ago when monkeys came down from the trees and humanity started and a new being was born. Again the moment is coming very close. It is a very dangerous moment, because there is every possibility…. It was possible that the monkey may not have survived on the earth, he may have died on the earth, but a few monkeys took the risk. And they must have been thought of as fools by other monkeys – mm? – who had always lived on the trees and were perfectly happy. They must have thought, "These people are going mad, crazy. Why in the first place are you going to live on the earth? Why create unnecessary trouble for yourselves? Our fathers and their fathers and their fathers have all lived on the trees."

Again the same situation is going to happen. Man has lived a long time the way he has lived. By the end of this century, a critical quantum leap is possible. Either man will die in the third world war or man will take the jump and will become a new man. Before that happens, a great Buddhafield is needed…where we can create the future.

Before he died, Osho predicted that he would be dissolved into his people, that wherever you met one of his sannyasins, or imbibed the tangible silence of one of his Buddhafield communities, there his presence would be, shining in the bright faces of his people, celebrating in their passion for life, and meditating in their silences. By establishing a Buddhafield that so far shows no significant sign of diminishing because of his death, Osho may be setting a new standard for all future gurus of the Aquarian Age. They may take his lead and dissolve any cult of messianic personality into the transpersonal phenomenon of their own versions of future Buddhafields.

The master in all of his actions is a means for remembrance. The future will gauge the success of masters of the Aquarian Age when their final gift, their physical departure from this earth, works to liberate the disciples from attachment to their bodies, and the danger of becoming just another distortion called "the Messiah."

THE GREAT PARADOX

The crises foreseen for the early to mid 21st century will be global. The only option for safety is to turn one's attention within to that still and silent point where a constant state of consciousness witnesses the storming and ever-changing world without fear or identification.

In the end, to save the world we must save ourselves. The forest, like the concept of humanity, is an abstraction. There is no forest, there are only individual trees. There is no humanity, there are only individual human beings. If enough people seek their individual enlightenment, and understand how they each contribute their individual portion of unconsciousness to the world's woes, then a great paradox can happen. If there are enough people who share this insight – if they turn their intelligence away from the forest, as it were, and train their full love, awareness, and understanding toward becoming individually healthy trees – then the whole forest called "humanity" will be saved.

Many think that they must first put their affairs in order and then serve God. This is not right: serve God every minute, every hour and in all circumstances. If you want to put your life in order before serving God, you will lose your present favorable conditions.... Always remember that you are cords as fine as a spider's web. If these cords are not united, they will not withstand external storms and winds. Thousands of cords combined into a whole make something solid and durable. If you each live for yourself without becoming united, your strength will be equivalent to the web and you will accomplish only as much as the spider. If, however, you become united you will carry out the necessary work, for God's work is being done by many people and not simply by a single person. Many people are predestined to accomplish God's work.

PETER DEUNOV (1935), ROYL

The soul of each individual is a portion then of the Whole, with the birthright of Creative Forces to become a co-creator with the Father, a co-laborer with Him. As that birthright is then manifested, growth ensues.

EDGAR CAYCE (D. 1945), NO. 1549–1

The ills attributed to an anthropomorphic abstraction called "society" may be laid more realistically at the door of Everyman. Utopia must spring in the private bosom before it can flower in civic virtue. Man is a soul, not an institution; his inner reforms alone can lend permanence to outer ones.

PARAMHANSA YOGANANDA (1945), AUTO

You are the world.... Be alert not to contribute anything that makes the world a hell. And remember to contribute to the world something that makes it a paradise. This is the whole secret of a religious man. And if every individual starts doing it, there will be a revolution without any bloodshed.

OSHO (1986), SRM

Good people from all parts of the Earth will lend each other a hand and will unite in the name of divine love, wisdom and truth. And they will bring in the new culture with all its benefits and achievements. Great is the future of the Earth. God is manifesting in the world.

PETER DEUNOV (1940), NWDY

You are the only hope! So don't keep your joy to yourself, spread it, make it available to anybody.

OSHO (1985), FTOT

The great unselfish love for humanity is bounded by none of these imperfect, semi-selfish bonds; this is the one perfect love, possible to all mankind, and can only be achieved by the power of the Divine Spirit. No worldly power can accomplish the universal love.
Let all be united in this Divine power of love! Let all strive to grow in the light of the Sun of Truth, and reflecting this luminous love on all men, may their hearts become so united that they may dwell evermore in the radiance of the limitless love.

'ABDU'L-BAHÁ (1911), PARIS 9:14, 15

Truth not only saves you, it also saves others through you. Truth not only becomes freedom to you, it becomes a door of freedom for many others also. If you become a light, it is not only your life that will be lighted – if you become a light then you also become a light for millions; many can travel and reach their goal through you. If you become a light, you become a representative, you become a Christ.

I don't want you to become Christians – that is useless, that is a lie. I would like you to become Christs. And you can become Christs, because you have the same seed.

OSHO (1974), MST

Mankind is the Avatar.

ADI DA SAMRAJ (1974), GARB

EPILOGUE:
CHILDHOOD'S END

There is one Eternal Law in Nature, one that always tends to adjust contraries, and to produce final harmony. It is owing to this Law of spiritual development superseding the physical and purely intellectual, that mankind will become freed from its false Gods, and find itself finally – Self-redeemed.

H. P. BLAVATSKY (1888), SCDOC

In this Aquarian Age, when minds become opened to the infinite, so much will be revealed as to make earlier strides seem puny indeed. Meditation unlocks the door, and those who learn properly to give themselves surcease and relief from turmoil through this quieting of the mind and spirit will progress rapidly.

SPIRIT GUIDES OF RUTH MONTGOMERY (1976), WBF

The ascent of man into heaven is not the key, but rather his ascent here into the spirit and the descent also of the spirit into his normal humanity and the transformation of this earthly nature. For that and not some post mortem salvation is the real new birth for which humanity waits as the crowning movement of its long, obscure and painful course.

SRI AUROBINDO (BEF. 1950), LFDV

[To] those then that are come into the new life, the new understanding, the new regeneration, there is then the New Jerusalem...not as a place alone but as a condition, as an experience of the soul. Jerusalem has figuratively, symbolically, meant the holy place, the Holy City – for there, the Ark of the Covenant in the minds, the hearts, the understandings, the comprehensions of those who have put away the earthly desires and become as the new purposes in their experience, become the New Jerusalem, the new undertakings, the new desires.

EDGAR CAYCE (D. 1945), NO. 281–37

It is possible that a time will come when we will forget that there was a Krishna, a Mahavira, a Christ or a Buddha – but religion will not be destroyed as long as man has the thirst and quest for bliss within him, as long as man wants to rise above unhappiness.

OSHO (1965), PTHM

It may be that one of the greatest conspiracies against human beings has been the programming that convinces us that we as individuals cannot influence our collective destiny. But the need for human survival runs deeper than all the conditioning of the past.

The claim will be made that humanity never needed to grow up until faced with the unprecedented challenges of the 21st century. Up to the new millennium we could get along with a social structure that needed people to be functional mediocrities, and so ignored their potential for genius and Christlike consciousness.

It is foretold that traditional solutions will be discarded in the 21st century. The humanity of the future will celebrate innovation and find the courage to embrace the unknown. Armed with this new understanding forged in crisis, they will find their way out of the apocalypse of ecological disasters, fire, and war in the 2020s. They will awaken from the messianic pathology imposed upon them by a past-oriented society that could exist only by exploiting people's limitations, superstitions, and fears.

The coming stresses are predicted to destroy such a society. Humanity will therefore face the death of its past so that it can have a future.

By the end of the 21st century, the Second Coming syndrome will fade away. We will see men and women of tomorrow, who have grown out of their childhood attachments to imaginary friends, gods, and sons of gods, and have matured into aware and responsible individuals.

Our descendants will have discovered that no messiah outside of themselves is coming. Instead the Messiah descends to earth from his hiding place behind their worrying eyes. He walks the earth using their own feet. He speaks in a billion voices. He saves the world through their actions, their love, and their willingness to abandon belief and trust in the unknown. Where they were once Christians, they now seek to be Christs. The Messiah is in actuality their collective awakening to their true natures.

At the dawn of the 22nd century, humanity comes of age – the Golden Age.

There will be a time when the world will have no use for armies, hypocritical religions, and degenerate art.

Life is evolution and evolution is development from the simple to the more complicated forms of the mind and body.

I see the passing show of the world drama in its present form, how it fades like the glow of evening upon the mountains.

LEO TOLSTOY (1910)

APPENDIX
SEERS' ENCYCLOPEDIA

Every prophecy in this book is followed by its source. This section contains a short biographical sketch for each prophet quoted.

'ABDU'L-BAHÁ (1844–1921) is the eldest son and successor of Bahá'u'lláh, the Persian founder of the Bahá'í religion. Upon the death of his father, he assumed full authority for the Baha'í movement as the interpreter of the teachings. 'Abdu'l-Bahá means "Servant of Bahá [glory]."

ADI DA SAMRAJ (b. 1939), born Franklin Albert Jones in Long Island, New York, studied philosophy and religion at Columbia University and Stanford University. In 1964 he met his first guru, American Swami Rudrananda ("Rudi"), and later took up spiritual practice with Rudi's guru, Swami Muktananda, in Ganeshpuri, India, where he underwent further expansions of consciousness.

He began teaching and giving darshan in early 1972, and in 1973 took the name Bubba Free John, inaugurating the second, more Tantric stage of his teaching work. In 1979 he dropped the casual "Bubba" for "Da" (an invocatory syllable derived from both Sanskrit and Tibetan Buddhist sources) and Da Free John took on a more formal and murtilike relationship with his devotees (that is, the guru acting as a living icon reflecting the forgotten divinity of the worshipers). By the mid-1980s, he had published some 40 books and established three ashrams, in Fiji, California, and Hawaii. Early in 1986 he underwent a transformation that he described as a fuller "descent" of the divine into his human vehicle. This inaugurated the third stage of his teaching, after which he called himself Da Love Ananda and, for a brief time, Da Kalki, suggesting that he is the fulfillment of Hindu prophecy of the tenth and final avatar (although he has since renounced some aspects of this association).

He currently lives in semiseclusion at Ruchira Buddhadam – his spiritual campus on the Fijian island of Naitauba. Devotees around the world live in communal houses, practice his teachings, and meditate daily before his picture. In 1995, he changed his name to Adi Da Samraj to celebrate a new deepening of the collective love and consciousness of his disciples.

ALI (602–661 C.E.) was the nephew of the Prophet Muhammad and founder of the Shi'ite sect of Islam.

AMBRES is an entity purported to be channeled by a modern-day Swedish carpenter named Sturé Johansson, who is known for his ability to pluck highly successful medical remedies and otherworldly insights out of trance states. Johansson obtained world renown during the 1980s through the patronage of Hollywood actress Shirley MacLaine. Ambres was introduced to the greater world through MacLaine's best-selling book and movie adaptation of her spiritual search, entitled *Out on a Limb*.

ANANDAMAYI MA (1896–1982). East Bengali mystic whose name in Sanskrit means "Joy-Permeated Mother."

SRI AUROBINDO (1872–1950). Bengali mystic, born in Calcutta, India. Educated in England, he graduated from Kings College, Cambridge, in 1892. Afterward he returned to India and became a political and spiritual revolutionary. In 1908 the British colonial government arrested him as a suspect in a bombing. After his release he established an ashram in Pondicherry in 1910.

BAHÁ'U'LLÁH (1817–1892), also known as Mírzá Husayn 'Alí. Iranian mystic who took on the Persian name meaning "Glory of God" after assuming the role of chief patriarch and spiritual messiah of Bahá'í, an offshoot of Islam.

THE VENERABLE BARTHOLOMAEUS VON HOLTZHAUSER was a 17th-century German professor of theology, pastor of St. Johann's Church in the Tyrol (Austria), and spiritual adviser to the court of Johann Philipp, Elector of Mayence.

H. P. BLAVATSKY (1831–1891), famous 19th-century Russian occultist, was born in Ekaterinoslav, Russia. After early marriage and separation, she traveled extensively, visiting temples, ruins, and centers of religious learning. In 1873 she settled in New York City, where she was the toast of spiritualist circles. During this time "Madame" Blavatsky met Colonel H. S. Olcott, with whom she founded the Theosophical Society. Later, the two moved to the society's main headquarters to Madras, India.

BUDDHA GAUTAMA SIDDHARTHA (563?–483? B.C.E.), the founder of Buddhism, was born Gautama Siddhartha near the town of Kapilavasta in what is now Nepal, near the Indian border. He was the son of an aristocratic Hindu chieftain of the second warrior caste. Astrologers predicted that he would either become a great world conqueror or a great Buddha (awakened master). At the age of 29, Gautama abandoned his protected, princely life and became a wandering mendicant. After six years of tremendous effort, he became enlightened, but only when he realized that all efforts to obtain realization are futile. As "the Buddha" (awakened one), Gautama taught that buddhahood is the birthright of all people. It is not an achievement, but merely a relaxation into the truth of one's being.

EDGAR CAYCE (1877–1945) was one of the most significant psychic healers and prophets of the 20th century. He was born near Hopkinsville, Kentucky. The Hearst newspaper syndicate labeled him "America's Sleeping Prophet" because he gave most of his psychic readings while reclining on a couch in a sleeplike trance.

DANIEL was an Old Testament prophet who may be a composite of several people. The first could be the King Daniel of an Ugaritic legend of the 14th century B.C.E.; the second, the example (along with Noah and Job) of a righteous man in Ezekiel 14:14; and the third, the wise man who knows secrets in Ezekiel 28:3. In Chapters 1-6 of the Book of Daniel, our prophet is a young Jew at a foreign court, divining royal dreams as a vizier of kings; yet in Chapters 8-12 it is the angels themselves who must interpret his own dreams.

DEGUCHI NAO (1836–1918) was a Japanese seeress and religious matriarch of the Omoto sect.

PETER DEUNOV (1864–1944) was a Bulgarian Christian mystic and proponent of a culture based on Christ's love and forgiveness rather than traditional dogma. By the time of his death his followers numbered over 40,000, and there were 144 study circles in and around Bulgaria.

DEUTERONOMY ("second law" in Hebrew) was the last of three books in the Old Testament transcribed from the final discourses that the aged Jewish prophet Moses (c. 1300 B.C.E.) addressed to his assembled people just before his departure from Canaan to seek the lost tribe of Israel. South Asian occultists and mystics claim that the bones of Moses are entombed in Kashmir, India.

EZEKIEL, a priest and prophet of the Old Testament, began his ministry in the final years of the kingdom of Judah, which ended in the Babylonian captivity following the destruction of the Temple in 587 B.C.E.

PROPHECY OF FÁTIMA is a remarkably accurate prophetic message delivered to the eldest of three Portuguese children, Lucia dos Santos, by a luminous spirit purported to be the Virgin Mary. The children regularly met "the lady" in a field near the village of Fátima during a series of sightings from May 13 through October 13, 1917. So far the mysterious "Lady of Fátima" has accurately predicted the end of the First World War, the rise of Russian Communism, and the onset of the Second World War.

JOHANN FRIEDE (1204-1257), an Austrian monk of the order of St. John "of Revelation" and noted late medieval Christian prophet, was an apocalyptic seer considered by his contemporaries to be a prophetic successor to the namesake of his order.

G. I. GURDJIEFF (1866? 1872?-1949) was born in Alexandropol in Russian Armenia. For some 20 years, Gurdjieff traveled throughout the remote regions of Tibet, Central Asia, and the Middle East seeking teachers and mystery schools in his obsession to understand the secrets hiding beyond all of life's odd and mysterious phenomena. Gurdjieff began collecting disciples in Moscow just prior to World War I; however, the Russian Revolution thwarted his efforts to establish his Mystery School there. In 1922 he emigrated to France and reestablished his Institute for the Harmonious Development of Man at the Château du Prieuré, near Paris. Two years later he survived a serious car accident and disbanded the school, devoting himself to recording his teachings in three volumes: *Beelzebub's Tales to His Grandson*, *Meetings with Remarkable Men*, and finally, *Life Is Real Only Then When "I Am."* From 1933 onward he lived almost exclusively in Paris, teaching a small band of dedicated disciples at nightly meetings in his apartment.

MAX HEADROOM is fake – and therefore a perfect candidate for the first virtual-reality TV personality. The pioneering cyber-pundit, conversationalist, and raconteur sound-bited and data-streamed his way on TV in 1985 in an edgy, cutting-edge TV show that bore his name. He was the fictional cybernetic alter ego of a fictional flesh-and-blood video camera reporter, rooting for news in the garbage heap of an ecologically defunct but computer-happy negative future utopia. The TV executives tapped the exit key on Max Headroom's show in 1987, but Max is now online. He has appeared inside TVs sitting on chairs in MTV rock videos, and cable TV has rebooted his show on reruns.

HERMES TRISMEGISTUS. The founder of ancient Hermetic mystery schools in Egypt, Trismegistus was a philosopher – or a series of philosophers writing under his name – living in Alexandria sometime during the first few centuries after Christ.

HINDU PURANAS. A collection of religious scriptures written between 3000 B.C.E. and 1000 C.E. that makes up the third and final foundation (after the Vedas and Tantras) of the popular creed of the Brahmanical Hindus.

ADOLF HITLER (See "Messiahs Gallery: The Nazi Messiah," p. 37)

HOPI PROPHECIES (See "Signs of the End Times: Final Signs," p. 69)

GRANDFATHER SEMU HUARTE (1904–?), contemporary Native American medicine man of the Chumash tribe of Ojai, California.

FIRST ISAIAH. Chapters 1–39 of the Book of Isaiah in the Old Testament are attributed to the first of at least three writers using the prophet's name. This "first Isaiah" – also called "Isaiah of Jerusalem" – was an adviser to four kings of Judah: Uzziah, 783–742 B.C.E.; Jotham, 742–735 B.C.E.; Ahaz, 735–715 B.C.E.; and Hezekiah, 715–687 B.C.E.

SECOND ISAIAH. Scholars believe that Chapters 40–55 of the Book of Isaiah were written by an unknown author generally identified as the "second Isaiah," who made his prophetic mark toward the close of the exile in Babylon (587–539 B.C.E.).

THIRD ISAIAH. The final chapters (56–66) of the Book of Isaiah are descriptions from diverse authors using the "Isaiah" pseudonym during the post-Babylonian exile period.

AHMAD IBN HANBAL was a noted 9th-century fundamentalist Sunni scholar and Islamic prophetic interpreter.

H. H. KARMAPA RIGPE DORJE (1924–1982). As the 16th incarnation of the Lord of Tsurphu (the living Buddha), Karmapa Rigpe Dorje was head of the Karma Kagyu, one of the four main sects of Tibetan Buddhism. He was the third most influential lama in Tibet after the Panchen and Dalai Lama. The 16th Karmapa Lama died in 1982, 14 years after making the pronouncement reprinted in this book. Tibetan lamas say that he has since been "reincarnated" a 17th time in the body of a poor Tibetan shepherd in 1984. The boy is currently undergoing religious preparation to resume his role as head of the Karma Kagyu sect.

DAVID KORESH (See "Messiahs Gallery: 'The Sinful Messiah,'" p. 25)

JOHN THE ELDER. The purported author of three letters in the New Testament. An early 1st-century Christian elder whose writing style has similarities to the Apostle John's, but whose identity is still disputed.

ST. JOHN OF PATMOS is the author of the New Testament's unique and thoroughly apocalyptic document the Book of Revelation, written around 81–96 C.E. A Jewish convert to Christianity, he wrote his revelations of doom in a prison cave on the Greek island of Patmos. Most scholars believe his writing style proves beyond a doubt that he is not the Apostle John, although a number of staunchly fundamentalist Christian scholars argue that John of Patmos and John the Elder are the Apostle John.

JOHN OF VATIGUERRO is a 13th-century Christian seer – one of many who share a collective vision of the destruction of the Vatican in what sounds like either a thermonuclear or ecological holocaust.

KATE-ZAHL (See QUETZALCOATL.)

KEIRO (also spelled "Cheiro," 1866–1936) was a professional pseudonym (from the Greek word meaning "hand") used by British spy, womanizer, adventurer, and most importantly, one of the early 20th century's most accurate clairvoyants, the noted palmist Count Louis Hamon.

KRISHNA (c. 3000 B.C.E.) is the flute-playing and life-celebrating 8th avataric incarnation of Lord Vishnu – the middle deity in the Hindu holy trinity comprising Brahma the Creator, Vishnu the Preserver, and Shiva the Destroyer. Krishna's standing as an enlightened master is to the Hindu religion what Christ is to Christianity, and as with Christ, historians find it difficult to separate the mythical Lord Krishna from the historical person. He was said to be royal-born, yet raised as a cowherd. He figures prominently in many Vedic Puranas and in the Mahabharata saga. In the latter he is best known for his famous dialogue on enlightenment and pantheism with King Arjuna known as the Bhagavad Gita.

J. KRISHNAMURTI (1895–1986), a south Indian philosopher, was born in Andhra Pradesh. English occultist C. W. Leadbeater "discovered" the frail 13-year-old boy on a beach outside Madras. He later convinced Annie Besant and other leaders of the Theosophical movement that the purity of the young Brahmin's aura made him a possible vehicle for the soul of Lord Maitreya, the great world teacher foretold by Madame Blavatsky. In 1929, at age 34, Krishnamurti rejected any ideas that he was Maitreya and abandoned the Theosophists. He spent the next five decades traveling the world, speaking about the need for the individual to experience truth (as the witnessing consciousness) through self-observation.

THE MAHABHARATA (Sanskrit for "the Great Story"). One of the two massive epics in Hindu literature (the other being the Ramayana) compiled between 200 B.C.E.and the 1st century C.E. The 18 books of the Mahabharata make it eight times larger than Homer's Iliad and Odyssey put together.

MALACHI. The Book of Malachi in the Old Testament focuses primarily on the controversies and hardships suffered by Judeans between 500 and 450 B.C.E., after their return to the Holy Land from the Babylonian Captivity.

BLESSED SISTER MARY OF AGREDA was a beatified 17th-century nun from northeastern Spain.

MEICHI NOZAMA. This modern Japanese mystic claims to be the successor and spiritual "channel" to Meishu Sama.

MEISHU SAMA (1882–1955) was born Mokichi Okada in a Tokyo slum. As Meishu Sama he became one of Japan's most significant 20th-century prophets and mystics. His prophecies, New Age teachings, and regimens for healing and meditation parallel those of his American contemporary Edgar Cayce.

MERLIN (5th century C.E.) is England's most illustrious prophet. Historical opinion is divided on whether the magician immortalized in the legend of King Arthur's court was a real or mythical person.

METHODIUS. 4th-century Christian saint.

MICAH, a minor 8th-century Old Testament Judean prophet, was a younger contemporary of First Isaiah. Scholars believe only the first three chapters of the Book of Micah were actually written by him.

RUTH MONTGOMERY (1912–) is a contemporary American spirit channeler, journalist, and author of *A Gift of Prophecy*, the best-selling book exploring the life of modern American seeress Jeane Dixon. In the early 1970s Montgomery became a spirit medium in her own right, publishing a string of prophetic books based on messages sent to her through automatic typewriting from "higher spirits" whom she collectively called her "guides."

MUHAMMAD (570?–632), the prophet and founder of Islam, was born in Mecca and spent much of his youth traveling with the Meccan camel caravans. At 26 he married Khadijah, a wealthy widow nearly 15 years his senior, who made Muhammad her business manager. One day, while meditating in a cave in Mt. Hira, he beheld the angel Jabril (Gabriel), who declared him to be the only Prophet of the Living God. With the angel's guidance Muhammad dictated the Qu'ran, the Islamic holy book. Fearing his growing popularity, many diverse pagan factions in Mecca planned to assassinate Muhammad. He escaped with his followers to Medina, where he remained for eight years before he reconquered Mecca as the head of a large army, made it his holy city, and ordered all 350 pagan images within the sacred Kaaba shrine smashed to bits. He granted amnesty to all his enemies and dedicated the Kaaba to Allah, the monotheistic God of Islam.

GURU NANAK (1469–538), Indian religious leader, founder of Sikhism, and compiler of its sacred texts. He grew up critical of formal ritualistic expressions of both Islam and Hinduism. In 1499, after his spiritual enlightenment, he took to preaching Sikhism in the Punjab, throughout India, and beyond until 1521, when he settled in a Punjabi village he himself founded, called Kartapur. There he lived until his death at the age of 69.

JOHN BALLOU NEWBROUGH, born in 1827 in Mohickinsville, Ohio, was a gold prospector in his youth and a resident doctor in an insane asylum in his thirties. He abandoned medicine to become a spirit medium in New York City. His contemporaries considered Newbrough the country's greatest 19th-century prophet.

NICHIREN (1222–1282). Buddhist reformer and prophet of Japan who founded the Nichiren school (or "New Lotus" school) of Japanese Buddhism.

NOSTRADAMUS (1503–1566), the Latinized nickname of Michel de Nostredame. A physician, author, cosmetics creator, and noted healer of the 16th century, he was responsible for almost single-handedly healing three cities afflicted with the bubonic plague in the 1540s. Nostradamus later retired to Salon, Provence, to write his enigmatic prophetic masterpiece, *Les Prophéties*. His prodigious output of nearly 1,500 predictions has made him the most famous and controversial prophet of the last four and a half centuries.

OSHO (1931–1990), a.k.a. "Archarya" or "Bhagwan Shree" Rajneesh, was born Rajneesh Chandra Mohan in Kuchwada, a small village in central India. He received his M.A from the University of Sagar in 1956, with first-class honors in philosophy. He was a professor at the Sanskrit College in Raipur and later was professor of philosophy at the University of Jabalpur. At the beginning of the 1970s, he took the name Bhagwan Shree Rajneesh and in 1974 established a spiritual commune in Pune, India, which attracted tens of thousands of seekers from the West.

In 1981 Bhagwan traveled to the U.S., where he lived among thousands of disciples in the eastern Oregon commune Rajneeshpuram (1981–1985). Christian fundamentalist elements in Oregon and in the highest echelons of the Reagan administration brought heavy political pressure to bear to prevent the expansion of the city. In 1985 Bhagwan was arrested without a warrant on charges of immigration fraud and was held without bail for 12 days. After being forced to plea-bargain, he was deported to India. His followers believe that he was poisoned in jail with thallium, a heavy metal that led to his rapid physical decline and death by 1990.

Between February and July 1986 he embarked on a world tour to share his vision. As a result of U.S. pressure and threats, 21 countries in Europe and the Americas either refused to grant him a visitor's visa or revoked his visa upon his arrival, in some cases at gunpoint. Bhagwan returned to India and resumed his discourses before thousands of disciples at the Pune Ashram.

In September 1989, nine months before he died, he changed his name to "Osho," signifying his complete discontinuity from the past. It is less a name than a sacred acronym for "Mr.," derived from Zen disciples' salutation to their masters; it also stands for the "oceanic" and orgasmic experience of spiritual enlightenment and refers to the one who experiences this state, the individual.

PADMASAMBHAVA was the 8th-century C.E. founder of Tibetan Buddhism. He was also known as the Lotus-Born, or the Precious Guru. In 748 C.E. he left the great Buddhist University of Nalanda to bring the Dharma to the Himalayas. He is also responsible for creating the Tibetan system of astrology.

THE PSALMS are a collection of 150 poems in the Old Testament said to be written by "the sages of Israel."

QUETZALCOATL (a.k.a. Kate-Zahl/Pale Prophet) was the pre-Columbian Aztec messiah and lawgiver who lived around the 1st century C.E. The Toltec Indians of central Mexico consider him their greatest prophet.

RAGNARÖK. Ancient Norse prophecy (c. 1000 C.E.), the Viking Armageddon.

NIKOLAS K. ROERICH (1874–1947) was a Russian émigré, explorer, poet, and artist who designed the costumes and sets for the premier performance of Igor Stravinsky's *The Rite of Spring* in 1913. Roerich developed an abiding interest in Tibetan mysticism and led several expeditions to the roof of the world. He was one of Tibet's first and most important Western emissaries. His many books and paintings helped spread the myth of Shangri-la and the prophecies of Shambhala to a wide Western audience.

SAUL OF TARSUS (a.k.a. St. Paul) was a Jewish Roman citizen from Cilicia, Tarsus, and one of the more zealous Pharisees aiding the Romans in persecuting and seeking the execution of Christians. While on his witch-hunt, traveling down the hot desert road to Damascus, he claimed to have had a vision of Christ and thereby made a complete conversion to Christianity. Although he never met his master in the flesh, Saul henceforth directed his prodigious zeal and charisma as. Christianity's first evangelist "Paul" (later canonized as "St. Paul" by the Catholic Church), and spread the faith to the Gentile (non-Jewish) world. Some scholars point out that Y'shua's twin brother, James, as well as most of the original Apostles, considered Paul a heretic for changing the focus of Y'shua's mission away from a Jewish religious revolution. Paul would later incur criticism from early Church fathers, such as Tertullian, for gaining Gentile converts by encouraging the incorporation of the pagan religious myths and customs they favored. Paul's credibility with the early Christian community was greatly enhanced when Simon the Zealot (a.k.a. St. Peter) sided with him. Paul made numerous journeys across the Roman world, preaching his reformed gospel through important letters. Both he and Peter faced martyrdom in Rome by Emperor Nero in 64 C.E..

THE PROPHECY OF SHAMBHALA is a set of apocalyptic prophecies of various Tibetan Himalayan, and Mongolian cultures appearing around 1,000 years ago. (See "Messiahs Gallery: King of Shambhala" p. 30)

SIBYLLINE ORACLES (2nd century B.C.E.–3rd century C.E.). In classical legend, a Sibyl is a woman inspired with prophetic insight by Apollo. During the Roman Empire certain prophetic verses known as Sibylline oracles surfaced. These played an important role in Roman religious thinking. A further wave of Sibylline oracles, written in Greek verse, came into the possession of Greek and Latin priests of the early Christian Church. They are said to come from an inspired prophetess from Babylon, and contain accurate predictions concerning the rise of Christianity and the coming apocalypse.

SIMON THE ZEALOT (a.k.a. ST. PETER). Apostle of Y'shua. New revelations in biblical scholarship suggest that Peter at first supported the succession of Y'shua's twin brother, James, as the Messiah after the presumed death of Y'shua. Peter later grew disenchanted with James and cast his influential lot with the more evangelical camp of Saul of Tarsus (St. Paul). Scholars theorized that Peter's action had a major influence in shaping the future of Christianity toward a "Pauline," pro-Gentile bias. In this way Peter fulfilled his destiny as Y'shua predicted by setting the foundation of the future Church. The Catholic Church considers him the first bishop of Rome, the place where he was crucified upside-down in 64 C.E..

THE SRIMAD BHAGAVATA PURANA. One of the 18 Vedic Hindu Mahapuranas (great narratives of ancient times). Compilation of the Puranic literature took place from 6th century B.C.E. through the 12th century C.E.

MADAME SYLVIA. Twentieth-century Viennese-German seeress (d. 1948).

TAMO-SAN (b. 1907), or the Reverend Ryoju Kikuchi of Kamakura, is well known in Japan as an enlightened mystic and early champion of ecology. Tamo-san is the founder of the Buddhist sect named Butsu gan syuu ("the eyes of the Buddha"), which was officially recognized by the Japanese government in 1951 – the first new religious sect to receive government approval.

THE APOCALYPSE OF THOMAS appeared around the 5th century C.E. and is considered part of the New Testament Apocrypha. Following the apocalyptic tradition of St. John of Revelation, a Christian mystic called Thomas recounts Christ's description of the last seven days of human life on earth.

THE BOOK OF THOMAS THE CONTENDER is a 3rd-century C.E. Gnostic scripture supposedly written by a Christian

mystic named Mathaias (the Apostle Matthew), who recorded a purported dialogue between his twin brother, Judas Thomas, and the resurrected Jesus Christ.

THE GOSPEL OF THOMAS. One of a number of Gnostic Christian and Coptic Christian scriptures written on papyrus, secreted away in a clay jar unearthed in 1945 from the Nag Hammadi region of Upper Egypt. The Gospel contains 114 sayings said to be those of Jesus Christ as transcribed by the Apostle Thomas.

RABBI HILE WECHSLER (1843–1894), an Orthodox Jewish rabbi from Bavaria, who published a pamphlet titled "A Word of Warning" in 1873. In it Wechsler tried to warn European Jewry of the coming Holocaust 60 years before Hitler and the Nazis took power in Germany.

PARAMHANSA YOGANANDA (1893–1952). This mystic from Calcutta, India – best known for his book *The Autobiography of a Yogi* – had come to the West to establish the "golden middle path" of Kriya Yoga, a yogic discipline helping its practitioners balance spirit and material energies in their daily lives. He spent the last 20 years of his life shuttling between India and the Western Hemisphere establishing a network of Kriya Yoga centers under the auspices of the Self-Realization Fellowship in India and America.

Y'SHUA BAR YOSSEPH, a.k.a. Jesus Christ, (4? B.C.E.–29? C.E.), believed by Christians to be the "only begotten son of God" and the Messiah. Y'shua the Christ reappears in biblical chronicles at the age of 30. After three years, his volatile ministry earned him condemnation and crucifixion in Jerusalem. The legend that he rose from the dead after three days is the foundation of all Christian belief. Most of Y'shua's prophecies were not written down until many years after his crucifixion, and there is every possibility that they were extensively revised by the Council of Nicaea. However, this would make the revisionists prophets in their own right, since many of Y'shua's forecasts resemble events in modern times.

FIRST ZECHARIAH. One of the most enigmatic of the Old Testament prophets, scholars believed Zechariah's first and second books were written by two different men. The first chapters (1–8) were penned in Jerusalem during the time following the exile to Babylon (c. 450–500 B.C.E.).

SECOND ZECHARIAH. The author of the second book (Chapters 9–14) wrote them after the Maccabean War, which drew to a close around 160 B.C.E.

SELECTED
BIBLIOGRAPHY

'Abdu'l-Bahá. *Paris Talks*. London: Bahá'í Publishing Trust, 1944.

_____. *Selections from the Writings of 'Abdu'l-Bahá*. Haifa: Bahá'í World Center, 1978.

_____. *The Promulgation of Universal Peace*. Wilmette, IL: Bahá'í Publishing Trust, 1982.

Adi Da Samraj. *See My Brightness Face to Face: A Celebration of the Ruchira Buddha, Avatar Adi Da Samraj, and the First 25 years of His Divine Revelation Work*. Middletown, CA: Dawn Horse Press, 1998.

Ambres. *Ambres*. Torsby, Sweden: A. B. Sturid, 1992.

Anandamayi Ma. *Shri, Matri Darshan, Mangalam*. Lautersheim, Germany: Verlag L. Schang, 1983.

Attar, Farid al-Din. *Muslim Saints and Mystics*. London: Arkana, 1990.

Aurobindo, Sri. *The Life Divine*. Pondicherry, India: Sri Aurobindo Ashram, 1996.

Bahá'u'lláh. *The Kitáb-Í-Íqán (The Book of Certaintude)*. Translated by Shoghi Effendi. Wilmette, IL: Bahá'í Publishing Trust, 1960.

_____. *A Synopsis and Codification of the Laws and Ordinances of the Kitab-i-Aqdas, The Most Holy Book of Bahá'u'lláh*. Compiled by the Universal House of Justice. Haifa: Bahá'í World Center, 1973.

_____. *Bahá'u'lláh*. Translated by Shoghi Effendi. London: Bahá'í Publishing Trust, 1991.

Barkun, Michael. *Religion and the Racist Right: Origins of the Christian Identity Movement*. Chapel Hill: University of North Carolina Press, 1994.

Barnstone, Willis, ed. *The Other Bible: Ancient esoteric texts including Jewish Pseudepigrapha, Christian Apocrypha, Gnostic Scriptures, Kabbalah, Dead Sea Scrolls*. San Francisco: HarperSanFrancisco (A Div. of HarperCollins), 1984.

Bernbaum, Edwin. *The Way to Shambhala: A Search for the Mythical Kingdom beyond the Himalayas*. Garden City, NJ: Anchor Press/Doubleday, 1980.

Blavatsky, H. P. *The Secret Doctrine*. Madras: Theosophical Publishing House, 1888.

Boissière, Robert. *The Return of Pahana: A Hopi Myth*. Santa Fe: Bear & Co., 1990.

Bonder, Saniel. *The Divine Emergence of the World-Teacher: The Realization, the Revelation, and the Revealing Ordeal of Da Kalki; a Biographical Celebration of Heart-Master Da Love-Ananda*. Clearlake, CA: Dawn Horse Press, 1990.

Boyd, Doug. *Rolling Thunder*. New York: Random House, 1974.

Brecher, Max. *A Passage to America: A Radically New Look at Bhagwan Shree Rajneesh and a Controversial American Commune*. Bombay: Book Quest, 1993.

Carrasco, David. *Quetzalcoatl and the Irony of Empire: Myths and Prophecies in the Aztec Tradition*. Chicago: University of Chicago Press, 1982.

Cheiro, Count Louis Hamon. *Cheiro's World Predictions*. Santa Fe: Sun Books/Sun Publishing, 1981.

Crowley, Aleister. *The Confessions of Aleister Crowley: An Autohagiography*. Edited by John Symonds and Kenneth Grant. London: Arkana, 1989.

Cumont, Franz. *The Mysteries of Mithra*. New York: Dover, 1956.

Donnelly, Ignatius. *Ragnarok: The Age of Fire and Gravel*. New York: University Books, 1970.

Ebon, Martin. *Prophecy in Our Time*. New York: New American Library, 1968.

Edmonds, I. G. *Second Sight: People Who Read the Future*. New York: Thomas Nelson, 1977.

Ellerbe, Helen. *The Dark Side of Christian History*. San Rafael, CA: Morningstar Books, 1995.

Elsmore, Bronwyn. *Mana from Heaven: A Century of Maori Prophets in New Zealand*. Tauranga, New Zealand: Moana Press, 1989.

Esslemont, J. E. *Bahá'u'lláh and the New Era*. Wilmette, IL: Bahá'í Publishing Trust, 1966.

Fisher, Joe. *Predictions*. Toronto: Collins, 1980.

Flynn, Ted and Maureen. *The Thunder of Justice: The Warning, The Miracle, The Chastisement, The Era of Peace*. Sterling, VA: Maxkol Communications, 1993.

Forman, Henry James. *The Story of Prophecy in the Life of Mankind*. New York: Tudor, 1940.

_____. *Garbage and the Goddess*. Lowerlake, CA: Dawn Horse Press, 1974.

Free John, Da. *The Enlightenment of the Whole Body*. Middletown, CA: Dawn Horse Press, 1978.

Gale-Kumar, Kristina. *The Phoenix Returns: Aquarius Dawns, Liberation Begins*. Hawaii: Cardinal Enterprises, 1983.

_____. *The Scriptures Are Fulfilled*. Hawaii: Cardinal Enterprises, 1991.

Gattey, Charles Neilson. *Visionaries and Seers*. Dorset, England: Prism Press, 1977.

_____. *Prophecy and Prediction in the 20th Century*. Wellingborough, England: Aquarian Press, 1989.

Gilbert, Adrian G. *The Mayan Prophecies: Unlocking the Secrets of a Lost Civilization*. Shaftesbury, England: Element Books, 1995.

Gilbert, R. A. *Casting the First Stone: The Hypocrisy of Religious Fundamentalism and Its Threat to Society*. Shaftesbury, England: Element Books, 1993.

Glass, Justine. *They Foresaw the Future*. New York: G. P. Putnam's Sons, 1969.

Goodrick-Clarke, Nicholas. *The Occult Roots of Nazism: Secret Aryan Cults and Their Influence on Nazi Ideology*. New York: New York University Press, 1992.

Gurdjieff, G. I. *All and Everything: Beelzebub's Tales to His Grandson*. New York: Arkana, 1985.

_____. *Views from the Real World: Early Talks in Moscow, Essentuki, Tiflis, Berlin, London, Paris, New York and Chicago as Precollected by His Pupils*. New York: Dutton, 1975.

Hall, Angus. *Signs of Things to Come*. London: Danbury Press/Aldus Books, 1975.

Hall, Manley P. *The Secret Teachings of All the Ages: An Encyclopedic Outline of Masonic, Hermetic, Qabbalistic and Rosicrucian Symbolical Philosophy. Being an Interpretation of the Secret Teachings Concealed within the Rituals, Allegories and Mysteries of All Ages*. Los Angeles: Philosophical Research Society, 1977.

Hansen, David, with Paul Owen. *Max Headroom's Guide to Life*. New York: Bantam Books, 1986.

Hansen, L. Taylor. *He Walked the Americas*. Amherst, WI: Legend Press, 1997.

Hassell, Max. *Prophets without Honor*. New York: Ace Books, 1971.

Haught, James A. *Holy Horrors: An Illustrated History of Religious Murder and Madness.* Buffalo: Prometheus Books, 1990.

Hazra, R. C. *Studies in the Puranic Records on Hindu Rites and Customs.* Delhi: Motilal Banarsidass, 1975.

Hitler, Adolf. *Hitler's Secret Conversations* (1941–1944). New York: Farrar, Straus and Young, 1953.

Holzer, Hans. *Prophecies. Visions of the World's Fate: Truths, Possibilities, or Fallacies?* Chicago: Contemporary Books, 1995.

Hussain, Jassim M. *The Occultation of the Twelfth Imam.* London: Muhammadi Trust, 1982.

Ions, Veronica. *Indian Mythology.* New York: Paul Hamlyn, 1967.

Jewish Publication Society of America. *The Prophets: A New Translation of the Holy Scriptures According to the Traditional Hebrew Text, NEVI'IM.* Philadelphia: Jewish Publication Society of America, 1978.

Jochmans, J. R. *Rolling Thunder: The Coming Earth Changes.* Santa Fe: Sun Books/Sun Publishing, 1986.

Kay, Tom. *When the Comet Runs: Prophecies for the New Millennium.* Charlottesville: Hampton Roads, 1997.

Kikuchi, Rev. Ryoju Tamo-san. *Moor the Boat.* Kamakura, Japan: 1960.

Kirsch, James. *The Reluctant Prophet.* Los Angeles: Sherbourne Press, 1973.

Knapp, Stephen. *The Vedic Prophecies: A New Look into the Future, Eastern Answers to the Mysteries of Life, Vol III.* World Relief Network, 1997.

Krishnamurti, J. *The Future Is Now: Last Talks in India.* San Francisco: Harper & Row, 1989.

_____. *Life Ahead.* New York: Harper & Row, 1963.

_____. *You Are the World.* New York: Harper & Row, 1972.

Lindsey, Hal. *The Late, Great Planet Earth.* New York: Bantam Books, 1981.

_____. *There's a New World Coming.* New York: Bantam Books, 1975.

_____. *The 1980's: Countdown to Armageddon.* New York: Bantam Books, 1981.

Lorimer, David, ed. *Prophet for Our Times: The Life & Teachings of Peter Deunov.* Shaftesbury, England: Element Books, 1991.

McGinn, Bernard. *Anti-christ: Two Thousand Years of the Human Fascination with Evil.* New York: HarperCollins, 1994.

Mayer, Jane, and Doyle McManus. *Landslide: The Unmaking of the President 1984–1988.* Boston: Houghton Mifflin, 1988.

Montgomery, Ruth. *Aliens Among Us.* New York: Fawcett Crest, 1985.

_____. *A World Before.* New York: Fawcett Crest, 1976.

_____. *Strangers Among Us.* New York: Fawcett Crest, 1979.

Osho. *The Book of Wisdom, Volume 1: Discourses on Atisha's Seven Points of Mind Training.* Rajneeshpuram, OR: Rajneesh Foundation International, 1983.

_____. *Christianity the Deadliest Poison & Zen the Antidote to All Poisons.* Cologne: Rebel Publishing House GmbH.

_____. *From Bondage to Freedom: Answers to Seekers of the Path.* Cologne: Rebel Publishing House GmbH, 1989.

_____. *From the Darkness to Light: Answers to the Seekers of the Path.* Cologne: Rebel Publishing House GmbH.

_____. *From the False to the Truth: Answers to the Seekers of the Path.* Cologne: Rebel Publishing House GmbH.

_____. *Glimpses of a Golden Childhood: The Rebellious Childhood of a Great Enlightened One.* Cologne: Rebel Publishing House GmbH, 2nd ed.

_____. *I am the Gate: The Meaning of Initiation and Discipleship.* San Francisco: Harper & Row, 1977.

_____. *The Mustard Seed.* New York: Harper & Row, 1975.

_____. *The Great Zen Master Ta Hui.* Cologne: Rebel Publishing House GmbH.

_____. *Showering Without Clouds.* Pune, India: Rebel Publishing House GmbH, 1998.

_____. *Socrates: Poisoned Again After 25 Centuries.* Cologne: Rebel Publishing House GmbH, 1988.

Ouspensky, P. D. *In Search of the Miraculous.* London: Harvest/HBJ, 1977.

Parfrey, Adam. *Cult Rapture: Exposé on the Oklahoma City Bombing.* Portland: Feral House, 1995.

Peterson, Scot. *Native American Prophecies.* New York: Paragon House, 1990.

Prieditis, Arthur. *The Fate of the Nations: Nostradamus' Vision of the Age of Aquarius.* St. Paul: Llewellyn Publications, 1982.

Qaddafi, Muammar. *Escape to Hell and Other Stories.* New York: Stanké, 1998.

Reavis, Dick J. *The Ashes of Waco: An Investigation.* New York: Simon & Schuster, 1995.

Robb, Stewart. *Strange Prophecies that Came True.* New York: Ace Books, 1967.

Roerich, Nicholas. *Altai-Himalaya: A Travel Diary.* Brookfield, CT: Arun Press, 1983.

Robinson, James M., gen. ed. *The Nag Hammadi Library in English.* New York: Harper & Row, 1988.

_____. *Shambhala: In Search of the New Era.* Rochester, VT: Inner Traditions International, 1930.

Schonfield, Dr. Hugh J. *The Passover Plot: A New Interpretation of the Life and Death of Jesus.* New York: Bernard Geis Associates, 1965.

Spengler, Oswald. *The Decline of the West: Form and Actuality, Vols. I & II.* Translated by Charles Francis Atkinson. New York: Alfred A. Knopf, 1939.

_____. *Prophecies & Predictions: Everyone's Guide to the Coming Changes.* Santa Cruz: Unity Press, 1980.

Timms, Moira. *Beyond Prophecies and Predictions: Everyone's Guide to the Coming Changes.* New York: Ballantine Books, 1994.

Tobias, Michael. *World War III: Population and the Biosphere at the End of the Millennium.* Santa Fe: Bear & Co., 1994.

Tsogyal, Yeshe. *The Legend of the Great Stupa: The Life Story of the Lotus Born Guru.* Translated by Keith Dowman. Berkeley: Dharma Publishing, 1973.

Vaughan, Alan. *Patterns in Prophecy.* New York: Hawthorn Books, 1973.

Willoya, William, and Vinson Brown. *Warriors of the Rainbow: Strange and Prophetic Dreams of the Indian Peoples.* Happy Camp, CA: Naturegraph Publishers, 1987.

Zimdars-Swartz, Sandra L. *Encountering Mary: Visions of Mary from La Salette to Medjugorje.* New York: Avon Books, 1991.

INDEX

A
Abbasid caliphs 67
'Abdu'l-Bahá 12, 85, 95, 162, 168, 171, 205–6, 212, 226, 245
Adi Da Samraj12, 104, 166, 200, 202, 245
Adventists 144
Aeon Child, the Occult Messiah 33
Age of Iron and Chaos *see* Kali yuga
Agreda, Bl. Sister Mary of 58, 94
al-Aqsa mosque *see* Dome of the Rock
al-Hillaj Mansoor 171, 205
al-Mahdi *see* Muntazar
al-Qa'im/al-Sufyani/al-Yamani 67
Alboim, Rabbi David Yosef 65
Alexander the Great 173
Ali, nephew of Muhammad 32, 93, 103
Allah 32, 169, 171, 172
Ambres 221, 225
Amida Buddha 35
Ananda 172
Anandamayi Ma 12, 218, 223
Andropov, Soviet Premier 132
Angel Moroni 26
Antarctica 56, 62
Antichrist 9, 59, 73, 76–7, 89, 95
    see also Beast, The
Apocalypse of Thomas 144
Applewhite, Herf ('Do') 142, 143
Arghati King, the Ruler of the World *see* Shambhala, king of
Armageddon 23, 59, 63–4, 79, 122–35
Ashahara, Shoko 134
Augustus, Emperor 84
Aum Shinrikyo 134
Aurobindo, Sri 12, 133, 246, 248
Aztecs 26, 28

B
Bahá'u'lláh 12, 113, 123, 168, 171, 181
Balder, the Viking Redeemer 24
Bartholomaeus, Pastor 92
Beast, The 76, 89–90, 91, 99, 125
    see also Antichrist
Berchtesgaden 60
Besant, Annie 104
Bethlehem 22, 84–5
Bible 12, 129
Black Elk 29
Blavatsky, H. P. 12, 104, 112, 246, 248
Bodhidharma 171
Boissière, Robert 108
Book of Mormon 26
Book of Revelation 25, 76
Branch Davidians 25
Buddha Gautama 35, 75, 101, 106, 145, 162–4, 169, 191, 207, 238–9
    death 112, 171
    prophecy abbreviations 12
    reinvention 172–4, 210–11
    salvation 186
    Second Coming 117
    union 225
    wheel of Samsara 201
Buddhafields 230–45
Buddhism 35, 49, 108, 112, 125, 172
Bush, President George 131

C
Carter, Jimmy/Rosalynn 143
Catholicism 58–60, 62, 93, 127
Cayce, Edgar 12, 60, 115, 165, 244, 246
Cheiro *see* Keiro
China 45, 55, 57, 66, 108

Christian Apocrypha 12
Christian Coalition 122
Christian Identity 134
Christianity 84–91, 142–3, 156–7, 173
    Armageddonomics 122, 125, 127, 130–2, 134–5
    Catholicism 58–60, 62, 93, 127
    Eastern 62
Clinton, President Bill 49, 131–2
'cobweb' prophecy 69
cohanim (the priestly caste) 65
Cold War 132
Columbus, Christopher 45, 62
Concerned Christians 134
Constantine, Emperor 172
Cortés, Hernando 28, 45
Crowley, Aleister 33, 39

D
Dalai Lama, 14th 66, 108
Daniel 89, 114, 152, 164
Deganawida 29
Deguchi Nao 232
Deunov, Peter 13, 167, 185, 227, 244, 245
Deuteronomy 22
Diaspora, Jewish 22, 64, 80, 88
'Do' (Applewhite, Herf) 142, 143
Dojobojo, king of Indonesia 36
Dome of the Rock 63, 64, 65

E
El Niño 53
Elijah (Elias) 25, 38, 60, 153
Enoch 25, 60
Eskimo Messiah 28
Euphrates River 79
European Union (EU) 45, 89, 91, 125
Ezekiel 103, 144

F
False Prophet 78–91, 95, 99
Fátima, Lady of 58–9
Ferdinand, Archduke Franz 105
Friede, Johannes 52, 54, 56
Friend, the *see* Maitreya

G
Gale-Kumar, Kristina 45
Germania 153, 159
Gessar Khan *see* Shambhala, king of
Ghengis Khan 204, 205
Ghost Dancers' Messiah 29
Good Horse Nation 111
Gorbachev, Mikhail 132
Great Barbarian King 59
Great Plains Messiah 29
Great Purification 109
Great Pyramid of Giza 33
Gulf War (1991) 64, 131
Gurdjieff, G. I. 13, 105–6, 192, 199, 201, 203

H
Hakuin 200
Hale-Bopp 68, 142
Hamon, Count Louis *see* Keiro
Hanbal, Ahman Ibn 72
Hand, Floyd 65
Heaven's Gate 139, 142
Heine, Heinrich 37, 38
Hermes Trismegistus 13, 50, 52, 56
Hermetic philosophy 104
Hindu holy trinity 34
Hindu Puranas 13, 34, 101

Hindu yugas 34, 42–57, 101, 112, 194
Hinduism 104, 125, 164, 171, 174
Hister (Hitler) 77
Hitler, Adolf 13, 37–8, 60, 74, 88, 117, 124–5, 150, 153–4, 159, 196
Hogue, John 77
Holocaust 88
Hopi Indians 27, 69, 102, 106, 108–10
Horus 33
Howell, Vernon Wayne *see* Koresh, David
Huarte, Grandfather Semu 114, 212
Hunter, Jeffrey 162, 212
Hussein, Saddam 64

I
Immanuel 22, 63–5, 78, 80, 84–91
India 106, 236
Indonesia 36, 53
Iraq 57, 131
Iroquois Messiah 29
Isaiah, the First 22, 63, 78–80, 85, 89
Isaiah, the Second 86
Isaiah, the Third 81, 158, 184
Islam 32, 63–5, 67, 125, 132, 172
Israel 63–5, 80, 89, 91, 116, 131–2, 134

J
Japanese Messiah 36
Javada *see* Kalki
Jerusalem 63, 64, 116, 134, 248
Jesus Christ 8, 59, 60, 92, 94, 127, 159, 240
    see also Y'shua bar Youssef
    advent 101, 116
    anger against 195
    death 171
    as False Prophet 78–89, 91
    Islam's recognition 32
    Messiah of the Gentiles 23, 172–3
    missionaries 62
    as Mormon Messiah 26
    as Nazi Messiah 38, 135, 153
    'Rapture' 143–4, 157
    recognition 162–7, 169, 180
    reinvention 210, 211
    resurrection 87
John the Baptist 21, 60, 85, 153
John the Elder 92
John Paul II, Pope 45
John of Vatiguerro 93
Jones, Franklin *see* Adi Da
Jones, Reverend Jim 74–5, 132, 142–3
Jonestown commune 132, 142–3
Judaism 63–5, 78–89, 91–3, 125, 144, 164–5
Judas Iscariot 86, 165

K
Kali-yuga 34, 42, 44–57, 101, 112, 192
Kalki 8, 34, 92, 101, 104, 117
Karmapa Rigpe Dorje 30
Katchongva, Dan 102
Kate-Zahl *see* Quetzalcoatl
Keiro 13, 50
Khidr, the Sufi Final Lawgiver 33
Kingdom of the Messiah, 1000 year 9, 23
Korea, North/South 57
Koregaon Park 242
Koresh, David 25, 75, 132, 140
Krishna 13, 16, 34, 74–5, 101, 169, 171, 207, 211–12
Krishnamurti, J. 13, 113, 124, 133, 159, 167, 198–9, 202, 212, 227
Kukami Monjo 36
Kukulcan *see* Quetzalcoatl

L

Lamb of God 146, 150, 154
Latter-Day Saints 26
Leadbeater, C. W. 104
Lindsey, Hal 88–9, 91, 143, 144

M

Mabus 68, 77
Mahabharata 53
Mahavir, Bhagavan 211
Maitreya 8, 35, 106, 112
Malachi 60, 85
Mao Tse-tung 30, 74
Maori Messiah 24
Matthew 84
Max Headroom 75
Mecca 67, 169
Meichi Nozama 112
Merkabah 144
Merlin 44, 47, 49, 50
Messiah, definition 21
Micah 84
Miller, William 144
Moctezuma, King of the Aztecs 28
Mondale, Walter 143
Mongol hordes 67, 206–7
Monongye, Grandfather David 108–10
Montgomery, Ruth 13, 38, 76, 140, 165, 246
Mormon Messiah 26
Moses 80, 164, 169, 171
movies of saviors 210–11
Muammar Qaddafi 74, 75
Muhammad 32, 92, 94, 114, 169, 172, 177, 192
   death 171
   doomsday 117
   prophecy abbreviations 13
   reinvention 174, 210–11
Muntazar, the Final Prophet of Sunni Islam 32

N

Nanak, Guru 117, 135, 169, 203
Napaulon Roy (Napoleon) 77
Native Americans 26–9, 65, 69, 102, 106, 108–11, 114
   Nazareth 84
Nazis 37–8, 60, 88, 135, 153–4
NBC (National Broadcasting Company) 63–4
Neo-Sannyas 240
Nero, Emperor 76, 91, 125
Netanyahu, Binyamin 91
Nevi'im 78, 80, 81
New Age Messiah 38
Newbrough, John Ballou 134
Nichiren 193
Noah's Ark of Consciousness 186–207
Nostradamus 64, 68, 103–4, 113, 188
nuclear warfare 59, 64, 131–2, 187

O

Orange People 240
Osho 13, 95, 102, 108–11, 113, 139, 226–7, 244–6
   Buddhafields 230, 234, 236–43
   chaos 184
   consciousness 187, 189, 191, 193–4, 206
   death 213
   family discord 47
   'free-sex guru' 238
   guilt 202
   Maitreya 112
   ordinariness 211, 213–16
   personal challenges 147
   recognition of the messiah 165–8, 181
   reinvention 175
   somnambulistic existence 197–200, 203
   trust 218

union 224
Osho International Commune 236–7, 242–3
Osiris, the Egyptian Savior 33
Ouspensky, P. D. 105

P

Padmasambhava 13, 29, 44, 49, 50–2, 54, 66, 108
Pahána see True White Brother
Paiute Indians 29
Pale Prophet 26, 29
Parashurama 101
People's Temple 142
Peter the Apostle see Simon the Zealot
propheganda 122–35
Pune 236–40, 242–3
Pythagoras 171

Q

Qa'im see 12th Imam
Quetzalcoatl 13, 27–8, 44–5, 102, 106, 113

R

Rabin, Yitzhak 91
Ragnarök 24, 42, 47
Rajneesh, Bhagwan Shree see Osho
Rajneesh Mandir 240–2
Rajneeshees 108–11, 113, 236–43
Rajneeshpuram 108, 109–10
Rama, Lord 101
Ramayana 101
Rancho Rajneesh 108
'Rapture, the' 23, 143–4, 156–7
Reagan, Ronald 110, 122, 131–2
red heifer 22, 65
Rigden-jyepo see Shambhala, king of
Rinpoche, Gomang Hhensur 108
Robertson, Pat 122, 143, 159
Roerich, Nicholas 30
Roman Empire 78, 80, 88, 172–3
Ross Ice Shelf 56
Rudra Cakrin see Shambhala, king of
Rumi, Mevlana Jalaluddin 204–6
Ryan, Leo 142

S

St. John of Patmos 23, 99, 150–1, 153–5, 186
   advent 114
   Antichrist 76, 90, 91, 125
   apocalyptic signs 79
   doomsday 116, 117
   UFOs 146–7
St. Methodius 93
St. Paul see Saul of Tarsus
Samsara, wheel of 198–203
Saoshyant, the Zoroastrian Messiah 31
Sarmad 171
Satan 144
Satsang 222–5
Saul of Tarsus 23, 92, 94, 138, 145, 162, 172–3, 176
Shahadah 92
Shambhala, king of 30, 59, 66
   Prophecy 13, 30, 57, 158, 168
Shi'ite Islam 32, 67–8
Shiloh, Shabetai 63, 64
Shore, Rabbi Shmaria 65
Shree Rajneesh Ashram 238–40, 242
Sibylline Oracles 116, 135
Sikhism 117, 169
Simon the Zealot 23
Sinful Messiah see Koresh, David
Sioux 29, 65, 111
Six Day War 63
Smith, Joseph 26
Socrates 162, 171
Soviet Union 31, 132

Space Station Alpha 69
Speer, Albert 153
Spiritual King, the Indonesian Messiah 36
Srimad Bhagavata 34, 42, 46–7, 50–1, 92, 101, 135, 164, 192
Students of the Seven Seals 25
Sudhiro, Swami 108, 109
Sufism 33, 204
Sunni Islam 32
Susano 36
Sylvia, Madame 102

T

Tamo-san 13, 49, 140, 234
Tara 58, 59
Tel Aviv 64, 131
Temple of Herod 22
Third Reich 153, 154
Third Temple 63, 64–5
Thubten Norbu 138, 151
Tibet 29–30, 58, 59, 66, 104, 108
Tolstoy, Leo 104, 105, 249
Tribulation, the 143, 188–9
True White Brother see Quetzalcoatl
Turner, Charles 215
Tzadok, Rabbi Ariel Bar 63–4, 78

U

UFOs 139–47

V

Veled, Bahauddin 204
Virgin Mary 23, 38, 58–9, 173
Vishnu 92, 100–1, 115
Vivekananda, Swami 104

W

Waduda, Ma 108–9
Watt, James 131
Wechsler, Rabbi Hile 13, 82, 92
White Buffalo Woman 65
White Burkhan 31
White Robe Brotherhood 236
World War I 105
World War II 68, 154
World War III 57, 64, 68
Wounded Knee 29
Wowoka He 29

Y

Yggdrasill 24
Yogananda, Paramahansa 13, 113, 244
Yom Kippur War (1973) 63, 131
Y'shua bar Youssef 16, 74–5, 82, 192, 200, 207
   see also Jesus Christ
   advent 98, 103
   awakening 21
   counterfeit Messiahs 72
   Elijah 60
   end of the world 42
   natural disasters 54
   ocean levels 56
   recognition 162, 168, 176–7
   salvation 93, 138, 140
   somnambulistic existence 202
   union 225
   war 57

Z

Zarathustra (Zoroaster) 31, 169, 171
Zechariah, the First 63, 87, 92
Zechariah, the Second 86, 87, 93, 116, 158
Zorba the Buddha 238

Author's acknowledgments

DEDICATION

To all that is divinely ordinary.

ACKNOWLEDGMENTS

I fold my hands together in blessing to all those individuals who continue to rediscover enlightenment, despite the efforts of religious hierarchies to dirty their minds with thousands of years of crippling dogma, and messianic nightmares. Bless *you*. And may you keep washing your brains clear and clean in each new moment, with each new breath.

COPYRIGHT ACKNOWLEDGMENTS

In instances not extensively covered by fair usage, every effort has been made to obtain permissions from holders of copyright material. If however – either through a mistake or through circumstances beyond our control – any copyright owner has been omitted, the author and publisher extend their apologies and undertake to rectify the situation at the next edition.

Grateful acknowledgment is made for permission to reprint material:

To the Sri Aurobindo Ashram Trust for excerpts from *The Human Cycle* by P. B. Saint Hilaire, copyright © by the Sri Aurobindo Ashram Publication Department, printed by the Sri Aurobindo Trust.

To the Bahá'í Publishing Trust (United Kingdom) for excerpts from *Paris Talks* by 'Abdu'l-Bahá, copyright © 1995.

To the Bahá'í Publishing Trust (U.S.A.) for excerpts from *Bahá'u'lláh and the New Era*, by J. E. Esselmont, copyright © 1999, by the National Assembly for the Bahá'ís of the United States; for excerpts from *Gleanings from the Writings of Bahá'u'lláh* by 'Abdu'l-Bahá, copyright © 1976, 1983, by the National Assembly for the Bahá'ís of the United States; for excerpts from *Kitáb-I-Íqán* (*The Book of Certitude*) by Bahá'u'lláh, copyright © 1931, 1950 by the National Assembly for the Bahá'ís of the United States; for excerpts from *The Promulgation of Universal Peace* by 'Abdu'l-Bahá, copyright © 1982, by the National Assembly for the Bahá'ís of the United States.

To Bantam Books (A division of Random House) for excerpts from *The Other Bible* by Willis Barnstone copyright © 1984.

To Coleman Barks, for excerpts from his English translation of "The Tent," a poem by Mevlana Rumi, copyright © by Coleman Barks; *The Essential Rumi*, HarperCollins*Publishers*, copyright © 1995.

To Edwin Bernbaum for an excerpt from *The Way of Shambhala* by Edwin Bernbaum, copyright © 1980.

To Butsugen-shu Enichi-kai (The Light of Cosmic Wisdom) for excerpts from *Look Here* by Reverend Ryoju Kikuchi (Tamo-san), copyright © 1960; and for excerpts from *Moor the Boat*, by Reverend Ryoju Kikuchi (Tamo-san), copyright © 1957.

To the Edgar Cayce Foundation for excerpts from the Edgar Cayce Readings, copyright © 1971, 1993, by the Edgar Cayce Foundation, all rights reserved, used by permission.

To Daniel Entin, Director of the Nicholas Roerich Museum, for quoting an excerpt from *Altai-Himalaya* by Nicholas Roerich, copyright © 1983, printed by the Arun Press (second printing, 1983) in cooperation with Urusvati Himalayan Research Institute, Naggar, India.

To Element Books Ltd., for excerpted translations in English of the works of Peter Deunov as they appeared in *Prophet for Our Times* by David Lorimer, copyright © 1991.

To Inner Traditions International Ltd., for an excerpt from *Shambhala: In Search of the New Era*, by Nicholas Roerich, copyright © 1990 by permission of the Nicholas Roerich Museum.

To the Osho International Foundation for permission to print excerpts from several published and unpublished works by Osho from their website: www.osho.com. Osho is the author of *The Book of the Secrets*, by St. Martin's Press © 1998; *Meditation the First and Last Freedom*, © 1997 by St. Martin's Press; and *Insights for a New Way of Living*, © 1999 by St. Martin's Press. Osho is also author of *The Book of Wisdom* © 1999 by Element Books Ltd., *The Mustard Seed* by Element Books Ltd., *Tantric Experience* by Element Books Ltd.

To the Osho International Foundation for also granting permission to print excerpts from *Beyond Enlightenment* copyright © 1986; *Come, Come, Yet Again, Come* copyright © 1980; *The Dhammapada: The Way of Buddha* copyright © 1979; *The Diamond Sutra* copyright © 1977; *Dimensions Beyond the Known* copyright © 1971; *From Death to Deathlessness* copyright © 1985; *From the False to the True* copyright © 1985; *From Misery to Enlightenment* copyright © 1985; *I Am the Gate* copyright © 1971; *Glimpses of a Golden Childhood* copyright © 1981; *The Goose Is Out* copyright © 1981; *Hallelujah!* copyright © 1978; *The Invitation* copyright © 1987; *Let Go!* copyright © 1978; *The Miracle* copyright © 1980; *The Mustard Seed* copyright © 1974; *The Mystic Experience* copyright © 1970; *The New Dawn* © 1987; *The Razor's Edge* copyright © 1987; *Sermons in Stones* copyright © 1986; *Showering without Clouds* copyright © 1976; *Ta Hui* copyright © 1988; *Take It Easy, vol. 1* copyright © 1975; *What Is Is What Ain't Ain't* copyright © 1977; *The White Lotus* copyright © 1979; *Zarathustra, A God That Can Dance* copyright © 1987; *The Zen Manifesto* copyright © 1989.

To Ray Palmer of Legend Press (9533 Clinton Road, Amherst, WI 54406), for excerpts from *He Walked The Americas* by L. Taylor Hansen, copyright © 1963; copyright renewed © 1991; twenty-first printing 1997.

To Sun Books/ Sun Publishing for an excerpt from *Cheiro's World Predictions* by Count Louis Hamon, copyright © 1981. Reprinted by permission of Skip Whitson, publisher.

THANK YOU ALSO

To The Dawn Horse Press for excerpts from the compilation of discourses celebrating the first 25 years of Avatar Da Samraj's teachings, *See My Brightness Face to Face*. The discourses include excerpts from *The ego-'I'*, copyright © 1980, excerpts from *Handle Business*, copyright © 1987, and excerpts from *The Way I Teach*, copyright © 1977.

To Dharma Publishing for excerpts from *The Legend of the Great Stupa: The Life of the Lotus Born Guru* translated by Keith Dowman, copyright © 1973 by the Tibetan Nyingma Meditation Center.

To Dover Publications Inc., for an excerpt from the *Bhagavadgita* (translated from the Sanskrit by Sir Edwin Arnold), copyright © 1993 by Dover Publications Inc.

To HarperCollins*Publishers* for excerpts from "The Gospel of St. Thomas (II, 2)," from *The Nag Hammadi Library in English*, copyright © 1988.

To HarperCollins*Publishers* for excerpts from *The Future is Now* by J. Krishnamurti, copyright © 1989 by the Krishnamurti Foundation Trust; excerpts from *You Are the World* by J. Krishnamurti, copyright © 1972 by the Krishnamurti Foundation Trust; excerpts from *Life Ahead* by J. Krishnamurti, copyright © 1963 by the K & R Foundation, copyright renewed 1991 by the K & R Foundation.

To the Krishnamurti Foundation of America for excerpts from *TRUTH IS A PATHLESS LAND: The Dissolution of the Order of the Star* (KFA Bulletin no. 53) by J. Krishnamurti, copyright © 1986.

To Mangalam Verlag S. Schang for excerpts from *Matri Darshan: A photo album about Sri Anandamayi Ma*, copyright © 1988–1997.

To Tatiana M. Nagro for excerpts from *In Search of the Miraculous* by P. D. Ouspensky, copyright © 1949 by Harcourt Brace Jovanovich Inc., (copyright renewed © 1977 by Tatiana M. Nagro: Harcourt Brace Jovanovitch Inc. and Penguin Books Ltd.).

To Penguin Books Ltd., for excerpts from *The Bhagvad Gita* by Gautama Buddha (translated from the Sanskrit with introduction by Juan Mascaró), copyright © 1962; for excerpts from *The Dhammapada (The Path of Perfection)* by Gautama Buddha (translated from the Pali with introduction by Juan Mascaró), copyright © 1973.

To Penguin Putnam, Inc., for excerpts from *Views from the Real World: Early Talks of Gurdjieff*, 1914–1924, by G. I. Gurdjieff, copyright © 1975.

To Penguin Putnam Inc., for excerpts from *Aliens Among Us* by Ruth Montgomery, copyright © 1985; for excerpts from *A World Before* by Ruth Montgomery, copyright © 1976; for excerpts from *Strangers Among Us* by Ruth Montgomery, copyright © 1979.

To Dick J. Reavis for quotes of David Koresh taken from *The Ashes of Waco* by Dick J. Reavis, copyright © 1995.

To Stanké (New York) for brief excerpts of two brief statements of Muammar Quaddafi in *Escape from Hell and Other Stories*, by Muammar Qaddafi, copyright © 1998 Stanké, New York.

To Berthold Strauss, for excerpts of Rabbi Hile Wechsler's statements from *The Rosenbaums of Zell*, by Berthold Strauss, copyright © 1962.

To STURID AB for excerpts from AMBRES by "Ambres," copyright © by Sturid Johannson.

To Thomas Francis Tarbet, ed., *From the Beginning of Life to the Day of Purification*. Taos, NM: Hopi Land and Life, 3d. ed., 1982.

To the Theosophical Publishing House for excerpts from *The Secret Doctrine* by H. P. Blavatsky, copyright © 1962.

To Weidenfeld & Nicolson Publishers (United Kingdom) for excerpts from *Hitler's Secret Conversations* by Adolf Hitler (with introduction by H. R. Trevor-Roper), copyright © 1952.